Community Power Succession

Community Power Succession

Atlanta's Policy-Makers Revisited

by Floyd Hunter

The University of North Carolina Press *Chapel Hill*

© 1980 The University of North Carolina Press

All rights reserved

Manufactured in the United States of America

Library of Congress Catalog Card Number 79-305

Cloth edition, ISBN 0-8078-1314-1

Paper edition, ISBN 0-8078-4067-X

Library of Congress Cataloging in Publication Data

Hunter, Floyd.
  Community power succession.

  Bibliography: p.
  Includes index.
  1. Atlanta—Social policy.   2. Power (Social
sciences)   3. Community leadership.   4. Decision-
making.   I. Title.
HN80.A8H86   301.15′5   79-305
ISBN 0-8078-1314-1
ISBN 0-8078-4067-X pbk.

In memory of
Louis W. Niggeman
and Granny Tuggle

Contents

Tables

Introduction

One must immediately differentiate this work from its earlier companion work, *Community Power Structure*, or Study I, as I shall call it. It was initially concerned with quite different questions from those which will concern us here in *Community Power Succession*. I shall use the term Study II to identify the second work.

Because Study I opened a new area, the empirical study of social power, questions of methods and scope had to be addressed. One substantive question of scope was: "Does Atlanta have, in terms of identifiable social roles, an informal as well as a formal power structure?" And importantly, in terms of the ultimate findings of the study, "What implications does such a structure have for the traditional concepts of American democracy?"

In continuous publication since it was written, Study I is now a quarter of a century old. Nevertheless, as I began Study II I assumed that my earlier findings were still valid, an assumption I confirmed almost immediately upon my return visits to the community. Indeed, an active, easily identifiable power structure was still in place. My questions then became: "How does it differ from that of 1950?" "What were the processes of succession?" "What has it been up to?" And, finally, "Is democracy better served by this structure than its predecessor?"

As will be shown in the materials to follow, I found a number of structural changes in Atlanta's power structure over time but little change in terms of its major functions or in its democratic implications.

A few correspondents acquainted with the host of studies that have accumulated since the publication of Study I have occasionally asked why I have never responded to various criticisms, positive and negative. To them I must say that I decided early after criticisms began that I would not answer *individual* critics. I have always felt that academic arguments are relatively fruitless, convincing to very few. I felt that the best general answers might lie in correcting in the succeeding works, with which I had been immediately occupied, any mistakes I recognized. Publicly, I have spoken with both positive and negative critics. And at last, I found that most of both kinds of critics had been answered by others; none of their answers, apparently, are pleasing to their opposites![1]

I feel that very much more time has been spent in the past two decades on methodological discussion than has been necessary and too little time on the more important issue of how democratic it is to have policy made by such limited groups as have been involved in policy-making in America for so long as one might remember. Thus, this work, in contrast to Study I, will be very much concerned with this political question and, what is more important, from a social science point of view.

At any rate, in the bibliography of this work, I do include the works of a number of people who I believe have made significant contributions to the study of community power in the past two decades. Otherwise, here I shall refer only to methods of community power study as they may explain the present work and which seem to me to have remained valid. I shall reserve the right to reply to any chronic criticisms at a later time and in more appropriate ways than by doing so in the introduction of a new work.

In the final chapter I will present in model form with accompanying discussion suggestions for what might be done to bring more balance into a situation now characterized by extreme political imbalance. A set of social and political hypotheses constitutes the essential base of reasoning behind the political discussion running through the whole work. These hypotheses, which are first stated in this Introduction, below, also will be referred to throughout the work.

This book views Atlanta in transition during two decades, 1950 through the 1960s, and into the major part of the third decade, the 1970s. The next to the last chapter of the work is intended to be politically critical, that is, critical of the drift and thrust of policy-making in a major urban center of America. The last chapter, critically positive, will present a balanced model of what might be done as a beginning toward solution of the many problems of the city created by the reigning imbalances. The suggestions are not utopian. They are set forth as illustrations of successful economic and political organizations that use alternative ways of raising and expending capital, which are at work today in both the United States and in other economically advanced parts of the world.

One of my recurrent assertions is that human behavior may be classified institutionally and observed within such a frame of reference. Political behavior, then, is one such classification. I have found that one can observe political behavior (policy-making behavior) best by observing men in action in collective association with one another, whether the association be public or private, formal or informal, in character. Associations are the visible manifestations of institutional value or belief systems. A number of my social and political hypotheses concerning power are framed in this context.

I will point out repeatedly that in the United States the system of institutional policy-making is gravely imbalanced, skewed in favor of economic institutional values. Any thinking person is in some degree aware of this skew. It is visible at all levels of societal life, community, national, and international.

I take issue with those who would obscure the fact that specific men holding specific positions in society make the major decisions that direct our lives. A majority of such decisions are directed from the control centers of the private enterprise sector of America, and to some extent by British and European systems (the Western bloc). This bloc keeps a wary eye on the Eastern one, and both follow the growing dictates of the rapidly formed but as yet undefined institutional set, the technological sector, in both of these societies. Many are weary indeed with the international paranoia and costly continuation of conflict between national states.

I also take vigorous issue with those who have claimed in this century that massive, unidentifiable irrational forces rule our lives rather than identifiable minorities of irrational men. Social irrationality in both instances arises from convictions based on false premises. The major false premise in world thinking is that either political or economic values alone are sufficient to guide the actions of men without reference to other vital institutional values concerning religion, the family, recreation, health, welfare, and education. There is a drumfire of negation or denigration of the values in these latter institutional clusters, values necessary to man's very survival. Many people know this intuitively, if not consciously, and many in recent times in the United States have acted upon it. The consistent, conscious aid given to the farm workers' unionization efforts in California by religious groups is a vivid case in point. Martin Luther King, Jr.'s religious base of operations is another. The conservation groups who have raised questions about the destruction of the environment is yet another.

Isolated efforts at piecemeal reform by political parties, however, do not go far enough nor do they appear to be well enough informed to attack the root of our national malaise, the institutional imbalance of which I am compelled to speak.

While one may also eschew the so-called conspiratorial view of the underlying cause of social ills, it is plain to many that the ceaseless flow of misinformation and invective directed against those who disagree with the present maladministration of social affairs is consciously orchestrated by well-organized partisans, including many academicians. I believe that the system is a political, a policy-making machine, a machine not always adroit, and certainly not always correctly informed, but a well-knit machine nevertheless. Its anchor points of power lie in industrial, urbanized society. Its shape has been broadly outlined in this and similar, recent works about the structuring of American power. Its class structure is defined in the closing analyses of this work as a patronage system.

One may argue that the American malfunctions of policy-making can be corrected by broadening the base of political participation. I firmly believe that is one sure way to success. However, such action must be guided by an adequate map of the whole structure if it is to be changed, else we may do little but run about briskly and fruitlessly. We are forced to make such a conclusion when we analyze the results of assaults upon the castle made by the ill-fated protest movements of the 1960s. Their tactics were mere charades of military maneuvers. The hope was that by creating social structures principally of protest and entreaty paralleling the existing institutional structures protesters could outflank them! These efforts failed dismally in the face of oaken clubs, tear gas, rumbling tanks, and more than all else, a wandering sense of purpose on the part of the protesting partisans, the "spontaneous" militants. Many of the problems remained standing while the partisans fell away and lapsed into silence.

One rightly may distrust any elaborate design to bring about social change. Social change occurs when men make up their minds that they actually want it in some parts of the social milieu identified by them as stress points. It comes when they really examine malfunctioning institutional schemes they have taken into their behavioral patterns without question. When such examinations occur, social change is bound to follow. New social structures are created to enforce the will of new makers of policy.

Part of the tactic of those who believe that the present mode of general political behavior is the best is to isolate those who openly question existing belief systems, to isolate and if necessary destroy such dissent. The individual in such a situation is hopelessly outnumbered, almost helpless. His help must always come from others, and in association with others.

As I said in Study I, the only recourse the individual may have in the highly organized life around him is to align himself with others of like persuasion if he wishes to engage in the pursuit of social change. Otherwise, he may find himself in a situation of enforced silence. He also may find himself thwarted if his support group departs too far from the norms of the community around him, strangely enough, the very norms he wishes to change! He must examine his strategies.

In American society we have a tradition of using associations for the achievement of social goals. Whether or not some associations are weak, or have atrophied from misuse, I must not take the time to argue now. I am convinced that in many instances we may have right at hand social devices and incipient social structures that remain unused. It is quite possible that very little elaboration may be needed to make the associations near us into viable instruments for policy definition and promotion, if not finally policy execution.

At any rate, it may be assumed with some certainty that basic institutional imbalances are not going to be righted by those who foster them. Nor will unorganized citizen apathy win the day. Imbalances of power and economic injustice will be righted only when there is insistent, consciously directed, democratic demand for it. I have long believed that one of the very effective devices for attaining economic democracy is cooperative endeavor. In many areas of the world, and in certain sections of the United States, the cooperative movement, without bloodshed and with quiet persistence, has actually turned many exploitive situations into equitable ones for both producers and consumers.

Within the past several years, it has been the author's good fortune to have lived in northern California in urban and semi-rural, small-farm communities where consumer, and to some extent, supporting producer cooperatives have been a vital force in community life. One is led to believe, through participating in the cooperative movement, that it offers one capital-producing alternative to the most flagrant exploitations of the American system by capital levy. It is quite possible that if the demand for such movements were to become more widespread, people could begin to work together and avoid the wasteful capital drain of either big-brother government or big-daddy corporations. Although most Atlantans do not know it, a very good model of cooperative performance operates only twenty or so miles north of the city, a cooperative with the unlikely name of Gold Kist.

For those politically inclined and determined to reform the corporate mode of operations, it may be that at some seemingly distant date, perhaps after a decade or two of hard political work, the corporations might be forced by law to make their governing boards subject to democratic procedures and public scrutiny.

Corporate charters, it may be remembered, are given by the people, and it would seem that many of them should be periodically reviewed and changed about. It might also be well for the public to have access to all corporate financial records through appropriate governmental bodies. Otherwise, we may never be able to answer such a simple question as, "How much does it *really* cost to build an automobile?"

Will the Atlanta power structure be moved by such words? No, perhaps not very much, but one may insist upon this: that if enough people in Atlanta and elsewhere want to know how much it costs to make an automobile, or even a bottle of Coke, they can with persistence and practice in the general art of politics, find out, just as, by the same methods, they find out many other things. The only practical advice one may give those dispirited about their condition lies in this: Be political; act politically persistently. Demand direct participation in the making of even the smallest of policies that affect your life. This may not always be easy, but there is currently, in the face of enormous consolidated power, no other way to redress the present imbalances of power.

One of the difficult elements in the American equation of power to explain to anyone is the institutional imbalance of power and its effect upon the population generally. It is the same kind of institutional imbalance that existed in the Middle Ages, when men were willing to tolerate the excesses of the church, the dominant institution of that era, because they believed that their souls would be damned if they did otherwise. In our era, as Weber has pointed out, a Protestant work ethic prevails; we believe that hard work will yield rewards both here and in the life to come, so work becomes a virtue for the poor and a super virtue of the rich, who co-opt the work of others. The poor hope for the opportunity to emulate the rich. Recent technological advances give many the illusion of catching up, yet the distance between the governors, public and private, and the people grows. While most look the other way, a coalition of business enterprise dominates.

The yearning for a more balanced life remains and has manifested itself in recent public revulsions against the public and private abuse of power. It is a mood reflected in the broad support from all parts of the nation for a Southern Baptist candidate for presidential office. The purpose of religion, to give meaning to life, struggles to overcome that of the economic institution, to provide the material means for life.

In order to be more readily understood, I have listed a number of hypotheses that I have developed over a number of years. They concern both social and political human behavior, and I believe they are held in mind, at least in part by most men, through institutional prompting by the family, our churches, the marketplace, and so on. Each may record imperfectly what he is supposed to hear about social behavior. These imperfect perceptions account for some of the institutional problems that run through society. On the other hand, some ideas gain or lose general credence as we move from one to another epoch of history. Acceptance of an idea today may have been impossible in an earlier day. Ideas change. However, the hypotheses I set down here seem to me to be those that customarily are now accepted in Western thought; they thus are useful guides to sociopolitical understanding of our immediate past history.

Hypotheses Concerning Societal Structures

Learned, habitual behavior practiced between members of any group constitutes a social structure.

Institutions are categories of behavior useful to the classifying mind as it deals with value and belief systems in society; the function of the belief systems is the maintenance of these systems and the survival of society. For example:

Institution (classified by behavior patterns)	Societal Survival Function
1. Familial	1. Preserve biological continuity
2. Economic	2. Provide physical means of life
3. Educational	3. Transmit social values and skills
4. Religious	4. Give meaning to life
5. Health/Welfare	5. Provide aid to needy and debilitated
6. Recreational	6. Provide a sense of balance and perspective to personal life
7. Political	7. Maintain order

The sum of institutional functions provides a buffer of reason and protection between the individual and society.

The individual internalizes the values of institutional belief systems, however imperfectly, and expresses these values by acting out the social roles available to him, e.g., fatherhood or motherhood, citizen, workman, churchman, city councilman, and so forth.

Behavior in conformity to institutional values is functional behavior, functional, that is, to the maintenance of institutional order.

Institutional behavior is deemed to be the only permissible behavior within societal limits. Deviance by ruling circles is often rationalized and later adopted by the masses, but initial deviance by the understructure of the population may be punishable in varying degrees.

Functional behavior can be observed only through inferences drawn from the objective consequences of acts of individuals or groups. The observation of it is, therefore, indirect.

Functional behavior may be manifest or latent. It tends to persist, while behavior dysfunctional to any given society may be excluded or destroyed.

Institutions, as belief systems, are subject to continual, even if not immediately discernible, change.

The various institutional belief and behavioral systems (familial, economic, religious, etc.) occupy varying positions of status from society to society and from epoch to epoch, the economic institution being the ascendant one in world technological society.

Variable learned attitudes toward personal and collective ownership of property may be classified, thus providing the behavioral basis of that which has become known as class (classifications) structures.

A community is the smallest societal, geographical area in which all institutional belief systems are functionally operative as associations and organizations.

Hypotheses Concerning Power in Society

Power can be precisely defined only as a social function, that of establishing and maintaining given institutional and societal modes of order.

Power functionaries are those who, in addition to their other societal roles, with formal and informal sanctions, carry specific roles in the maintenance of any prescribed differentiated social order.

A power structure is a coordinated system, public and private, formal and informal, of learned and repeated power roles and relationships, the function of which is the maintenance of any prescribed, differentiated social order.

A community power structure is one such order and is linked by its power functions to larger societal power systems. Other such power systems include organized labor, partisan political blocs, leg-islative management systems, etc., often linked to larger parent, national, and international systems of power superior to them.

A substantial portion of families with ascendant status and prop-erty interests appear sequentially in community power structures by decades and some of them appear in longer epochs of social history.

Local power structures vary in size and composition according to their coordination function, which they perform for both public and private centers of power internal and external to them.

Those ascendant in any given power structure assume its policy-making function.

Bureaucracies in modern technological society perform the in-vestigative and enforcement tasks inherent in delegated authority.

Bureaucratic functionaries are decision-makers who take care of details of policy-making and direction; they thereby indirectly affect policy made by policy-makers superordinate to them.

Power roles, however covert or overt, are always performed with symbolic displays of pomp, ceremony, pageantry, and ideological cuing.

Ceremonial centers of power display may range in size and complexity from personal ritual space (a place at the head table, teepee posts or ceremonial stools, depending upon the society), to plazas, squares, pyramids, holy of holies, and skyscraper executive suites.

Power in American society is reflected in associations, which are the visible apparatuses of institutions. These associations have vary-ing gradations of status.

The manifest function of formal American government is that of adjudicating various institutional claims regarding their rights and the rights of their individual members, but because of the ascendancy of the economic institution, a bias at this time exists in its favor.

Economic institutional values are present in both private and public power centers in such degree that they, in effect, form a dual, coordinate system of de facto power, existing constitutional govern-ing theories to the contrary.

A societal power system, commonly called "the system," repre-sents the sum of all cultural, institutional, and technological policy-making actions within given territorial limits. These elements extend internationally as differentiated power blocs. Direct association pro-vides the nexus of such power.

Dominant world power structures are at present national, em-bracing multitudinous, subordinate internal and external systems, communities and cities being their anchor points of power.

The means of power are modes of material, money, and symbolic patronage which, at root, are processes of inclusion and exclusion. The processes of control range in intensity from mild persuasion to financial and bodily coercion, to personal murder, and to the genocide of war.

The historic, now cumbersome, function of money as a medium of exchange in production and distribution and ultimately as an expression of corporate book-capital is being superseded in practice in technological society (as electronically distinct from agrarian and mechanistic societies) by computer functions, which supply instant control mechanisms in systematic capital accumulation, retention, and dispersal of goods and services among the population.

Monetary policy control is centered on monopolistic price management (including inflation management controls), which in either so-called private or publicly controlled societies results in overcapitalization of production centers (corporations or politbureaus) and in chronic undercapitalization of the vast majority of the world's population.

Institutionally reinforced, systematic biases favor centralized monetary controls which, because of a preoccupation with building capital structures dysfunctional to human life and well-being, transform the social functions of production for consumer uses into capital aggrandizement, thus creating an imbalance among institutions that is detrimental to the full realization of life-enhancing activities of every individual in the world.

These hypotheses and propositions will be referred to throughout the text to follow.

The bibliography lists the many works that have contributed to the study of power since 1950. With most of them I in most part agree. With some I am in radical disagreement—with the so-called pluralists, for example—but they have been quite adequately answered by others, even though a false duality has been erected between my work and theirs, which harmfully for the field of study continues to exist. In any case, I must insist: power in the United States, from localities to the great power centers, is centered in too few people for the good of the whole people. This fact needs to be turned completely around.

Floyd Hunter

Sonoma, California

Community Power Succession

A Central City Rebuilt

After twenty years' absence, I returned to Atlanta to restudy its power structure.

As the airport limousine in which I was riding sped along the broad, new expressway leading from Atlanta's busy airport, I could see flashes of an amazing panorama of new skyscrapers. The beautiful foliage of north Georgia's Piedmont plateau, a mixture of evergreen- and fall-colored softwoods, alternately hid and revealed what appeared to me to be an essentially new central city.

Yet, even with the preparation of the sweeping, distant view, I was not prepared for the shock of disorientation that awaited me as I stepped to the ground on downtown Peachtree Street, the city's main street, which I had known intimately some years previously. For a few moments I literally could see nothing with which I had been familiar. On each side of the street, a giant cluster of newly designed buildings rose in a great bulk twenty-five or thirty stories into the clear autumn air. I learned later that I had been looking at John Portman's development, Peachtree Center, a $100 million multiple construction containing 5.1 million square feet of office, hotel, and commercial space. Set back, exposing sculpture and greenery at its several entrances, the center buildings on either side of Atlanta's main street are connected by soaring aerial walkways. It is built, even with its massiveness, to give a feeling of light and space throughout. One can walk from its center to any point at its periphery in seven-and-one-half minutes. One enters its 800-room Hyatt Regency Hotel at street level, but one's eye instantly is carried upward past twenty or more floors of vine-covered balconies to the roof of the lobby.

At first glance, a typical reaction is, "My God, look at all of that wasted space!" Then one remembers that the hotel has 800 rooms (and was then in the process of adding 200 more), all of them reached by exposed, glass-capsule elevators that give their riders a view of the whole lobby as they silently ascend and descend. At ground level, as a part of the lobby, skillfully arranged outdoor, indoor restaurant tables, snack areas, and notions facilities give one the impression of Parisian street cafes and shopping grottoes. One becomes quickly accustomed to the space around, loses awe of it, and likes the feeling of expansiveness it gives.

To my right, before entering the hotel lobby and looking north beyond the Center, I saw another building of equal height rising near a point where I thought the prestigious Capital City Club ought to be. (I learned later that the club is still where it ought to have been, but it was hidden by a new monolith, that housing the Coastal States Life Insurance Company.) Beyond, for a few blocks, one after the other, clusters of contemporary motels beckoned. These were resolved at the horizon by an enormous, cylindrical tower of reflecting glass occupied by a branch bank of the Citizens and Southern Bank system. It stands as a work of technological pop art on a spot that previously had been a desolate area of decaying, transitional, one- and two-story buildings. I looked at the freshness of the new view with growing conviction and appreciation. Downtown, at least, had experienced more, much more than just a facelift. The castle had been rebuilt!

To my left stood an upended, rectangular headquarters of the Fulton National Bank, and at last, beyond that, I saw my first familiar point of orientation, the old Candler Building, a building built in 1906 by Coca-Cola money but more recently owned by Emory University. Somewhat irrelevantly, I recalled interviewing Howard Candler at some length in his small office on the top floor of the building at about the time he was considering giving the building to Emory as a tax benefit to his own estate. Candler, an old man then, is now dead. As a matter of fact, many of the men of the 1950 power structure have died or were inactive by 1970. This is not surprising considering that the average age of these men in 1950, twenty years earlier, was fifty-three years.

I entered my hotel determined, after checking into my room, to return immediately to the street in order to get a better view of Atlanta's dramatic physical changes. More importantly, perhaps, I wished to quiet a persistent sense of dislocation in this city where my mind told me I should be on familiar ground.

Presently from my hotel room I gazed out the window to the east toward a great arc of a freeway and over a huge new stadium surrounded by considerable parking space as well as open space. To the southeast, in an area previously inhabited by a slum of blacks, I tried unsuccessfully to distinguish Auburn Avenue, the black main street. In its vicinity, perhaps to the left of it, stood a lone skyscraper, ten to fifteen stories high. "Do the blacks have a token high-rise building?" I wondered. The following day, I was indeed assured that the blacks had their first high-rise office building a bit off Auburn Avenue, a building under the control of the first black bank, the Citizens Trust, which occupies very impressive, open space on its first two or three floors. A second such building, a denial of tokenism, I was told later, was in its planning stages.

The bank, I observed upon visiting it the next day, occupies the first floor of the building, a first floor of impressive proportions, including a huge open space and a massive chandelier. A carpeted stairway leads to an executive balcony. One of the inner offices of the balcony into which I mistakenly stepped appeared to be occupied by two or three giggling on-the-job trainees. Below the balcony, banking operations were being carried on at functional and colorful counters and desks. I was reminded of some of the new buildings and their operators that one may observe in former colonial capitals, newly independent. The signs of problems yet to be solved, blight and decay, human and physical malaise are everywhere within sight of new, showcase buildings. However, one must not detract too greatly from the new bank structure. No matter for the moment the continuing problems around it; for thousands of blacks, it stands as one of Atlanta's new business pyramids, a magnificent status symbol where none had stood before.

Around the corner from the new building, the Atlanta Life Company, a fully black-owned insurance company, capable financially, I was told, of building another high-rise building, conservatively maintains its operations in a structure built in 1915. Ornamented in front by two Grecian columns backed by two sets of wooden casement windows with papers piled on their ledges, the building was an avenue landmark, but some of the residents of the area called it an architectural disgrace. It was abundantly evident that the street had not kept pace with central downtown development, nor with the lead of the new Citizens Trust. Rotting interstitial housing, ramshackle commercial buildings, and empty lots filled with refuse still characterized the whole scene. Some of the buildings serving civic enterprises were old, beyond repair. The nationally famous Southern Christian Leadership Conference, founded by Dr. Martin Luther King, Jr., operated in a building that decidedly appears to be a firetrap; a large portion of its staff were working in poster-filled, windowless, stale-aired rooms in its basement.

In the days that followed, I observed another, deeper malaise of Auburn Avenue, one that no amount of fixing up or painting up could remedy. By design or accident, the gigantic freeway system surrounding the city had cut the black business area away from its hinterland of residential areas. It now sat between massive downtown development and a wall of concrete which, although a few underpasses had been furnished, effectively isolated the traditional main street from its historical neighborhoods. Further, higher-income black population had continued to move west. Local neighborhood facilities were still small. White-controlled, larger regional shopping centers catering to the total population were serving those blacks in large numbers to whom automobile transportation was readily available. It seemed possible that Auburn Avenue, whether black or white in character, may finally become an integral part of downtown Atlanta's Manhattanization. Certainly, it seemed quite unlikely that it would ever again be the teeming, boisterous downtown of Saturday-night black Atlanta of a decade or two ago. Black Atlanta may have become too sophisticated for that, but regardless, the builders of the new Atlanta have made it physically impossible. By 1980 Atlanta Life had built a new building for its headquarters, segregated from downtown Atlanta.

Certainly, as later I moved about among the white leaders and association personnel of the city in order to reconstruct its power scene, I heard over and over proud statements about Atlanta's phenomenal growth, and actually I could never quite get over the shock of wonder at seeing what had been accomplished downtown. Yet, the obvious relative position of blacks in the scheme of progress never quite measured up to what one might expect of a technology that could rebuild downtown so completely. This gave me pause. It suggested subtle, hidden problems, wisps of continued social disparity that tended to spoil the whole picture of well-being touted on every hand downtown.

One comes to understand in community life that hearing what men say is often less important than observing what they do. Clichés tend, in many instances, to be stated as great, unshakable truths. Statistics quoted at length may at last state only half-truths. American businessmen, especially, operate in syndromes of action in which great injustices are perpetrated in the name of astute decision-making and many disastrous results of such activities are covered by pious pronouncements rather than deeds of restitution. Few see beyond the short-range advantages that may come their way nor may they wish to, for in the long-range view dire consequences of present acts may become apparent. A whole language-set accompanies all this: "You win a few and lose a few." "It's a whole new ball game." "It's how the ball bounces!" (Possible remarks after "driving another to the wall"—bankruptcy.)

Whatever its shortcomings socially, the Atlanta business community *had* produced a new downtown, a visible manifestation of great power over the general technology. My task in restudying the power structure actually lay in finding out whether or not the new building surge was reflected in the composition of the power structure of 1970 as it may have been related to the power structure of 1950. A first step in such study would be, as it had been in Study I, to begin, not altogether with the words of men, but with a closer examination of what they have built around themselves physically and to what purposes.

Power and the Physical City

The physical characteristics of Atlanta are of primary concern to the people occupying power positions within the city. Where to put streets, utility lines, shopping facilities, office buildings, warehouses, factories, recreation facilities, sewage treatment plants, airport installations, rapid transit systems, houses, and freeway interconnections from time to time are among the many physical projects facing any set of policy-makers in urban areas of our time. What gets done and what must remain in abeyance is of continuing concern to the men of power of any particular time. The roles played by these men are rather precisely defined by law and custom, both of which are guided by the societal function of the production and exchange of goods and services peculiar to the cities within which they operate.

In Atlanta law and custom are guided by the fact that the city is a gateway city, a service city catering to a large regional hinterland, especially the southeastern coastal plains. It provides financial, commercial, transport, storage, record-keeping, fabrication, and manufacturing services to the southeastern portion of the United States and to some parts of the world. In this it is an anchorpoint of power in regional exchanges. Both the size and shape of the city and the area of its power reach is determined by its functions as a national and world city. The rank order of the urban functions listed above are a part of such determination. One sees "fabrication and manufacturing" placed at the end of the listing of functions. Were the city under discussion Detroit, "fabrication and manufacturing" would be placed at the beginning of the list, and by this placement one would expect to find somewhat different physical and social characteristics in that city. By the same token, the theocratic papal city of Rome has characteristics very different from those of a Middle East oil capital, in terms of both their physical aspects and their relations with peoples of the world.

Atlanta's geographical location at the crossroads of the south-eastern United States has given it a natural advantage for transportation operations and financial transactions both within and beyond its region. Commercial transactions supply goods to an extensive hinterland through storage, assembly, and distribution activities. Raw materials supplied by the hinterland make possible many branches of both light and heavy industry. The position of Atlanta makes it a national center of exchange devoted to finance, commerce, and industry, in about that order of importance. The activities centered in these areas engross most men of Atlanta from Monday through Saturday of each week.

By day there is a constant roar of traffic over the vast network of freeways lacing the central city to a great rim of superhighways by-passing it some twenty to thirty miles away. This giant system of transportation resulted from work by Atlanta's power structure of the early 1950s on a major community project and was used in Study I as an example of community power. The power structure was involved in both the initial planning stages of the project as well as in its subsequent development. During Study II, Tom Cousins said that the superhighway system has proven its worth a thousand times over or more. It has helped to usher in an unprecedented era of overall growth of the city, especially in the late 1950s and the entire decade of the 1960s. The highway traffic running in, under, over, and around the city symbolizes (along with its recent surge of high-rise buildings) the dynamic, ever-moving quality of the community.

The economic indicators used to illustrate the magnitudes of activity and growth of the city in Study I, indicators stressing rail-car loadings, bus schedules, and building permits, now seem quite dated, old fashioned. Local pride in Atlanta's economic achievement demands growth figures in percentages, especially the figures of the golden years between 1959 and 1970. All progress now seems dated by these years, although a little digging into history would indicate a similar pride in earlier years, a time in which Coca-Cola built its empire, the Georgia Power Company expanded from Atlanta throughout the state, the first high-rise commercial buildings, the Candler, Hurt, Healey, and Haverty buildings, were constructed.

One story regarding those old buildings suggests the personal, small-town character of the community then. One morning, so the story goes, Asa Candler (new Coca-Cola wealth), was seen directing a black man with a mule and plow turning up the earth on a lot he owned near the center of the city, and upon which it was rumored that a new skyscraper would be built. Candler was noted for his frugal ways, and one of his downtown business neighbors had stopped to ask, "What are you doing, Mr. Candler, putting in a corn crop?"

"No," replied Candler, "I'm softening up this ground so that, when they dig the basement for my building, they can go faster."

The activities of two people during the early stages of the 1960–1970 building boom are illustrative—those of Charles (Chuck) Palmer and Ben Massell, both large-scale purchasers of downtown real estate. They stand out as persons who consciously helped to get the boom underway. They were imaginative "movers."

Chuck Palmer early recognized the moribund state of Atlanta's downtown building inventory and the growing need, even before World War II, for office space. Because of growing shortages he decided to renovate run-down downtown office buildings, the Palmer Building being one of the first of his successful ventures.

He also had been successful in bringing one of the first slum-clearance projects to Atlanta during the same period. He had happened to read a phrase in one of the early New Deal recovery laws that allowed for such activities for private interests and proceeded to put a large project together near the Georgia Tech campus. His activities were closely watched and admired by the circle of entrepreneurs of the central city who had learned by Palmer's example that with government help it was quite possible to convert heretofore unprofitable properties into good investments.

No one was more aware of this than one of Palmer's contemporaries, Ben Massell, a member of Atlanta's Jewish community and a quiet and persistent buyer of downtown properties. He was, by 1950, reputed to be the owner of the largest share of such properties of any of his real estate competitors. In some quarters it was said that Ben Massell could win no popularity contests, but his skill at valuable acquisitions in the central city was admired by those who became aware of them.

In spite of the volume of recent building in Atlanta, one must not leave the impression that it leads the nation in this regard. Prior to World War II, Detroit had begun to plan, mainly through the efforts of the power structure there (the "Big Five," four industrial companies and a major department store, plus, in this instance, the backing of the giant local labor unions) to renovate its grimy downtown civic center on a big scale. Pittsburgh's power structure, dominated by the Mellon name and interests, had begun to redo on a massive scale its Golden Triangle. The New York Rockefellers had boldly moved far up on the Manhattan map to place its great cluster of Center buildings, which helped to revitalize many others near it.

Immediately, at the end of World War II, the Rockefeller family also helped put together the land and money to revitalize the slum area now occupied by the United Nations and the properties around it. San Francisco, a conservative and relatively slow-moving city, had begun to talk about its wasted Embarcadero area, its Bay waterfront, and although it had accomplished much, until very recently, it largely was still talking. William Book, of the Indianapolis Chamber of Commerce, was moving all around the United States preaching the gospel of thrifty bargains contained in the whole concept of redevelopment —especially as it contributed to central city development and the aggrandizement of capital structures there. Downtown urban rebuilding was in the air, and urban leaders across the nation began to take notice. Certainly Ben Massell had made ready for Atlanta's forward surge in the 1950s.

Looking at the preview map of one of the early studies for development of the proposed freeway system that was to encircle the city, one of the prominent owners of downtown land is said to have exclaimed, "It's just like the Chicago Loop! Everything inside the circle will be 'chicken salad'! Everything outside, 'chicken shit.' " As it has turned out, a lot outside also has been "chicken salad," almost as delectable as the inside. No matter, the expressed enthusiasm has been proven to be justified for those who have benefited most.

In 1950 Atlanta growth statistics of the Chamber of Commerce prominently featured the volume of railroad activity. By 1970 air traffic was so featured, but construction industries topped all.

Giant, impersonal earth movers grunt and growl over grounds in Atlanta almost daily even now and passing citizens hardly look up. A song popular for a while, "They're digging up Peachtree again" (a main thoroughfare), is all but forgotten. The digging is routine.

For the years indicated, the percentage indicators of change are indeed impressive: population increase, 32 percent; nonagricultural employment, up 61 percent; construction, up 141 percent; retail sales, up 97 percent; bank clearances, up 133 percent; and per capita income, up 80 percent. Even with the percentage rise in income, the average per capita income had climbed only from a little under $2,000 to slightly more than $3,000, and housing, another indicator of personal satisfaction in the economic picture, had an increase in private units of only 8 percent. When these figures are compared with the others, they indicate social problems underlying the roaring boom in central city building. For example, when population has increased 32 percent and housing units only 8 percent, some families are bound to have a struggle finding living accommodations.[1] Or when average income is only a little over $3,000 when the national poverty line had been determined to be just under that figure, there is liable to be restiveness. Technological employment also leaped, but unemployment for the young and the unskilled, particularly among blacks, also presents an uncited and under-discussed problem in the community. Various groups of organized citizens were pounding on the doors of City Hall asking that lands being taken for high-rise buildings be allocated to neighborhood development. City Hall, and those behind it, consistently denied such pleas.

But this is not the point at which one should underscore problems. (I shall later.) The advance in rebuilding downtown was of particular pride to the powers of the city, largely responsible for it, and it visibly indicated a massive surge of activity between Study I and Study II. The point here is to indicate that power is connected not only with cleaning the streets, organizing police activities, and emptying the garbage pails of Atlanta (City Hall activities), but also with the movement of goods and services in and toward the private sector. Indeed, this last far outweighs and continually overshadows the other policy-making processes of the city.

Because of all of the physical activity involved in moving goods and services in the complex system, Atlanta, it is obvious that a social order, or system, must be maintained. Broadly speaking, the maintenance of this order falls in some small measure to the lot of almost every man in the community, but the establishment of major changes in the old order falls to the lot of relatively few. In a city as old and as large as Atlanta, the existing order is the result of a cumulative process. It has been handed down to the present generation by the past. Consequently, the men in power in Atlanta may be said to have inherited its present order. But new times bring new problems, and decisions have to be made concerning changed conditions. Policies have to be formulated and made effective.

The physical community plays a vital part in maintaining the existing order by helping to differentiate men from one another. The men of power and policy decision in Atlanta have definite places in which they are active. Power has its ecology. There are certain places in which men of power make decisions and formulate policies to meet the many changing conditions that confront them. In locating these men of power in a community one finds them, when not at home or at their regular work, dividing their time between their clubs, the hotel luncheon and committee rooms, board rooms, and other private and semi-public meeting places. And the appearance of a man's surroundings is very considerably determined by the kind of work he does, the money he is paid for it, and the status his occupation has in the community.

Because of the great variety of physical activities performed within the city, direction and coordination on a corresponding scale is required. The functionaries of power also are distributed among the population according to the implied need. Since most such services are directed in centralized hierarchical fashion, the directors of urban order, public and private, are located—at least during rush, business hours—downtown. The nature of their daily activities is coordinated with the postulates set out in the preface of this work and may be made explicit in regard to the ordering of affairs in the physical city. One may take the policy question of extended freeway systems as a case in point.

In regard to downtown redevelopment, and especially to the routing of traffic, one study after another had been made for a decade or more, the last of the major ones being the Lochner Plan, prepared about 1945. It laid out an impressive, if very expensive, system of expanding and interconnecting circles of freeways in and around the whole metropolitan complex. Many of the inner-city connections were to be depressed or tunnelled beneath the existing street level, and major connections of the radial spokes to the great circular arcs at some distance from the then-existing outskirts of the city appeared to offer room for an orderly expansion of the whole region. As a matter of fact, it has done just that for the commercial and real estate development of the community, and as we shall demonstrate at the appropriate time, it also expanded the existing power structure to accommodate the new functions of urban building involved. New names in the power complex, Portman and Cousins among many others, were to appear in newly created architectural and developmental roles. The postwar eras of the past—Civil, Spanish-American, and World War I—had witnessed polyglot growth for short periods of time and produced in erratic spurts a jumbled assortment of architectural forms ranging from wedding-cake Victorian to Shriner-Byzantine, or as one put it, "from Missouri Gothic to Oklahoma Renaissance." This has now been succeeded by a massive, sustained era of growth of contemporary box architecture. After viewing it critically, as it appears in one city after another throughout the country, one may be bound to feel that it lacks distinctiveness, if not quality—the quality lacking in all mass-produced products.

As hypothetically demonstrated in Study I, a minuscule number of men in relation to the total population made the basic policy decisions regarding both the planning and execution of the great project of highway expansion.[2] To be sure, there were other coordinate parts to the Lochner Plan, namely airport expansion, rerouting of utility lines, expansion of urban limits to correspond with actual urban growth, and so on, but here for clarity we shall continue with the one major activity of highway planning and construction.

While it is undoubtedly true that the discomfort and waste implied in the traffic problems of the community may have affected nearly everyone adversely, only a handful of men, as law and custom prescribed, were involved in settling the problem. The "custom" to which we refer is that defined in the Preface hypothesis, *Learned, habitual behavior practiced between members of any group* (in this case the Atlanta community) *constitutes a social structure.*[3] In Atlanta, as will be shown especially in the case of the history of elite policy-making groups, the policy-makers are few in number, and generally the underlying population has acquiesced to their decisions regarding actions affecting the whole community.

Aside from periodically and rather mechanically voting for the mayor and a few other elective officials, most citizens of Atlanta have little to do with decisions regarding its physical development. Even official planning groups are influenced by the expressed points of view of a handful of downtown policy-makers, not by the opinions of the whole body politic. The relationships of specific individuals, especially those occupying positions in five or six of the major corporations and City Hall, are in essence a network of roles that are habitually interrelated in their policy-making activities, and thus in our terms, form a "structure."

Ordinary citizens of Atlanta have generally, if somewhat vaguely, assumed that a group, "they," somewhere downtown would, as a matter of course, see to getting those things done downtown that needed to be done. It was rather widely suspected that among the "they" would be representatives of at least the Coca-Cola Company, the Trust Company of Georgia, the Georgia Power Company, the First National Bank, the Chamber of Commerce, Rich's department store, the mayor—a list sometimes expanded more recently to include the fast-moving Citizens and Southern Bank, and a half-dozen other names.

It will be noted that most of these names represent larger economic organizations and corporations serving the community. In our society this phenomenon is taken for granted, that is: by the very nature and size of corporate groups, their leaders will of necessity be concerned with any large-scale developments in community life. These organizations now have dual roles in the scheme of social direction. They perform in two distinct functions of societal affairs, namely, that of *providing the physical means of life*, and *maintaining order in societal life*. While all other institutional groupings in society, e.g., the family, religion, educational sectors, also have coordinate roles to play in the activities of everyday life, none in our time have the predominate position of business and industrial organizations in the dual roles they play in shaping the destinies of the ordinary citizen.

An ordinary citizen, Joe Bloke, assumes as a natural phenomenon the greater powers of the urban scene. The whole is so immense as to be almost meaningless to Joe. "Someone, somewhere," he may muse, "must be in charge." He knows that it is not he, nor does he believe it is any of his friends. He knows that he votes now and again, but he has little if anything to say about another skyscraper going up, nor does he make the vital connection related to that event: that in time he will be required to pay his proportion of its cost!

The social roles of power, like other roles, are awarded to some, not to others. The roles arise, as indicated in our hypotheses, as behavioral guides arising from institutional values: *The individual internalizes the values of institutional belief systems, however imperfectly, and expresses these values by acting out the social roles available to him, e.g., fatherhood or motherhood, citizen, workman, churchman, city councilman, etc.*

The words above, "social roles available to him," are of importance in differentiating power roles as well as other social ones. Many who read only the traditional textbook descriptions of American society are led to believe that power roles are equally and potentially available to every citizen. This supposition is based largely upon the premise that power exists only in the formal institutional loci of power, in city hall, the state capitol buildings, or in federal legally designated locations. All one need do to occupy any one of these sites is to join one of the two major parties, get elected, and be sworn into office. One can then legally perform roles of power, roles admittedly few in number.

But power in American society, according to our definition of it, is based on roles performed in the marketplace, in the counting houses, and in the fabricating plants of the nation as well as in city hall, Congress, and so on. The private sector dictates our national direction as surely, and often more surely, than elected officials through both formal and informal actions. Raising the price of butter may be as effective a reduction of Joe Bloke's income as raising his taxes. Such illustrations are endless. Current news accounts are filled with illustrations of how the private sector bends public officialdom to its will, protestations of dual governance to the contrary. The major difference in governance by the two institutional systems lies in the fact that the private sector governs the nation indirectly, while it lays its hands directly upon the citizen when it is deemed necessary.

In asking ourselves "How can this be?" we may refer to another of our hypotheses: *The various institutional belief and behavioral systems (familial, economic, religious, etc.) occupy varying positions of status from society to society and from epoch to epoch, the economic one being currently ascendant in world technological society.*

During the Middle Ages, for example, the church, the organization based on religious institutional values, was dominant over all other institutions. In our day, the economic institution, made manifest in business and industrial organizations, holds center stage. Most social roles, even absolute, monarchical roles, pale in magnitude before the powers of the leaders of our larger monopolistic corporations. Furthermore, such functionaries *are those who, in addition to their other societal roles, with formal and informal sanctions, carry specific roles in the maintenance of any prescribed differentiated social order.*

The matter may be simply put this way: While hundreds of thousands may leave their homes in Atlanta each day and go downtown, the roles of each in their places of occupation may vary extremely. If one thinks of power as defined by its function, that of *establishing and maintaining given institutional and societal modes of order through patronage and force* (another correlative hypothesis), he might compare and contrast the roles of the patronage decisions available to the president of large corporations in the community, like Coca-Cola, with those available to the mayor of the city, admitted by all to be a man of power. With his aides, the president of the soft drink company conceivably might choose to buy another company if such a move were compatible with profit motives of the parent company. Such a prize might be worth as much as the whole city budget for a five-year period. The proper signature on a Coca-Cola contract would bind the deal, a transaction enforceable in law and granting to the purchaser vast patronage powers which in effect are bound to substantially affect the city of Atlanta and any number of cities and plants outside its sphere. On the other hand, the mayor in his role would never have the possibility of committing the city to such vast expenditure—a new bureau here, an administrative building there, perhaps, but the expenditure of a sum five times the annual budget? Never! Herein is a vast differentiation of powers, a differentiation reflected in deference patterns toward each individual, the lifestyles of each, the retinues behind each, and the roles either may play.

A file clerk or even a middle-management employee of either City Hall or Coca-Cola affects his environment in inverse proportion to his employer. Both are excluded from the living area of their respective employers by the fact of their employment with its rigid financial and social restrictions. Their places of dining downtown differ markedly from those of their employers, their places of recreation have a different quality and price tag, their educations are likely to be inferior, and many other roles in their lives differentiate them from the more socially affluent, the more powerful than they. Neither might ask for a seat at the head table of any civic banquet, a seat assumed to be available by custom to any mayor or corporate president in the community. Line employees have no such options. None would seem to quarrel with these facts. They are taken for granted, assumed as a proper order of social events.

In Study I, considerable attention was paid to the ecology of power: eating space, office appointments, building occupancy, neighborhood areas, clubs, and homes. By many illustrations it was pointed out that: *Power roles, however covert or overt, are always performed with symbolic displays of pomp, ceremony, and ideological cuing (board meetings in posh settings, on private yachts; the testimonial dinner; expressions of pleasure or displeasure during meetings by grimaces, finger tapping, and so forth).*

Study I also demonstrated, along the same lines of display, that size and grandeur made for status differentiation of space. Our hypotheses sum this up as: *Ceremonial centers of power display may range in size and complexity from personal ritual space (a place at the head table, teepee posts, or ceremonial stools, depending upon the society) to plazas, squares, pyramids, holy of holies, and skyscraper executive suites.*

In any of these centers the means of power *are modes of material, money, and symbolic patronage which, at root, are processes of inclusion and exclusion. Such processes of control range in intensity from mild persuasion to financial and bodily coercion, to personal murder, and to the genocide of war.*

I shall not repeat the detailed reasoning which accompanied these items in Study I, but I shall evaluate their durability over the time span between Study I and Study II, nearly a quarter of a century.

A description, therefore, of the physical features that surround the men of power, such as their offices, industrial plants, or commercial establishments, as well as their clubs, homes, and other personal living quarters, seems quite pertinent. Men are ranked and classified by other men, in some degree, by the physical elements around them. An office with soft carpeting, wood-paneled walls, and rich draperies immediately suggests that the man occupying it is more influential than the man who walks on composition concrete floors and looks at plasterboard walls each day, and whose only window decoration is a pull-down shade. Such physical characteristics may give accurate pictures of power.

While the general physical facts of location still remain true, air conditioning is no longer the status symbol it once was, and many offices of hundreds of minor public and private officials on the surface look very much like the more plush offices of a decade or two ago. Synthetic material now readily available at little relative cost gives the appearance of hardwoods and brocades, perhaps a little telltale shiny, but neat in their presentation.

The present status symbol very hard to beat is that of being able to sit in the executive suite of your own private skyscraper and look out upon the panorama of the busy city and the vast greenbelt around it!

Earlier, besides special parking and other transportation privileges, two of the men of finance portrayed in Study I had private elevators that carried them directly to their offices, making a trip through their outer offices unnecessary. The pattern more generally now is that of the use of an express elevator to the executive suite floors of one's skyscraper. Status is measured by the number of the floor upon which one spends his days, or whether or not he eats in the executive dining room. Rugs on one's floors still separate the influentials from the rank and file.

Even in the vast terraced and multistoried expansion of the local branch of the University of Georgia system, one of the city's major projects of the 1950s and 1960s, professorial offices and subadministrative offices remain small, sterile cubicles of operation, neat and plastic but very compact and often overcrowded.

Welfare and other social management officers (income up some two or three times over the 1950 level) still live out their professional lives in beige, green, or blue painted (practical colors which do not show dirt) warrens in second- or third-rate buildings hugging the center of town. As mentioned previously, a building containing famous civil rights offices in the black community has so many crowded basement offices that it looked both unsafe and unsanitary to me. One who operated in such quarters, Andrew Young, occupied (at the time this was written) more elegant space in the United Nations

Building, a fact attesting to his meteoric rise and partially symbolizing the very rapid change in political relations both within and beyond the city of Atlanta in a very few intervening years.

Yet, in spite of better times and the upward thrust of so many skyscrapers, wallboard paneling is still common in many other underprofessionals' offices. The buildings in which they conduct their work are also third rate, if they are judged on a rough-and-ready scale of values. One professional office, housing some of the community's social service agencies (now located in lower-rental buildings), could only be entered by a freight elevator that formerly served a warehouse. The location is now that of a new office building for business.

Meetings in Atlanta are still generally held in the downtown hotels and super-motels, in boardrooms, private business auditoriums, several civic centers, in private clubs, or in fraternal halls. The "top flight" meetings—those of a high policy nature—are held in the private clubs' business rooms or in private homes. The club meetings are famous in Atlanta, and the leaders of the community were often referred to as "that Capital City crowd," this organization being, in 1950, one of the exclusive clubs in the community and a place where many decisions affecting the future course of events took root.

By the 1960s the Capital City Club had lost some of its exclusiveness. Its membership had a high proportion of the "gerontocracy," those top business leaders who had retired, staying perhaps on a number of overlapping financial and industrial boards as honorary stations, and using the old club as a luncheon spot to visit with old cronies. Current power structures usually consider a man retired as one who has lost much of his clout. If he has been a hired manager of any one of the corporations, he has lost much of the patronage power he once may have had. Those who still own a major portion of their company's capital, for example, R. W. Woodruff or Richard Courts, may continue to earn respect from any power structure of the moment. These kinds of men—Woodruff, who had retained power over the financial committee of Coca-Cola, and Courts, who has sold a thriving investment company to a New York house and who had reinvested his gains in one of the famous older buildings of the town —are cases in point.

The majority of comers, climbers, and strivers of the power structure, however, had joined Mills Lane, president of his family bank, the Citizens and Southern system, and had formed a new club, the Commerce Club, nearer downtown. This club, with some thirty or forty charter members, the roster of which read like a listing of the 1960s power structure, immediately became one of the new "in" places to eat and do business. The older Capital City Club still has a devoted clientele, but its rooms appeared to be a little shopworn, and the vast renovation of its portion of downtown has left its architecturally dated building standing isolated and alone, surrounded by a number of parking lots which are waiting for new building development when times for additional building may be propitious. Changing power structures may periodically, in keeping with the times, change their architectural skins.

Private homes also still serve as places where decisions of considerable consequence are reached. When asked about his social contacts, in Study I, one leader stated that he had no purely social contacts, that all his contacts related to business. Generally, he had people with whom he wanted to do business visit his home, whether that business concerned him or the community at large. Homes were mentioned by others as being important places of contact for informal decisions.

One of R. W. Woodruff's attorneys, Hughes Spalding, Sr., told me that Woodruff would often call him and perhaps one or two others late at night and ask them to come over and help him think through some proposition that was depriving him of sleep. He indicated that Bob, as he called Woodruff, usually had something of importance on his mind and thus no one grumbled about late hours.

The results of one such meeting were related to me by Federal Circuit Judge Elbert Tuttle. Prior to his appointment to his federal post in the Atlanta district, Elbert Tuttle had fulfilled the expectations of many in several important roles: high-ranking officer in World War II (he once told me that he had seen such a waste of brave young lives that he decided, if he came out alive, to try to do something for his community and nation), successful attorney for corporate groups in Atlanta, a member of the 1950 power structure, and leading Republican among business groups favoring that party.

He told me that one evening he had a call from a friend of his, Bobby Jones [the famous golfer], who said that a good friend of his (whom Tuttle was supposed to know by reputation) was standing beside him and wanted to talk to Tuttle about an important job that needed to be filled in Atlanta. Jones said that after his friend talked to Tuttle, he'd put another man on the line to help clinch his arguments.

The next voice identified himself as Bob Woodruff [whom Tuttle had met but did not know well]. He said that he was calling to ask Tuttle to consider, with the "go signal" from the president [Eisenhower], a federal judgeship. He continued for a minute or two, speaking of the importance of the job at that time, then he said that he would like to assure Tuttle that the place was ready and waiting for him. The next voice identified itself as that of the Secretary of the Treasury, George M. Humphrey, who outlined how the appointment would come about. Tuttle would take a job in the Treasury department, which would embody him with a "political patina," and after a time he would be moved to the Federal bench.

Tuttle told me that he asked for time. The job, especially in the Treasury, would not have paid him enough to retire as he had anticipated, and he said as much, but was immediately assured that money should not stand in the way of his decision. He was told to think it over and make his decision within a very short time. He decided soon that the post had so many possibilities for civic action that he took it. He told me that he has never regretted it, but that was the way it had happened.[4]

For any who may cling to the notion that there is no overlap of policy-making between government and the private sector, please note! One could continue such a recitation, but in these post-Watergate days the newspapers are filled, day by day, week in and week out with such accounts of policy exchange, public and private.

Woodruff's current successor, J. Paul Austin, was once quoted as saying that he did not intend to try to be another Bob Woodruff and become too deeply involved in Atlanta affairs, yet, he and three or four of his upper-drawer townsmen of the current power structure for many months, during the touchy period of civil rights disturbances, met regularly with top leaders of the black power structure in each other's homes, homes still separated by considerable geographical and social distance.

The hotels continue to cater to the Chamber of Commerce type of large, "community-wide" meetings. Many leaders may be involved in the endless luncheons that go on in the hotels. One leader described the men who attend the hotel meetings regularly, whether they be the like of Rotary, Kiwanis, or privately sponsored gatherings, as men who belong to the "luncheon circuit." It is common knowledge that the same men are seen over and over again in the same places. This frequency of contact makes for community solidarity among the leaders, a solidarity which springs partially out of carefully selected meeting locations. Places tend to center activities. Luncheons and meetings differ in their fundamental purposes, and those devoted to policy matters are usually held in the places already described.[5]

Professor William Domhoff, with his interest in interlocking elite memberships in clubs, boards, "old school tie" associations, clearly shows that the basic policies that guided the New Haven committees of redevelopment were formulated, among other places, at the local, prestigious Quinnipiac and Lawn Clubs, and attended by local, interlocking economic and political notables, some of them of the "old school tie."[6] To be sure, the New Haven mayor was in attendance at these meetings helping to formulate policy that at least was administered through daily decisions made in the subordinate redevelopment committees of that city.

Professional and other groups still tend to hold their meetings in establishments less pretentious in appearance and serving relatively inexpensive meals. However, one set of community professionals, those with expense accounts or with the larger salaries among others, may be an exception. A few of the associations of immediate use to the general power structure may be peopled with personnel well able to afford luncheons at any of the prestigious hotel dining rooms. Upper-echelon Chamber of Commerce executives, the director of the Downtown Improvement Association, and a group recently established to analyze census figures and other statistical data are examples. The latter group came into being partly because the businessmen have long been at odds with the Community Welfare Council (under whatever names over the years); consequently, through the United Fund organization which supports the council, the traditional function of analyzing demographic data was taken away from them and put with the newer association, which resides in one of the new insurance skyscrapers. The location is closer to the other skyscraper dwellers who use the figures and is a pleasanter place to visit than the cramped, rundown headquarters of the Community Welfare Council.

While the development of downtown Atlanta is almost unbelievably impressive, and the outer suburban areas look like middle America everywhere, from tract housing to rolling one-acre carefully attended suburban plots, one is bound to say that little has happened to the huge spaces occupied by the ordinary population in between. These remain areas characterized by progressive deterioration bordered by pockets of social desolation.[7]

Some persons of liberal persuasion took me on an extended tour of the city briefly after my first arrival to restudy it, and they stressed over and over the vast differences between the city of 1950 and the city of today. I was driven through a very large area of one-acre and half-acre plots upon which some very fine homes for black people had been developed. The fact that blacks had been able to gain political offices at all levels of government was stressed. The magnificent achievements of central city development were lauded and unfolded.

The fact that the power structure of 1970 had failed to upset the election of Samuel Massell as mayor was hailed by at least those in general opposition to it as the "demise of the power structure of Atlanta." Mayor Massell, for his part, knew that the power structure, of which he was a part, was still quite alive. He quickly extended an olive branch to those who had opposed him and thereafter continued to curry its favor during his brief administration.

William Miller, a young attorney who had been keeping his own tally of the city's power structure, took a great deal of time in helping me visit various areas of the city. Two reform groups invited me to speak to their members, and I was invited to the homes of some of those in "loyal opposition" to the power structure. Julian Bond also invited me to his home for an afternoon with a number of his supporters. Later, I spent a day with him and others in the Georgia legislature. I also walked alone through several of the city's neighborhoods and revisited some of the nearby communities in the line of urban expansion and talked with a few of those who had not yet been swallowed up in the local land boom.

With all of this, and in spite of the charm and "good housekeeping" correctness of the developing black areas, I still was aware of the many areas of the city peopled with blacks and whites who had not moved forward in the great city but had seemed to have moved backward, or who at best, like the labor officials of two decades ago, had managed to barely tread water. I was more convinced than ever that many middle-class critics of the systematic failures of power are also easily led to positions of rationalizing inevitable progress. Many of their associations are dependent upon money furnished to them by fund drives among the affluent, or at the beggars' windows of their charitable foundations. It is easier to catch flies with sugar, many feel, than with vinegar.

A new comparison was made of living areas occupied by professionals and power leaders. It leads one to the old French adage: "The more things change, the more they stay the same!" Great gulfs of territories still divide predominantly black and white areas. The leaders in either case live in the same areas they cohabited with the more congenial of their followers in 1950. The basis for their harmony is not necessarily their closeness in rank of power. It is the psychological similarity of class attitudes that makes them comfortable together. Any given status factor, such as residence, remains merely one functional variable of power, and not necessarily a decisive one.

The one professional nominee of power rank (1950) in the Buckhead area (north on Peachtree Street, an elite area in 1950 and 1970) had been joined by two others by 1970, certainly not an avalanche of movement. The 1950 professional was an educator admired by his neighbors. The 1970 additions are from associations favored by the powerful. These new residents, like many other persons of lesser power, have their homes in a historically exclusive area, but there are signs that the overcrowdedness of nearby commercial facilities and the encroachment of other newcomers who are inflating local land values will ultimately cause the larger estates to be broken up. One couple, old-timers there, indicated that they were becoming too exposed and did not feel safe anymore. There were considering buying into a condominium of more congenial people, one that would have built-in police protection, gates and so on. They also indicated that they have a number of their art works under lock and key elsewhere. Local rioting downtown in the 1960s had badly frightened them.

Office space in the unions and in their council headquarters had continued to hold their own in their historical physical transformation toward improved working space outlined in Study I.

The newer breed of union leader in mid-1970, like many professionals downtown, wore sports coats or jackets and had long sideburns and slightly longer hair than they had worn a decade before. As before, they spoke of advances, this time in terms of organizing the chicken industry in Alabama. And as before, they knew some of the top leaders downtown merely by name as persons who guided the policies of their professional negotiators and labor attorneys.

Labor relations have been very largely institutionalized by law and custom on either side of any given conflict. Southern unions still have to fight for what they get, but they do so battle by battle. The war declared in the 1940s has long since been abandoned as a strategy. The rank and file are satisfied with modest wage gains and periodic changes in one or another of badly aligned working conditions. Their social philosophy is well summed up by the current clichés of big business.

Some of the older areas of traditionally middle-class housing had begun to show signs of the blight of age and lack of systematic repair. One could see the slow evaporation of a lifetime of savings of many families. With inflation eating up savings, a form of dispossession accelerates. In contrast to 1950, modern, multiple apartments and condominiums of modest price have begun to dot the area.

The financial interests, who make plans for the people, including plans for their housing, and who themselves live in well-trimmed, broad acres on the outer limits of the city, are beginning to say that the trend to multiple housing for the average family is inevitable.

The future of those so patronized indeed looks bleak if the present is any indication.

As before suggested, the black population of Atlanta still remains largely segregated. It still tends to fan out in an east-west axis from the central city, the west and southwest perimeters being areas of more affluent living facilities. The leaders of the black community have been joined by many hundreds of their relatively better-off contemporaries into the choice segregated neighborhoods, neighborhoods in which the mortgage-debt, credit-card syndrome helped to make them feel that they have entered the mainstream of the American system. Some of them now live in quiet terror, as do so many of their white counterparts, that these privileges of credit might be shorn from them by some term of misfortune. At least the old stereotypes of blacks have surely disappeared from these neighborhoods.

One or two of the black construction companies have profited handsomely in the changing course of housing patterns, but the core of unrehabilitated properties still attests to the differences between affluence and poverty in community life, more so in the black community than in the white. The circular problems—poverty, ill health, unemployment, and crime—will not go away in some neighborhoods regardless of how the facts about them may be glossed over as minor sags in an era of unprecedented improvement.

With the exception of the new bank building and two or three smaller ones, the office buildings along Auburn Avenue, in spite of a decade of discussion about rebuilding the area, remain relatively inferior in construction and design. Most of the buildings are apparently twenty-five to thirty years old. They are drab in appearance and poorly maintained. Space in all of the black offices seems to be at a premium, and even in the newer buildings the private offices of the power leaders are cubicles compared with the offices of some of the leaders in the larger community. Meeting places for blacks, with the possible exception of facilities in local black colleges, tend to be as colorless as the meeting places of the majority of professional, civic, and social personnel in the larger community.

The Butler Street YMCA, long a general meeting place for political gatherings of any size, has an enlarged auditorium, but it cannot compare with any of the central city facilities. It is still relatively small and isolated. To be sure, it is still packed on occasion. Jimmy Carter was running for the office of governor during my first return visit to the community, and he spoke, seemingly comfortably, to an overflow crowd of black people and white liberals regarding the concerns for black welfare, a happening that could not have occurred in 1950.

One has the feeling, however, that Auburn Avenue, around the corner from the YMCA and a main street for blacks, is living on borrowed time, that it may never experience the renaissance some of its leaders envision. Viewed objectively, it appears redundant. Some black leaders now are openly recognized by the central city power structure and are for all practical purposes a part of it, as I will point out in some detail in a discussion of black politics. Also, as previously mentioned, Auburn Avenue was cut off from a major portion of its hinterland by freeway construction in spite of earlier successes of black leaders to keep the freeway from running down the middle of Auburn Avenue. Removing the freeway construction two or three blocks away did not make that much difference. The freeway itself is used by blacks, who now shop uninhibitedly at any one of the scores of huge shopping centers at the freeway interchanges.

Many of these, probably a majority, would never return their patronage to Auburn Avenue even if it were renovated. Its era as a center of community life for its sector of the community is probably past. It could contain a number of new buildings, to be sure, that would vastly aid the appearance of the area, but those buildings undoubtedly will reflect any number of changes in the objective movements of Atlanta's black and white populations. The prevailing tendency, at the moment, in spite of some setbacks and unevenness of progress, continues to be toward greater integration of the races in Atlanta.

As more black leaders move into the general power structure of greater Atlanta, such leaders will reinforce status distance between themselves and their black, as well as white, compatriots, just as their home locations now give them exclusiveness in relation to the mass of black residents. The leadership has opted to run the course with the system, abjuring separatism, the separatism that Auburn Avenue historically has represented in the community as a whole.

It was stated in Study I that a significant result of the various locations of Atlanta's top leaders lay in their isolation from the problems of the average citizen. This remains true. They daily shuttle by automobile between their homes, their work, and their meeting places. The streets over which they travel pass through many blighted areas, but the sights of poverty are hidden from view along most of the routes by a crush of new cars and the sterile monotony of freeway shrubbery.

One other spatial feature of Atlanta that was appraised in Study I must be mentioned. The city spreads over a large area. It remains a metropolitan community. Its growth has pushed its natural bounds

into large portions of contiguous outlying counties. The city boundaries have never caught up with the ever-widening population distribution of the metropolis. As population has moved into the outlying
areas, city services such as water supply, gas supply, fire and police
protection, and road construction and maintenance were demanded
of the local units of government. The city charter did not allow the
city government to go beyond its corporate limits in providing such
services, and consequently the county government was called upon
to take on functions that are normally considered within the jurisdic-
tion of a city.

Because of the present voting power of blacks surrounding the
central city, unified regional government, the long-term goal of the
power structure, seems further from reality today than it did in 1950.

Although many questions had been asked about social conditions and political inequalities in the policy-making process during
the insurgency over civil rights, public debate on the matter was kept
very largely in the arena of voting rights. When it showed signs of
moving into more relevant matters, such as economic inequality, the
whole matter was taken care of by ridding the movement of its top
leadership, moving the so-called debate to the back pages of the
press, and picking up policy items such as those related to homo-
sexuals and their life-styles, women's lagging rights, and in Atlanta,
whether or not Martin Luther King, Jr.'s portrait should be hung in
the halls of the legislature. He had not, of course, ever been elected to
the legislature, and the debate therefore had some grounds, even if
slight ones.

Problems of the environment, important problems, did make
headlines, however, and were quickly acted upon, and almost as
quickly ignored. As Andrew Young has so rightly said, "Nothing is
illegal if one hundred businessmen decide to do it."[8]

Few critical questions have been raised in recent years regarding
the burgeoning computer-controlled technology and communications
networks that are making obsolete so many forms of social life,
including the cities from which information pours forth. In spite of
the cancerous wounds at the core of most cities, and the quiet revul-
sion of their people, the policy-makers choose to pretend they hear or
see nothing amiss. Marshall McLuhan's "global village"[9] would seem
to be their reality with their grandiose dreams of wall-to-wall cities
stretched along highways from coast to coast, gobbling up fertile
lands and fragile desert lands. This reality exists so that the energy
charts and financial charts of the policy-makers may continue to spurt
beyond the ceilings of corporate board rooms.

These same policy-makers might at some time choose to use their latest tool, the computer, to address more fundamental problems rather than to further enrich those who are already overcapitalized. One can only speculate about this. No one indicated in my interviews that such a golden age had dawned upon my interviewees' consciousnesses, but it has of course dawned upon those of others, and is being held back. Presumably the technology has been developed to bring a reverse to either ignorance or perversity in such matters.

The concern here has been with the physical structure of the community studied. It is obviously impossible to speak about structure without becoming concerned with social organization and action. In describing the physical structure of Atlanta in some of its aspects related to power personnel, one notes movement. Men move over highways to and from their homes. They attend meetings. They talk about one another. The community is a thing of perpetual motion and change, but as often as not it may change physically while social relationships within it remain relatively fixed.

Atlanta's Historically Powerful Families

Having found early in my fieldwork for Study II a continuity between family members as well as indications of carry-overs of the names of power leaders from one decade to another, the question arose, "Do these same names go back into Atlanta's more distant past?" and "Do major institutional organizations or corporations aid in moving names from epoch to epoch as well as from decade to decade?"

Either too much power appears to be attributed to the favored names in social history, the Astors, Rockefellers, and so on, or such history may become a lament over the notion that the fine old families are losing their grip, going to seed. They can no longer elect Junior to the city council!

I do not place too much credence in any theories of charisma, including the aura of historical worth and respect due those whose forebears may have got to our shores early, or who may have lived in the community, say, three or four generations. I come from a part of the country, Kentucky, where perhaps a majority of families in some of the eastern counties of the state may have been in residence for the prescribed number of generations to be called venerable, but the press generally refers to them as hillbillies or mountaineers. Most of them do not even have tombstones recording their generations. It has been my repeated observation that unless a family has accumulated capital, its deeds are seldom recorded. Even members of families who may earn considerable fame, unless that fame is transformed into goods and chattels, transferable generation to generation, memories become frail about just what it was that had been done in the first place. Scrapbooks bolster a few egos in such instances and bore the importuned listener.

Yet, if any family saves a bit, and "acts right," it has a leg up, so to speak, in the power escalator. It may in a few instances be on the way to becoming a part of America's ensconced, corporate money aristocracy.

All history records the activities of elites. The history of Atlanta is no exception. The major function of history, in terms of social power, is to bolster processes of inclusion and exclusion, to stress ingroup/outgroup values, and to bolster current policy-making stances. One of such stances is framed by the contemporary phrase, "We now live in a mature economy," meaning that no change is necessary, desirable, or even possible. There is a synchromesh of elite names in current power structures, as we shall see, with those of the past.

A substantial proportion of the names in the current structure of power in Atlanta have persisted historically year by year, decade by decade, or, as we shall see, in a few cases from one epoch to another. As may be observed at the national level of civil life, where a core of people make up a family/corporate/money aristocracy very much taken for granted in our society—Astors, Byrds, Cabots, Crockers, Dodges, Dollars, Duponts, Harrimans, McCormicks, Rockefellers, Stephensons, Tafts, Vanderbilts, Whitneys, and so on to a few hundred names—local counterparts of such families everywhere are blurred over in the rhetoric that recounts their aristocratic ways in the day-to-day governance of the republic or any given community. Such people are presumed, in any case, to be above the ordinary scramble for place and position. They have ascribed status in contrast to those who may have achieved status, a relatively lower order to the same social value. They are, on the whole, a nonstriving, assumptive class of people, whom I prefer to call the ownership establishment—the patrons—in contrast to the power structures' strivers.

Some, whose forebears may have achieved fame and fortune for them, may be content merely to enjoy their established positions, make those policy decisions in community life that aid in holding their goods and reputations free from harm so that they may live quietly and enjoy the fruits of labors of others as well as their own. Only their bankers and best friends may know their monetary worth. Such leisure-class characters are scarcely visible in American life in which "hustle" is the word. Even those who disappear in the sameness of suburbia busy themselves with pretense occupations, often claiming early retirement and chairing first the rose jamboree and then the Elm Grove music festival before vacationing for the winter in Aqua Azure Bay. Some of these, less content with doing little, may hold honorific legal, medical, or even business titles and positions that enable them to move about among community doers with ease, or dabble in this or that as they may choose. Some of these bitten with the bug of power may act as officiously as strivers and achievers. In any case, they remain a model of emulation in American society for the strivers, who hope that one day they or their sons may be so endowed, that is, have the ultimate freedom of doing or not doing, as they choose.

A large proportion of any power structure, however, remains strivers. Through a restless urge for more money and position, so often available to them, they chop away at the day-to-day problems of power and often seem as pleased as children when the knick-knacks and plaques of community honor fall to them.

Because of the often-repeated notion that families of power weaken and fade out, I wished to make some test of this matter in Atlanta and began my quest for information, not as a historian, but first of all as a collector of oral history. I called Robert (Trot) FOREMAN,* whom I had known a number of years before, and told him I would like to go over some points of history with him, especially as it might relate to current and past power structures of Atlanta. Trot, a retired insurance broker, met me for lunch and talked in an amused but interested way. His mother, incidentally, was a HOWELL and was related to the GRADYS of post–Civil War newspaper fame; both families had accumulated and kept enough goods and chattels to still be well spoken of in the community. Trot denied being much of a history buff, but he talked easily about it while retaining his amateur standing. He put me on the track of several other history buffs in town, who were also very helpful. One of them was Franklin Garrett, with whom I had corresponded and who pulled together everything he could find on Atlanta's elites in 1954; Garrett is the author of a comprehensive history of Atlanta.[1] I was also told that an account of 1960–1970 called "Amazing Atlanta" had been published by the Atlanta *Journal and Constitution* in 1970, which might be helpful.[2] For my purposes, both publications were indeed.

All I wished to do in this phase of study was either to interview local historians or scan local historical summaries, with a list of 1970 power structure figures in hand, and see whether they or their forebears appeared. I had no intention of rewriting local or state history, whether the exploits described be the conquests of Sherman or the views of Henry GRADY on the New South (which I had always considered merely a continuation of the old one, changing as the national moods and technology changed). This chapter is a record of that

*In this chapter historical names will be carried in small capitals to differentiate them. Also so designated will be any who have occupied a place in power structures for two or more decades.

scanning process. It does show, I believe, that contrary to prevailing belief in some quarters, a number of families survive and participate in two or more decades of continuing power structures; some of them have survived since the middle 1800s, when the city was founded.

From the available sample of historical Atlanta names (white and black), those that also appear in at least two of the power structures between 1950, 1960, and 1970 include: ADAIR, ALEXANDER, ALLEN, ALSTON, BORDERS, CANDLER, DOBBS (one black; one white), GRANT, HAVERTY, HEALEY, HERNDON, HOWELL, HURT, INMAN, JONES, KING, LANE, LANIER, MASSELL, MAYS, MILTON, POST, RICH, ROBINSON, SCOTT, SMITH, SIBLEY, SPALDING, TROUTMAN, WALDEN, and WOODRUFF.[3]

The chronological emergence of these names in history reminds one of the episodic depiction of action in many oriental scrolls. Between episodes, space indicates passages of time as well as space itself. In scenes of furious action, men on foot and horseback rush pell-mell into and over each other to storm a palace raging with battle, smoke, and fire, while in the foreground a peasant may be concerned only with making his ox go; yet a few inches away, scholars might be taking tea, tailors making clothing. One may be reminded of merchants waiting on the fringes of Atlanta for the smoke of the Civil War to clear so that they might enter the city for trade. From time to time the same faces reappear, or the same names do.

I shall merely excerpt bits of history relevant to present leaders. Blacks and whites are included in the historical list. Some of the blacks and a few whites of Atlanta are aware of white-black liaisons of earlier days, from which the blood of those generations flows in the veins of the living, leaders and nonleaders alike. This factor is not generally recorded in southern history. Haley's *Roots* may set a new trend.[4]

Before a clearing, 1820, a white man, a transient, watched some Indian squaws till nearby corn-patches slashed out of surrounding forest growth. It now seems strange to think that the footpath trod by them wended along a way now known as Alabama Street, today a wide, well-paved downtown thoroughfare.

To the southwest, at Columbus, Georgia, about 1828, George Waldo WOODRUFF, father of one of the owners-to-be of the famous COCA-COLA Company, built a grist mill on the Chattahoochee River and invested in numerous other enterprises; he died a millionaire at the age of ninety-one.

Five years later, 1833, Hardy Ivy arrived, the first permanent white settler of the Atlanta area. Upon 160 acres of land leased from the government (early establishing the practice of give-and-take between public and private enterprise), Ivy erected a log cabin. Around him lay a vast wilderness, occupied only by the earlier settlers who lived on the game and fish of the region, and by tribes of Creeks and Cherokees, tribes already begun to be decimated by hunters, trappers, and other frontier adventurers.

Little else is known of Ivy. Evidently he did not make much money. A secondary street leading into the central city bears his name. The spot upon which he built his cabin is now covered by one of the administrative buildings of SOUTHERN BELL TELEPHONE Company, which did make a lot of money. The grave of this earliest settler is covered with the asphalt of a parking lot nearby.

By 1850 the original seven families who had populated the settlement town of Terminus, later Marthasville and finally Atlanta, had expanded to a community of in-migrants numbering 2,500. By the time of the Civil War, 1861, this number had quadrupled to 10,000.[5]

Leading citizens at mid-nineteenth century, elated by urban growth and feeling that they had been too hasty in the selection of the rather pedestrian name "Marthasville," began to cast about for a more suitable one. Richard PETERS, among them, heartily agreed. He thought the name "Marthasville" was too long and advocated something snappy and suggestive of a progressive community.

The man of the hour to come up with a name turned out to be J. Edgar Thomson, chief engineer of the Georgia Railroad, who wrote to PETERS, "Eureka—Atlanta, the terminus of the Western and Atlantic Railroad—Atlantic, masculine, Atlanta, feminine—a coined word, but if you think it will suit, adopt it."[6]

Other railroaders of the time, besides the ADAIR and PETERS families, who undoubtedly approved the new name were the ORMES and GRANTS; they also have extended their early railroad money into affluence and influence in community affairs.

Another family name, HOWELL, also began to emerge at this time, its fortunes ultimately long bound up with the famous daily newspaper, the Atlanta *Constitution*, a post–Civil War publication that had the name Henry GRADY at its masthead for many years. In the minutes of the meeting at the Atlanta City Council of April 1852 one reads: "Clark HOWELL resigned from the Council, as he removed from the city."[7]

Councilman HOWELL did not go far. The city finally grew out to the place where he settled and where he continued to be a power in Atlanta. He established residence upon newly acquired land on

Peachtree Creek and erected a grist and saw mill upon it. The place, besides serving its normal, utilitarian first purposes, was to become and remains a famous place-name, HOWELL Mill Road, a fine address in the exclusive Buckhead region. At the time of his death Clark HOWELL I owned some four thousand acres of this increasingly valuable land. In 1921 Howell was to complete one of the earlier high-rise buildings of the community, the building of a six-story building at Broad, Luckie, and Forsyth streets.

George Washington ADAIR practiced law for two years, then restlessly moved to the operation of a mercantile store for two more years. By 1859, committed to the Confederate cause, he established a newspaper, the *Southern Confederacy*, to publish Southern sentiment.

Upon returning to Atlanta after serving in the Confederate army as colonel on the staff of General Nathan Bedford Forrest, ADAIR found his house destroyed and his fortune greatly diminished. After a brief return to the practice of law, he entered and stayed in the real estate business, where he founded another fortune upon the remains of his earlier fortune. The family has remained in the business up to the present.

On the second night of the Battle of Chickamauga, Clark HOWELL II was born, 1863. His mother had fled Atlanta, fearing General Sherman's advance marauders. Soon after, feeling reassured by the general's slow progress, she returned to the home of her father-in-law, Judge HOWELL, on the Chattahoochee River, only to have to flee again farther south to Sandersville, where she and her infant son remained until the end of the war. The HOWELL home on the Chattahoochee from which she again had fled was the first to be burned as Sherman advanced toward the city. Former city councilman Clark HOWELL had by now become Judge HOWELL.[8]

While it is probable that briefly during Sherman's march to the sea, Atlanta may have remained that "pure military garrison" he had commanded that it be, subsequent history tells us that its citizens did not take long in returning to the city, nor were they averse to welcoming covertly the forces of trade and commerce that no military order could hold in abeyance. The legend goes that even before General Sherman's torches had cooled, the post–Civil War version of the Chamber of Commerce was back in town proclaiming that "things could be worse." Social reality, including the favorable items, a kindly climate, a key rail location, and a grim determination on the part of many to rebuild the city, combined to give it a head start back to a greater prosperity than it had ever known. Traders and rebuilders, along with notorious carpetbaggers, swarmed into the city to enrich themselves and to help Atlanta again rise as the Gate City of the South. Ever since, a phoenix rising from ash and flames has been the official city symbol.

Two families stand out among those who came soon after the war, those of Morris RICH and Julius M. ALEXANDER, each connected with the commercial growth of the city.

Morris RICH, beginning in 1867 in a rough-hewn building, established a department store which by 1973 was to be doing some $180 million worth of business. It takes but three names within the RICH company to span more than a century of growth: Morris RICH, the founder who died in 1928, was succeeded by his heir to the business, his nephew, Walter RICH, who died in 1947. For two years Frank Neely became the store's third president. Richard RICH took over the management of the business in 1949. He remained active in the business until his death in 1975.[9]

Richard RICH, at age seventy-four at the time of my last interview with him, 1973, still retained control of the important finance policy committee of his corporation. He had been active throughout his business career in major community developments, having been a key figure in the Plan of Development, a major project before the community during Study I, and during the early part of the present study he was chairman of a commission devoted to developing a rapid transit system for the metropolitan area. He will be spoken of again with particular reference to his policy-making roles over a number of years.

The other merchant of historical note, Julius M. ALEXANDER, founded in 1865 a hardware business that eventually provided a fortune from which a number of other family businesses sprang, all of them related to steel and other construction supplies. In Atlanta's present power structure, an heir to the founder's enterprise is the successful architect Cecil ALEXANDER, Jr.; his father had carried on and expanded the family business enterprises. As well as being renowned members of the larger community, both the RICH and ALEXANDER families are respected members of the local Jewish community.

Among other families named in the present Atlanta power structure, those who can trace their ancestry back to figures of power and influence in the immediate post-Civil War period include ADAIR, ALEXANDER, DOBBS, HIRSCH, RICH, SPALDING, SIBLEY, and ROBINSON. These were to be followed in a decade or two, 1875 to 1890, by the names of ALLEN, CAMPBELL, CANDLER, GLENN, HAVERTY, HEALEY, HURT, INMAN, JONES, MADDOX, and MASSELL.

These names in each generation since the Civil War have represented family principals busily engaged in either new or older expanding businesses and professions: law, banking, commercial enterprise, industrial development, real estate, and insurance—in brief, the technology of any given period. Older names are joined in each generation by a few new people, who reinforce the American dream of making it big. One begins to see in all of this an emergence of elites who, at least for some time, tend to remain elite. To be sure, some few of the "old money" people, generation by generation, unless the line may end, withdraw into lives devoted to arts, literature, or plain leisure-class functioning. They may no longer contend in the marketplace for power and position. Their positions, again, are ascribed, but they remain few in number in working America, and some of those seeming inactive for a generation or two, as in the case of the WOODRUFFS, suddenly may become active again. As a matter of fact, the ADAIRS in the 1950s (because of temporary business conditions) were judged to be "second-raters" in the power scheme, but with the onset of much urban building in the community in the 1960s the family name, through Jack ADAIR, jumped again to a "first-place" rating.

The nostalgic sentiment so long embedded in the literature of post–Civil War history of the South arose from distortions regarding a way of life that probably never actually existed at any place at any time. Plantation life, in spite of a few beautiful manifestations of architecture looking backward to classical design, was on the whole a hot, earth-grubbing, bitter struggle for all concerned. More sweat and tears were involved than all the sentimental writing of Margaret Mitchell can ever erase. Blacks were often more courageous and heroic than any knew. They have had to write their own history.

Professor Dwight Billings in a concurrent, independent study of Southern leaders has come to view Southern history generally as elite control contained within the South. The ruin of the Southern planter and the subsequent rise of a wholly new set of dominants remains largely myth.[10]

One begins to sense rhythmical periods of growth related to the national extension of technology. The WOODRUFF family is a good case in point: When George Waldo WOODRUFF came to Georgia from the central Atlantic states, he evidently brought with him either money or the ability to raise money. He soon established two of the technological necessities of his day, a saw mill and a grist mill. His less affluent neighbors were obliged to trade with him and during the next half-century made him rich. Some of his fortune (late 1800s) was invested, according to my informants, in the rising industry, cotton spinning, near the outskirts of Atlanta. Later investments at the turn of the century included shares in the developing electrification of Atlanta, electric lines, and transit systems, technological improvements burgeoning at the close of last century. At last, in the 1920s the steadily increasing family fortune found a most lucrative mark, COCA-COLA, where it has assumed astronomical proportions. Other family fortunes have followed almost identically this technological route, some of them centering at last in banking, real estate, or manufacture. The suggestion here, contrary to many who lament that the old families are dying out and a new breed is taking over, is that many of them have lasted, at least in Atlanta, for a number of generations and have indeed been quite active in one power structure after another. While any group of the institutional power structures may have to move over in any given generation to make room for aggressive newcomers like Portman, Cousins, or Russell, they do not move very far—just far enough to refresh the general systematic structure.

The Marxian dictum concerning the invariable evolution of historical processes—that is, that feudalism is overtaken by capitalism and ultimately superseded by socialism—does not seem to fit the history of Atlanta. Within that system, at least, it would appear that each leadership system has overlapped another, all now running side by side. Feudalism has never died. The landed feudalists there have invested in the developing technologies; many, thereafter, have merely changed one title, landlord, for another, say, president of a corporate realm in America's interlocked corporate feudalism. If it has a large enough share of the economy, when the corporate realm may run into trouble of great magnitude, government will at last bail it out—socialistically!—i.e., general public taxes will support the subsidy. Such is another facet of our many-faced system, and in the Atlanta area the local Lockheed (military) aircraft bail-out by the federal government at around $1 billion is a recent case in point.

At last, I asked about the history of interchanges of highly placed politicians and various power structures over time. The specific question was:

Do political leaders, who arise in relation to a particular issue, move from high office into business power structures?

In order to answer the question, I secured a list of the governors of Georgia between 1920 and the early 1960s in order to find out what happened to these men—or their descendants.

The list included Hugh Dorsey, Thomas Hardwick, Clifford Miller, L. G. HARDMAN, Clifford Walker, Richard RUSSELL, Ed Rivers, Eugene TALMADGE, Ellis ARNALL, Herman TALMADGE, Melvin Thompson, Ernest Vandiver, Samuel Marvin GRIFFIN, and Carl SANDERS (honorable mention in the 1970 power structure).

The names in capital letters indicate that these men emerged from issues that thrust them into high office in the Atlanta or another community power structure in the state or nation following their tenure of office or that inclusion of one of their descendants in a later power structure was partially assured by the achievement of one of these men.

Of the fourteen names, I could not get information relating to my question on five. Leaving nine for which I could account, six of them or their descendants went into business (Hardman came out of and went back into business) or political power structures of note; two of these, RUSSELL and TALMADGE, moved on to the U.S. Senate; three went into major business positions which thrust them into local power structures and beyond: ARNALL, law practice and insurance, HARDMAN, back to Harmony Mills and other powerful corporate boards, GRIFFIN, newspaper, Bainbridge, Georgia, SANDERS, powerful corporate boards, Atlanta.

From the above, with the possible exception of Hardman, it must be said that while election to high office is not a guarantee of transition to a place in a private power structure, a substantial portion of those in power either had moved themselves to such positions or their heirs had. A public political triumph certainly would not appear to thwart one's chances for such succession.

Within the framework of national power, such historical local names as have been noted as counterparts in Atlanta remain as members of that greater power, although as a part of the undergirding of that whole. The same processes of capital accumulation and historical reference are at work within the whole system of highly integrated national and international power. This facet, however, of the family role in power processes must be tempered with other facts.

While I found, as the Introduction hypothesis states, that a *substantial portion of families with ascendant status and property interests appear sequentially in community power structures by decades, and some of them in longer epochs of social history*, in a very real sense those of family wealth appear to be a rather functionless appendage in a computer age that instantaneously can assess the whole condition of capital requirements, if its managers are so inclined—without the assent or dissent of those of presumed wealth. Their wealth, one can say, is partly true, mostly myth. They have but a tentative legal lien on the resources of most of the nation, and they remain but models emulated by their hired managers who naturally insist upon the relevance of their patrons. However, the family as an institutional power seems to have become a limited, ingrown relationship. In the whole of community life, it is rarely visible as a power. Even families of some notoriety become for the most part the basis of accepted myth rather than realities of power in its structural sense.

Giving computer addresses to the main flows of the nation's capital, and choosing police and managerial forces with which to guard their accumulation, may at last appear uneconomic in contrast to the expense of this socially archaic form.

At this point in time, however, the same families of which I speak have had and continue to enjoy the talents of John Portman, Herman Russell, Jesse Hill, Thomas Cousins, and Julian Bond, among many others, to help them in the old ways now decked with newer appurtenances. These men do not yet share the same platform as their historically elevated neighbors. Because of their skills, they have been picked up and carried along with the moods of current social history; their own elevation in history may be possible, but at present it is far from assured. They have architectural, organizational, or political skills—and, yes, racial characteristics—readily of use to the current power structures of Atlanta and of the nation. Their use of their skills, so far as I can determine, has been well within the shape of the prevailing historical mode of enterprise.

Lastly, I shall argue that family power, as such power is perceived by those in charge, may not only be an archaic form of social construction, and patronizing to say the least, but that it is also dysfunctional to modern man. I will suggest alternate forms of capital development and distribution more suitable to the requirements of these advanced technological times and more directly responsible and democratic in character.

4

The Atlanta Structure of Power in Continuity

The continuity of which I speak here means simply that although changes in personnel are apparent in the Atlanta power scene and in the observable new structures such as those concerned with downtown renewal, the basic pattern of circular, self-selected leadership remains. Community-wide policy is determined by a handful of men in the larger private corporate groups, who prod a smaller handful of public and private bureaucrats from time to time and who are in accord, generally, on what is wanted or needed by the corporate powers.

I had determined at the beginning of the study in Atlanta that I should not repeat in detail the kind of study that I had made in 1950. By 1970 it was evident to me that many had accepted the view that a power structure operated there in the general terms in which I had earlier described it. As a matter of fact, many had used the concept and its living structure in a variety of community practices that attested to the validity of the earlier findings.

Public relations men and association personnel told me that they had referred to the power model in extending their business enterprises and in organizing the community for civic purposes. One of the major public educators in higher education had raised prodigious sums of money for his institution using top power people to influence state legislators and private donors in the power structure. The civil rights movement used the concept as a text, and along with a great show of courage among a mass of people, black and white, had moved hitherto recalcitrant processes of power in their favor. Businessmen involved in high-rise building development benefited by the fact that some of the financiers of New York and Dallas had come to admire the cohesiveness and strength of the Atlanta power scheme and had felt that Atlanta would be a safe place for investments. Among the hundreds of books devoted to the subject of power since 1953 was a book by one of Atlanta's prominent businessmen, Ivan Allen, Jr., who used the concepts of power in writing his memoirs. More recently a novel about the city threaded through with concepts of power structure and rather pulpy love themes seems to be selling well. The difference between the past history of Atlanta and the present of the sixties and seventies, in these instances, appears to lie in an increased public awareness of the reality and shape of its power processes and in a growing ingenuity of the ways to use such knowledge.

Thus I did not feel compelled to repeat in detail the 1950 study effort. However, in order to assess successive processes of power, it was necessary for me to obtain basic data regarding the power structure of 1970 in some detail so that they might be compared and contrasted with my earlier model. Such efforts gave me a baseline of material from which I could evaluate current power performances over time. I had completed the basic power structure evaluations by 1973. Thereafter, I followed Atlanta happenings in the news and revisited the city on different occasions to interview and review changes that may have occurred.

After preliminary efforts and with lists of power structures in hand—historical, intervening, and current—I was able to interview knowledgeable people among the current power structure to determine, more than all else, whether or not it had been a critical factor in the major boom of rebuilding downtown Atlanta. If not, the study would have ended there. The whole concept of power structure would have been invalidated. I must say, however, although I would have been willing to accept such invalidation, it never seriously occurred to me that such would be the case.

For any unfamiliar with my methods of study, I used a routine reputational assessment of the power structure; that is, I asked major groups in the city for nominations of top-rated power wielders, and I followed those queries with interviews with the principal policymakers to determine their roles in policy-making. I also used a power scale to measure power-weight members of the structure in order to compare and contrast them. Such a scale had not been used before in power studies, and it is important, therefore, to explain it briefly here. At the end of the chapter, I shall more concretely illustrate the dynamics of power through the use of interview materials. The interviews from 1973 on concerned the preoccupation of the top leaders in the 1960s with the massive redevelopment of downtown that took place during those years. The status organization in this gigantic effort came to be Central Atlanta Progress, Incorporated, peopled largely by prominent businessmen, predominantly white but with a few blacks for a show of post civil-rights-days solidarity.

Early in my examinations of power relations, as early as 1955 during a study of Salem, Massachusetts, I began to ask informants to indicate to me how those within a given power structure might be measured according to status, roles, and personal and other characteristics, which might, taken in total, differentiate them from persons of lesser power. For Study II, at last I was ready to experiment with the scale, which was constructed from a composite of answers and from insights of my own.

I wished ultimately to have an instrument that might be used to gather in summary form information about individuals previously recorded in one of the reference works on prominent people: *Who's Who*, business-evaluation publications such as Moody's indexes, Standard and Poor's, individual biographies, histories, and the like. I also wished to so construct the instrument that additional information could be gotten from any who might know any particular individual well so that interviews with a whole panel of knowledgeables would not be necessary. I felt that such a scale should reflect the normal status position in community ratings of an individual. If a man is rated high in a poll soliciting nominations for power leaders, something would be quite wrong with the new scale if it grossly lowered or raised that rating. Finally, I intended to use as a base for the questions many of the ideas already referred to in the listing of social and power hypotheses in the Introduction to this work. I assumed that roles and role performances are observable in published arrays of such performances. I wished to capture this "visibility" in a scale and, in the present case, to use it as a further test of the validity of the overall method of study.

Both status and role positions of men are, at bottom, evaluations of themselves and of those around them. Each person carries in his head an image of himself as he compares himself with others. He has role expectations for himself, and can measure others in terms of their visible role in performances. The social milieu in which he lives, the training he may have had as a child as well as an adult, and the acuteness of his observations may vary from others, but when his judgments are added to others an average can be arrived at. It has been suggested that no one factor of measurement, reputational, positional, cultural, or personal, may accurately describe men of power any more than one single factor can describe anyone. Added together with other factors, a personal and even a group profile may be constructed to reveal certain fundamental characteristics of behavior and social position.

Answers to such questions as "Where does one live?" "What does he do?" "Where did he go to school?" begin to suggest status measurements. All people use them when meeting or judging others. With additions, such stored knowledge reveals a good deal about one's own or another's power status.

Over the years I have worked such questions into the scale shown in table 1. Using the scale, one may, I believe, measure with some accuracy the power position of individuals. Answers to the questions have varying weights. The sum total of all weights indicates a man's power rating; by using the scale, we can even compare one group with another. The weights used were +1 to +4 or −1 to −4 for each whole factor. I have listed the items used in scaling in an array for convenient reference rather than in the form used in operating the scale.

It will be readily seen that the scale is more comprehensive in its coverage of factors than the usual device of judging a man to be powerful by naming one to two factors, e.g., mere fame or fortune. It allows for points in relation to business, politics, and professions singly or in combinations. It is a device that includes facets of activity and passivity, giving weight or demerit as the case might be. One may use the scale to measure his own power with that of his contemporaries, at least those in Atlanta.

The average score of all Atlanta leaders nominated by others as top power leaders was 94. Individual scores within this array of persons ranged between a top figure of 144 to a low in the 30-point range. Those scoring above 80 points include persons from a wide variety of business and political backgrounds, but dominated by the banking interests. In descending order of points, the leading names in 1973 were: Mills Lane, Jr., Ivan Allen, Jr. (combining both political office and ownership of a local corporation, a high-scoring combination, even though Allen's business is in the middle range), Richard Rich, J. Paul Austin, Rawson Haverty, Richard Courts, Edward D. Smith, Cecil Alexander, A. H. (Billy) Sterne, George Craft, Gordon Jones, R. H. Dobbs, Arthur Howell, John Portman, Jack Adair, Noah Langdale, R. W. Woodruff (even though incapacitated, still retained financial control of Coca-Cola), Thomas Cousins, Allen Hardin, and Jack Tarver.

In the same scale, white politicians scored an average of 72 points, while their black counterparts scored 56. Black businessmen

Table 1. Hunter Scale: Leadership Power Weights*

1. Rating as a local power (weight by reputation)
2. Independent judgment as member, leading corporation
3. Independent judgment as executive, leading corporation
4. Will to exercise power (public/private)
5. Interest in general policy matters beyond own organization
6. Consulted on policy in own organization
7. Consulted on policy outside own organization
8. Leader recent project affecting body politic
9. Member other recent policy-making committees
10. Member prestige association(s)
11. Officer prestige association(s) or committee(s)
12. Member corporate board(s)
13. Officer corporate board(s)
14. Member prestige club(s)
15. Officer prestige club(s)
16. If extraordinary, institutional rating (education, church, family, welfare)
17. Bridging cultural leader
18. Policy-maker beyond local: state to national or multinational
19. Personal qualities:
    Peer acceptance
    Prime age
    Who's Who listing
    Society book listing
    Status schools
    Church prestige (local standard)
    Area residence
    Interaction with others
    2d, 3d generation
    2d, 3d generation ownership establishment
20. Media relations
21. Occupational quarters
22. Wealth:
    moderate means   1
    $10 million   2
    $10 to $100 million   3
    above $100 million   4
23. Uses wealth politically
24. Community residence:
    relative newcomer   1
    long residence   2
    most of life   3
    life   4

Table 1. (*cont.*)

---

25. If corporate affiliate: control of business
    outside owned   1
    local and outside   2
    local owned   3
    local owned and managed 4
26. If corporate affiliate, size of corporation (*Fortune 500* = very large)
    small   1
    medium   2
    large   3
    very large   4
27. Family succession in business organization or profession (if yes, +1 to +4)
28. Corporate chain "nomad" (if yes, +1 to +4)
29. Control corporation expenditures
30. Number employees under direction:
    under 100   1
    100 to 500   2
    500 to 1,000   3
    over 1,000   4
31. Professional status (besides business/industry)
32. Control finances beyond own organization
33. Run for public office
    successful   +1 to +4
    unsuccessful   −1 to −4
34. Recent political appointive office, by prestige
35. Political participation party politics (nonprofessional) (+1 to +4 or −1 to −4)
36. Political popularity (if professional politician in office)
37. Party affiliation by local majority or minority
38. Broker politics/business
39. Other items, by positive or negative weight points

Note: Applicable items are graded +1 to +4 or −1 to −4.

*I am well aware of the fact that I could have called upon scaling experts and extended the study and perhaps the usefulness of the scale, but I did not wish to use that much time at this stage of work. If it seems to have value, others will pick it up and develop it further. Otherwise it will remain as it is, the methodology used in the present study of power structure succession.

scored slightly better than the politicians, 58. Black professionals, highly visible in Study I, dropped behind both black businessmen and politicians to a score of 43. The scores of black politicians, particularly Maynard Jackson and Leroy Johnson, followed the general order of their immediate past political fortunes. At the time of interviewing on this topic, the scale measured, in descending order: Maynard Jackson, Julian Bond, Leroy Johnson. Johnson had not yet lost to Jackson in an Atlanta mayoral race, but the profile poll suggested that the weight of public opinion would be in favor of Jackson.

Corporate nomads, regional managers likely to be moved from the city by national businesses, scored but 54 points compared with the average in the power structure, 94 points. Civic lay leaders and civic professionals trailed everyone else on the list by scoring an average of 45 and 38 points respectively.

The scale, as indicated, is in a developmental stage; it has not been standardized by repeated testings and use by others, but nevertheless it points to the fact that power may be rated and measured more precisely than seemed possible heretofore. It represents a beginning. Such scaling, when standardized, might make possible economies in time and expense in finding and polling top leadership in communities and in the nation. The differentials in the point scores would appear significant and in accord with more casual observation.

The scale average score of all power structure nominees in the study stood at 94 compared with a score of 60 for those not so nominated but who were scaled for comparison. Such are the "placements" of some in relation to others. The process involved in such mental placement is psychological reference and differentiation.

Our scaled ratings of power structure members agreed with the assessments of author Ivan Allen, Jr., an insider who also asserts that power structure leaders are mainly businessmen drawn from the major banks, industrial concerns, legal firms, utility groups, and the media. In a sense they represent a cross-section of the top executives, plus a cross-section of well-recognized corporations, plus the top-ranked personnel of government. Such a configuration may be expanded and contracted according to the policy or development under consideration at a given time.

Another test for structure was made—a test to assess the interrelationships between power-structure nominees. Some fifty-six persons were analyzed for primary relationships existing between them, i.e., for business, professional, and political relationships. Within the fifty-six names used, four major, sociometric clusters emerged, each with a "star isolate" to whom all of each cluster were related. Each cluster, in turn, could be related to all other clusters by primary, mutual relationships, and these in their turn tied all fifty-six together as a structure, one derived from a habitual exchange of ideas and mutual effort. The largest group contained thirteen persons; the smallest group contained five.

Some twenty persons could be said to have been peripheral to the clusters analyzed. They were those who may have had only one primary relationship to the cluster and hence to the whole larger structure. Those who occupied the central positions within clusters, the star isolates, were without exception those who were major financial, industrial, or business leaders of the community—the patrons of the city who dispensed money, jobs, and other types of emolument and benefit upon those surrounding them and occasionally on the community generally. Those peripheral to these persons were patronized by them and consisted largely of upper-bracket professionals, loner or lesser industrialists, racial comers, and elected and appointed politicians. The great majority of the whole was further interrelated by multiple overlapping club and community projects of civic and ceremonial virtue.

As in Study I, one of the largest of the patrons within the system also remained peripheral to all sociometrically derived groups, but could be shown to be integrally connected secondarily, through managerial and upper-professional agents, to the system as a whole. Such facts must be determined through empirical, experiential inquiry. This, then, also describes the power structure. It remains a structure in continuity. Some enter, some leave, decade by decade, but its function remains in place: to maintain order by a few of the many—generation after generation.

More than anything else, however, and whatever its size and composition, the power structure represents a dominant voice concerning any matter of interest to a majority of businessmen. Although it has a few educators and politicians at the periphery of the circle to show institutional solidarity, the weight of the whole scheme veers unerringly toward the goals of business and the business-dominated technology. Its rallying cry against anything it does not approve carries the notion that income, jobs, or even the system itself may be in jeopardy were the other side to win. The power of this social solidarity rests absolutely upon current institutional values, belief systems, which give priority to continuing the superordinate position in our society of business. A change of institutional cultural values would change the whole picture immediately, but the leadership of urban and national America loses little sleep over such a peril. Sociologist William F. Ogburn, one of my teachers, rightly said that institutional belief systems and values change slowly: something like twenty years is required for a complete turnabout. Within such a time span, those leaders who wish to hold onto power have ample time to convert to new postures or coopt their opposition.

The total configuration of power in which metropolitan Atlanta operates is, of course, the national power complex of the United States and the world, a fact that is stressed in this narrative. However at this point we are mainly concerned with local relationships.

By the time I had returned to Atlanta, and after several more such studies and an empirical national study of power, I had defined the concept of power structures (Introduction hypotheses) more precisely than I could have in Study I:

A power structure is a coordinated system, public and private, formal and informal, of learned and repeated power roles and relationships, the function of which is the maintenance of any prescribed, differentiated social order.

A community power structure is one such order and is linked by its power functions to larger societal power systems. Other such power systems include organized labor, partisan political blocs, legislative management systems, etc., often linked to larger parent, national, and international systems of power superior to them.

Local power structures vary in size and composition according to their coordination function, which they perform for both public and private centers of power internal and external to them.

As suggested, I returned to the city quite convinced that, as in 1950, I would find a power structure in place in 1970. I came especially to note changes in its structure and in its interests and thrust. I knew that blacks had begun to put men into political positions in City Hall and in the state legislature, a feat that would have been deemed impossible by most knowledgeables but a dozen years ago. By 1970 they were trying for federal office, which Andrew Young at last succeeded in attaining in the U.S. House of Representatives in 1972. I had learned through reading about it and through correspondence that the city had elected a new mayor in 1969, Sam Massell, nephew of Ben Massell, one of the big realtors of 1950. Sam Massell, however, who owned no big fortune, claimed to be a liberal who had been elected by a coalition of blacks and white liberals, in that order. He was opposed in his candidacy for office by a number of the traditional power structure. By 1973, Atlanta had a black mayor.

Among other notable changes, even though the majority of all blacks continued to move west in the city, some high-salaried black professionals and businessmen had begun to move eastward in Atlanta, defying the traditional ghetto restriction of movement. The city of Decatur and Dekalb County, to the east and heretofore reserved for white middle-class suburbanites, had begun to change complexion.

An important fact, according to one of my correspondents, Robert Foreman, a civic affairs leader in my earlier study, was that democracy *within* the power structure was at work. Two self-made men, Thomas (Tom) Cousins and John Portman, now major real estate operators and urban developers, had begun their careers in modest circumstances and, within a very few years, each had become eminently successful professionally and financially.

More importantly, perhaps, I found during the course of my second study that a few prominent blacks would also be included in Atlanta's overall power structure, particularly at the corporate board level of affairs. Atlanta blacks' achievements were being watched with excited interest by other blacks across the nation. Many have asked why women don't make top billing in most power structures. My answer is simply, white male chauvinism in those power structures.

Later (1970) I was told, with some negative headshaking, that Atlanta had a hippie population and an underground newspaper, *The Great Speckled Bird*, which then had a circulation of about twenty thousand per issue and was sold along the main street of their freedom colony, 10th Street. By the middle 1970s, I understood that that movement, as were its counterparts across the nation, was in eclipse.

When comparing historical power names with present ones, I found that twenty-nine families had connections in both business and civic affairs—these were families that had come through history and had become part of the power structure of the last three decades. The 1950 list of power nominees yielded connections between thirty-eight organizational and historical affiliations. The power-generating organizations that provided thirty-eight historical connections between the earlier period and 1950 included the following: the Atlantic Coal and Ice Company, the Atlanta Street Railway, the banking industry (various names and consolidations), Coca-Cola, commercial enterprises of large magnitude, the cotton industry, educational administrative units, government, insurance, legal firms, military units, the news media (by various names), railroads, real estate firms, and utilities.

Power-structure names from a poll conducted in 1950 included the following: Allen Albert, Ivan Allen, Jr., Harllee Branch, Jr., Oby Brewer, Virginia Campbell, Asa Candler, James Carmichael, Richard Courts, John Wesley Dobbs, R. (Shorty) Doyal, Hal Dumas, Robert L.

Foreman, Carlyle Fraser, William B. Hartsfield, Clarence Haverty, Mrs. W. T. Healey, Norris B. Herndon, Clark Howell, Joel Hurt, Ira Jarrell, Harrison Jones, Mills B. Lane, Jr., Julius McCurdy, Robert Mc-Dougall, N. Baxter Maddox, Ben Massell, Charles Mathias, Benjamin Mays, L. D. Milton, Richard Rich, Hugh Richardson, James Robinson, C. A. Scott, James Shelor, John A. Sibley, Harry Sommers, Hughes Spalding, Sr., R. G. Tabor, Robert B. Troutman, Jr., Elbert Tuttle, A. T. Walden, R. W. Woodruff, Cator Woolford, and C. R. Yates.

The power-generating organizations that, by analysis, connected the 1950 power-structure names with those of 1973 included the following: Adair Realty Company, Ivan Allen Company, Atlanta Gas Light Company, Atlanta Life Insurance Company, Atlanta Newspapers, Incorporated, Atlantic Steel, the *Atlanta World Newspaper*, Beers Construction Company, Citizens and Southern Bank, Citizens Trust Bank, Coca-Cola, Cousins, Incorporated, Davison-Paxon, Delta Airlines, First National Bank, Fulton National Bank, Genuine Parts Company, Georgia International Corporation, Georgia International Life Insurance, Georgia Power, government, Haverty Furniture Company, Healey Company, Hurt Building (now Atlantic Realty), Muse's, National Bank of Georgia, Oxford Industries, Portman, Incorporated, Retail Credit, Rich's Incorporated, Russell Companies, Selig Enterprises, Southern Bell Telephone Company, Trust Company of Georgia, and J. M. Tull Metals.

My data provided one hundred connections between these organizations and the powers of 1950 and 1973. They are categorical relationships, to be sure, but as such, they do show the processes of inclusion and exclusion of specific individuals within the inner circles of power. They also show closure between individuals and organizations within power circles as they relate to the larger remainder of the population. As we shall see in subsequent analyses they show individuals within the current power structure interacting on current matters of policy concern to the community and to themselves and their organizations. This is what social scientists mean by the term *relationships*.

In 1973 the analytical array of power names, some lesser, some greater in scale, utilized for the above purposes included the following: Jack Adair, Cecil Alexander, Ivan Allen, Jr., Philip Alston, J. Paul Austin, Joseph E. Birnie, Julian Bond, Henry Bowden, Harold Brockey, Lee Burge, Richard Courts, Thomas Cousins, George Craft, R. H. Dobbs, Jr., Charles W. Duncan, L. L. Gellerstedt, Allen Hardin, Edwin I. Hatch, Rawson Haverty, Vivian Henderson, Jesse Hill, Arthur Howell, Maynard Jackson, Leroy Johnson, Gordon Jones, Mills

B. Lane, Jr., Noah Langdale, Jr., Sartain Lanier, F. M. Malone, Samuel Massell, Rolland A. Maxwell, John Portman, Allen Post, L. E. Rast, Leonard Reinsch, Carl J. Reith, Charles Reynolds, Richard Rich, Herman J. Russell, C. A. Scott, Simon Selig, Jr., Opie Shelton, James Sibley, Edward D. Smith, Hughes Spalding, Jr., A. H. Sterne, Jack Tarver, Pollard Turman, A. W. Vogtle, Jr., Q. V. Williamson, R. W. Woodruff, C. R. Yates, and Andrew Young.

In order to further test the inclusion/exclusion processes in community life, the ranking power nominees were connected by membership in the following community prestige associations: arts and music societies (general), the Capital City Club, Chamber of Commerce, various ranking civic clubs, the Commerce Club, hospital boards, Peachtree Golf, the Piedmont Driving Club, the Standard Club, out-of-town clubs (well-known extra-city clubs), other social inter-city clubs, and university boards. I was able to find some seventy-seven memberships belonging to fifty-six members. Only a dozen power nominees had no such membership data available for analysis. Of those recorded, fourteen had multiple memberships, two or more. These persons may be characterized for the major part, as higher ranking business (twelve) and professional (two) persons. Public politicians were conspicuously absent from the available listings, and minority members, apparently, by preference or otherwise, remained in their own historical placement in clubs and other prestigious community associations.

In the historical listing one can find links between many of the families from their early point to some point in time in 1950 or beyond. For example, one could relate the Robinsons to an earlier family, English, each cogently related to Atlanta banking. Or one might trace the newspaper families involving at least the Gradys, Howells, and Foremans, but these ultimately become exercises of history. Each link in the network, it may be said, had such facts behind them. No such tracing was possible for the hundreds of thousands of persons who were contemporaries of these people and who like Hardy Ivy may lie in unmarked or paved-over graves and for whom the pen of history was never dipped. I asked Atlanta historian Franklin Garrett to go over my list of historically prominent names that I could link to latter-day power structures, and he conceded that he could cull no more from memory.

When one moves into the listing of power-structure names and power-generating and club organizations of the era 1950 on, one notes an increase in both the number of power-generating organizations and the power-structure names of 1973. The boom of downtown redevelopment and the ascendancy of names from the building and real estate industries nominated by community knowledgeables account in large part for the increase. Also, names of ranking professionals of major associations were included on the 1973 list. They remain, I found once more, subordinate people to the top policy-making groups in community life.

Anyone familiar with the lists of power-structure names would recognize most of the professionals as well as other individuals to be of different weights in any scale of power. Coca-Cola representatives outweigh a good many other names on the list. That company remains a high-status organization in Atlanta's power scheme. As a financial power, however, it has been topped by Citizens and Southern Bank. One would know that banks, like community churches or other organizations, have varying status weights, and consequently the representatives of the more esteemed groups reflect this fact in being nominated to the lists. A cloak of history, at least two or three generations of it, lends an aura to such names as Adair, Alexander, Candler, Dobbs, Foreman, Grant, Haverty, Healey, Howell, Hurt, Inman, Massell, Rich, Richardson, Spalding, Woodruff, and Yates.[1]

Of the top leaders, Ivan Allen, Jr., and Mills Lane, Jr., were considered to be "comers" in 1950. By 1970 they had certainly arrived. Because of Lane's rather flamboyant personality as a younger man, some reservations had been expressed to me in 1950 concerning his ability to master the mechanics of carrying on the large banking operation left to him as an inheritance. By the 1970s the bank had moved from one of some $300 million to one of more than $3 billion. I heard no more regarding his qualifications as a banker. Instant credit, personalized banking, and the ability of its officers to think big and daringly had stopped all criticisms. He had become one of the biggest men in town. He could be very decisive, very sure of himself when he backed any community project—and often nearly alone in the initial policy decisions. Others followed his decisions.

During his mayorship, Ivan Allen had scouted the possibility of acquiring a baseball club to round out the city's metropolitan image as well as to relieve the boredom of some of its citizenry. He had visited the officers of major leagues, and they in turn had looked Atlanta over, but they were reluctant to come to Atlanta because no adequate stadium facilities were available there. It at last occurred to Allen to approach his friend Lane.

Upon taking Allen to a site for the proposed stadium, Lane spent about thirty seconds looking it over, then turned to Allen and asked him how much he really wanted it. Assured by Allen that it was no passing fancy on his part, Lane said in effect, "Then this is it!" Lane went on to suggest that Allen revive the old Stadium Authority, which had languished, make Arthur Montgomery chairman and Lane treasurer, and Lane in turn would thereupon swing the full credit of Citizens and Southern Bank behind the project. If that wouldn't get the job done, he exulted, then it probably could never be done.[2] Of course, redevelopment land was in the picture.

In his book Allen goes on to explain how he and Lane swung the current power structure behind the smaller policy-making group and how the job was indeed done, and with dispatch.

Mr. Allen's description of the initiation and carrying through of this project is reminiscent of "James Treat's" analysis of similar processes described in Study I.[3] Treat had outlined the formation of an international trade center, which has now culminated in the development of the gigantic Omni-International development. Although not all projects get off the ground so easily, many of them sponsored by ranking members of any current power structure do. The structure itself provides for a continuity of interest in policies sponsored by powerful principals even when the projects may have to stand in line to become operational. Projects are picked up around the circle on a back-scratching basis of agreement about priorities.

Besides those just mentioned, none had given more stability to the Atlanta power structures for the past three or four decades than R. W. Woodruff of the Coca-Cola Company and Richard Rich of the Rich's department store. I wish to give special mention to each of these outstanding power leaders before turning to a summary of a continuity of power names at the end of the chapter.

By 1970, R. W. Woodruff, a community prime mover in 1950, had given up most of his community activities, holding on to the major corporate post, however, chairman of the Coca-Cola executive financial committee. In that position he had but recently conferred a new library upon Emory University, one of his beloved institutions, and an open-area park near the downtown Five Points, donated by him, which led everyone to rephrase the sentence: "Donated by Robert Woodruff, Atlanta's most famous anonymous donor." Nevertheless, because of age, for the first time in more than two decades, the Woodruff name failed of top billing in power polling.

When I visited Emory University, I rode through a subdivision that was once the pride of the metropolis, through miles of aging, dispirited, wage-earner housing that melded into white-collar housing, and at last crossed a campus garden bridge leading to the new Woodruff library. A small brook flowed under the bridge, and rather appropriately in one of its eddies floated a red paper cup proclaiming "Coca-Cola" to the world. Upon entering the building, I saw a bust of Woodruff, apparently cast near the time, around 1950, when I knew him briefly; the bronze face stared timelessly into the space of the library rotunda.

It is well known that no major community project was executed in Atlanta during the 1940s and through the 1970s without Woodruff money.

One of the most enlightening interviews in Study II in 1970 and 1973 was given by Richard Rich of the largest department store complex in the Southeast. I had known Rich since the mid-forties when he and I were both active in USO affairs. His interest and enthusiasm for needed civic services never waned during that period or in the years to follow. He drove himself hard in his business and in civic projects until his death in 1975. Because of his business interests, as one may see, he was a champion of downtown improvement. While enlightened self-interest may have motivated his activities, one is led to believe because of Rich's very many civic works that he was moved by an especially deep-seated generosity toward his community. Venerable, easy to meet, friendly, twinkling eyes, and redoubtable are words that quickly come to mind as I think of Dick Rich.

As I walked toward Rich's department store one fine morning, historical structures evoked any number of memories. Nearing Five Points, a central business district intersection not far from Hardy Ivy's grave (Ivy was Atlanta's first white settler), I stopped for a moment to view the broad, open point of entry of downtown streets. Without too much interest I looked up toward the bird-whitened statue of Henry Grady at one end of the plaza, then toward the opposite end, now opened into an urban park provided by the destruction of a valuable city block fronting the new headquarters building of the Trust Company of Georgia, a park made possible by an $11.5 million grant from R. W. Woodruff. On one side of the plaza, out of a sense of nostalgia, I looked for an old landmark, the Ivan Allen-Marshall building.[4] Gone. Gone too, the once nearby Kimball House Hotel, a gathering place for nineteenth- and early twentieth-century power structures. Admittedly more beautiful buildings had sprouted up in their places, a new set of towers of the First National Bank, towers which, it was said, helped spark the 1960s renaissance of building around the square. Near where an earlier transient had stood and watched two squaws work in their corn patches, I turned into Alabama Street, then lined with any number of cheap-side stores, pawn shops, dark, grease-filled air in its restaurants, trash and glass-strewn sidewalks, littered gutters. Many blacks loitered along the way. Definitely a transition area. (Rich, unhappy about the street, prophetically indicated later that soon all of that area "would go," that is, would be redeveloped.) Plans had been made for tearing out a whole block along Alabama Street to provide a corridor that was to lead past Rich's store and tie into a huge complex, the Omni-International development, later built on more than fifty acres of land then occupied by the historically unsightly railroad switching yard called Railroad Gulch. A rapid transit stop had been designated for the area, a multibillion dollar project in total. (Later question: Did Rich involve himself and others with the project, others such as the Courts Company, the Cousins Company, City Hall, and so on? The answer is that Rich and a good many others in the store did become involved in the project.)

About a block before reaching Rich's main entrance, going past some railroad tracks lower than street level, one becomes aware of an earlier Atlanta, a portion of which ground is now covered by a series of over-street viaducts up to the second story of many of the older buildings. For a while, great numbers were drawn to this underground area, a nightspot and tourist shopping area nurtured by nostalgia, but recently the underground digging for rapid transit has interfered with this recreation spot. With transit construction completed and out of the way, the promoters hope it will revive.

Despite the exceptional expansion of his department store, Rich had remained a careful and thrifty merchant. He also had remained an inveterate downtown developer until recently. When I last interviewed him he was in his seventies, alert and keen about details of his business and civic activities. Over mid-morning coffee in his tastefully furnished but relatively small office, he explained his current positions regarding his business and the city.

He had moved many of the burdens of the store operation to his business associates, but he had retained control of the finance committee of the company board. He said that for a number of years he had been very cautious about expanding the store beyond downtown into the many neighborhoods now served by the new freeway system, a system he had helped to build. He had always felt that downtown should be fully redeveloped before any great effort should be made by downtown merchants to develop outlying shopping centers.

From the point of view of his own business, he had held to the principle that one should establish a sound enough financial position that any such move would not jeopardize the original, highly successful downtown operation. He produced a number of financial reports and other historical documents to illustrate his points. At the time of our first discussion, he said that the store was earning some $160 million a year and was, in his opinion, at last in a firm enough position to make the steady moves already begun into outlying areas. The business, he said, had moved from $5 million a year to its present earnings in the three decades he had been in command of operations. He seemed very pleased, and I, with the politeness of the moment, commended him on his success.

He continued by saying that he had not only taken into account the success of his own business but had also carefully watched the progress and expansion of other community facilities. He stressed that his own activities may have been beneficial to community development, but that such development, to him, was another justification for expansion of his own business. He listed his expectations of the community as follows: (1) Atlanta had to have its freeway system essentially completed before Rich's would expand. (2) Atlanta must have more than a million population. (3) Downtown merchants and the city should have insured the continued existence of a viable central city by the construction of a 1,250-car parking garage. (4) Rich's would join with other merchants in outlying expansions only when all were prepared to spend enough on them to make them attractive and to keep them up to date.

He continued by saying that actually Rich's had moved to its first outlying location, Lenox near Buckhead, in 1959 at a cost of some $10 million. By 1970 they had expanded to six centers with more than forty top executives to whom central management had given considerable local autonomy. A seventh center was then under way at Phipps Plaza, across the street from Rich's and within the perimeter of the major freeway circle around the city. The neighboring operation, he said, had been New York–financed and was scheduled to include a Lord and Taylor's, a Saks, a W. & J. Sloane, an I. Miller, and a Tiffany outlet. The exclusive stores in the area in terms of fashionable personal items would enable Atlantans to buy almost anything locally that they could in New York. For the first time, he felt, the city would have become a major national city in this regard.

Urged to speak of his community activities, he said that his own source of power in community projects was quite closely connected to his business interests. He laughed lightly and said that he and some of those immediately around him had been accused of being selfishly motivated in all that they did, but he said that while he would have to admit a bias in favor of the business in all that he did, he had also tried to think of the good of the whole community as he took on projects. He joked that he was not entirely motivated by greed.

When asked if any particular projects had brought up specific criticisms, he said that some people had said that he worked on the rapid transit proposal for the obvious reason that its construction would benefit his downtown store. In response, he contended that although he would be the first to admit the value that rapid transit would have for the store, the system would have beneficial effects for all downtown properties and business establishments; it would also help those who need a rapid and relatively inexpensive way to get to work and to come to the city to shop. One must weigh all factors.

Rather in passing, he mentioned the connection of Robert Troutman, Jr., whose law firm helped to get the Railroad Gulch project underway, and in response to my questions he verified the helpful interest of Richard Courts and Tom Cousins in that project. He had worked with each of them in various ways over the years. After a minute or two of thought, he added Rawson Haverty's name to his list of notables as an ardent champion of rapid transit and as a hard-working volunteer then heading that movement. He said that the transit project had taken years of discussion and planning to become a reality. Most good things, especially the big ones, do not happen quickly, he said. Allen Hardin was then mentioned as another enterprising power structure member whose work as a volunteer in the Chamber of Commerce had brought him to the attention of many. He had expanded greatly a construction industry begun by Hardin's father. According to Rich, Hardin and Cousins had worked closely together.

The $3.5 billion, which had then been voted by the federal government for local rapid transit systems, was of considerable interest to local leadership, and Atlanta's top leadership had a small bureaucracy working on how they could get their share, and more, of it. The first referendum on rapid transit failed before the voters because it had asked for a property tax increase. The project actually got under way with the help of two of the black leaders in the state legislature, Leroy Johnson and Julian Bond, who had pushed a measure allowing a levy of a local sales tax. This was much easier than trying again to get property taxes increased.

Dick Rich's opening statement to me on my second visit to him, 1973, concerned labor troubles he was encountering. He indicated that there were a few Black Panthers in town, meaning Dr. Ralph Abernathy (!) and a group that was striking Rich's for union recognition as well as fair practices in employee upgrading. An account in the morning press had indicated that Abernathy and a number with him had been arrested the day before in front of the home of Harold Brockey, Rich's general manager. All were out on bail.[5]

Rich, seemingly deliberately, turned his attention immediately to other matters. It was apparent that he did not wish to give the impression that the strike activities bothered him very much.

He spoke of his continued involvement in rapid transit. Prior to the inception of the program, he was on the Chamber of Commerce Committee for rapid transit for some ten years—indicating that it takes a long time to move these things. The legal basis for rapid transit was created by three out of four adjoining counties. Cobb County to the north was against it while Fulton (Atlanta's county) and Dekalb (east) led the sentiment for it.

He repeated that after failure of the property tax referendum, the legislature put through a 1 percent sales tax that applied only to counties involved. It was then a pay-as-you-go measure; interest had to be paid on bonds. This, he said, was better for taxpayers. The original schedule would be in effect maybe ten years. He indicated that once a tax is taken for granted, the politicians are always reluctant to give it up.

Some construction people, those building San Francisco's rapid transit, were to build here: Brinkerhoff and Bechtel. The federal government had been expected to pick up 50 percent of the tab.

He spoke again of the importance of the nearby Alpert and Cousins Omni development, a project that would probably take another ten years, and of some struggle between the Portman group who built Peachtree Center at another axis of the city and the Cousins group, including himself. Portman contended that the Center at upper Peachtree was not yet fully developed. Rich contemplated that Portman felt that the Omni-International Center would have been better located near the Peachtree Mart and other facilities. The question was now moot; Cousins' Omni-International Center for trade shows and other developments had been built over Railroad Gulch. The Omni development had helped Rich's, said Dick Rich,* with its rapid transit connection and the corridor from it to Five Points, plus greatly increased parking space.

He then spoke of "new town's developments" around the perimeter of the city, Cumberland Mall to the northwest then being one of the latest, along with Peachtree City to the south. On Highway 285

*But by 1978, the Omni itself needed help. It was reported to be in the hands of receivers.

to Marietta, Cumberland had four department stores: Rich's, Davison's (Macy's), Sears, Penney's—the first time all four of these stores had been put in one center.

As against $160 million three years before, Rich's sales were then running at over $280 million a year, up $20 million in the last quarter. Atlanta's airport was then the third largest in the nation. Portman had completed his tallest hotel building in the world in expectation of ten years' growth in international trade. Everyone was optimistic. (Actually most businesses in building and real estate activities were a bit on the down side then, and very much so later.)

Who was paying for it all? Rich indicated that it was mostly private money and some state money. That combination was particularly true of the Omni project, in which the state put up a major building, the World Congress Center.

Our second interview ended pleasantly over a cup of coffee. Two years later this fine citizen of Atlanta was dead. His place in the power structure has been taken by executives of the chain of Federated Stores, which has since bought Rich's. Their power roles cannot ever exactly coincide with the many carried previously by Richard Rich. Even the enterprise will change pace and scope in accordance with their wishes, but the very system will demand their espousal of a responsibility for helping others in Atlanta to maintain a system of order comfortable and profitable to those who make power decisions at all circumferences of power. None that I talked to felt, beyond their feeling of loss related to Dick Rich's absence, any sense that the Atlanta situation would worsen with the entrance of the Federated Stores system.

Dick Rich had been a leader, if not in the front position, of every major community project in Atlanta since at least the 1950s. It was he who assumed first the leadership (Study I) of the Chamber of Commerce in order to push from that vantage point the finally successful freeway redevelopment project of the early fifties. He led a successful drive for a comprehensive fine arts building program in the city; he found himself involved in furthering Mayor Allen's ambitions for a sports stadium; and at the time of my last visits with him, he was the leader of the movement to bring rapid transit to Atlanta. In such projects, he always enlisted the interest of various sectors of any given power structure of the time. The process is well established.

In a city or two in the nation, investigators of power relations have felt that they had to conclude that all projects of importance had been initiated and brought to conclusion by individuals who had had little if any contact with one another before. It was said that business-men certainly did not call the shots in relation to policy-making in those cities.

However those cases may have been, Atlanta is quite opposite. As Rich himself pointed out, he was involved over and over again with many of the same persons, persons whom he trusted implicitly to help in first one project and then another for at least three or four decades of civic and business endeavor, both being closely entwined in relation to public and private objectives. Often Rich was called upon to head a project largely because all knew that he would recruit personnel among the existing power structure, plus one or two talented newcomers to help him. Bureaucratic help from the many voluntary associations and governmental agencies was always available to him and to others with him.

In these ways, the Atlanta power structures have historically kept a strong hand on the community policy-making function, whether a given project may have been rapid transit, a new art center, a university complex, a coliseum, or a new skyscraper. For years Dick Rich was known to many as "Mr. Atlanta." He wore the title gracefully, quietly, and with the stout heart of a genuine civic booster.

Leaders come and go. But withal, the new and old act much the same. Their feet stand firmly upon an institutional base of economic expansion coupled with a determination, now more than a century old, to bring all other institutional elements of society into accord with it. The central goal in all mechanized societies of the world is capitalization, whether the goal be set by private or state collective forces. All institutional forces compliantly bend to the dominant will of centralized economic organizations peopled by countless directors, professional manipulators, academicians, technologists, military and police forces, legislators, and sectors and waves of ordinary working people.

The concerns of the Atlanta leadership most recently have been divided among innumerable activities: building business buildings and factories, stadiums, university facilities, skyscraper hotels, and condominiums, yet their reactions to matters of public policy could be said to have been contained in a mold of conformity to self-interest that has coursed through the history of the city and the republic. I saw little evidence of any loss of continuity of the general power structure of the city in all its history. That grip has deep roots in the habitual responses of most citizens, in their institutional attitudes and values; they hold them whether or not such attitudes contribute to their own well-being. The determination of black people, as will be seen in a chapter to follow, to enter a few into the ranks of that power structure and to leave in uneasy abeyance some of the remaining chronic educational, work, and welfare problems is a case in point.

Among the many "community-wide projects" taken into account by the city's policy-makers, none was more dramatic than the developments of the Peachtree Center, the urban university center, the stadium, the Omni-International project, and rapid transit. Any one of these projects might have been investigated with some thoroughness and it would have been seen that in each some (not all) of the members of the overall power structure would have been involved in numerous tasks contributing to its eventual success. Building tall buildings downtown by far exceeded all other community efforts in the city during and preceding the time of this study.

In order to underscore the importance given to the massive effort of rebuilding downtown, I shall presently list members of the governing board of Central Atlanta Progress, an organization of the highest prestige in the city during the 1970s. Power-structure people who have been previously mentioned in this book will appear in boldface type.

Much about what a community values can be discovered by reviewing the honors that men bestow upon themselves. Merely belonging to an association may give a modicum of honor to some, but when one finds the larger proportion of a community power structure belonging to the same association, and furthermore when such association expresses a listing of values and goals in its by-laws the very aims to which a large portion of the community has most recently been devoting itself, one must assume that such an organization may bestow great honor to its individual members. Atlanta's distinguished association, the Central Atlanta Progress, Inc., is in just such a position. Table 2 is taken from one of the brochures published by that association in 1973. Its bestowals of honor are self-explanatory. For the purpose of identifying members of the power structure and power-generating organizations put into nomination for positions of overall community power, I have added emphasis to certain names by putting them in small capitals.

One would expect that through their organizational behavior many of the top leaders, over time and in succeeding phases of organization, would belong to major, civic policy-making groups devoted to building and urban development, while keeping a tight watch over policy formulations. As we shall see, this hypothesis proves to be valid.

Thus, I have been able to make note of an important fact: the

Table 2. Central Atlanta Progress, Inc., 1973*

Officers of Central Atlanta Progress, Inc., 1973

John C. **Portman**, Jr., President
William L. **Calloway**, Vice-President
Thomas G. **Cousins**, Vice-President
Harold **Brockey**, Vice-President
George S. **Craft**, Treasurer
Mills B. **Lane**, Jr., Executive Committee Chairman
Robert W. Bivens, Executive Director
Richard C. D. Fleming, Associate Director
Roy F. Kenzie, Urban Design Director

Board of Directors of Central Atlanta Progress, Inc., 1973

Jack **Adair**, Adair Mortgage Company
Ray **Alden**, Vice-President, Genuine Parts Company
Cecil A. **Alexander**, Finch, Alexander, Barnes, Rothschild, and Paschal
Ivan **Allen** III, President, Ivan Allen Company
J. Paul **Austin**, Chairman, The Coca-Cola Company
Joseph E. **Birnie**, The National Bank of Georgia
Henry L. **Bowden**, Chairman, Trustees, Emory University
Harold **Brockey**, Chairman, Rich's
W. Lee **Burge**, President, Retail Credit Company
William L. **Calloway**, President, Calloway Realty Company
Alvin B. **Cates**, Jr., President, Adams-Cates Company
Fletcher **Coombs**, President, Mutual Federal Savings and Loan Association
Thomas G. **Cousins**, Chairman, Cousins Properties
Joel H. **Cowan**, President, Phipps Land Company
George S. **Craft**, Chairman, Trust Company of Georgia
James E. **Cushman**, President, Cushman Corporation
L. G. **Dewberry**, Jr., President, Atlantic Steel Company
R. Howard **Dobbs**, Jr., Chairman, Life Insurance Company of Georgia
J. J. **Doherty**, Jr., Vice-President, Western Electric Company
Milton G. Farris
Richard A. Fritzsche, Manager, The Equitable Building
Steve H. Fuller, Jr., Chairman, Underground Atlanta
L. L. **Gellerstedt**, Jr., President, Beers Construction Company
Elliott Goldstein, Powell, Goldstein, Frazer, and Murphy
Hix H. Green, Sr., Chairman, Hix Green Corporation
Robert P. Guyton, President, **The National Bank of Georgia**
Allen **Hardin**, President, Ira H. Hardin Company
Joseph F. Haas, Haas, Holland, Levison, and Gilbert
Edwin I. Hatch, President, **Georgia Power Company**
Rawson **Haverty**, President, Haverty Realty Company

Table 2. (*cont.*)

Francis J. **Heazel**, Jr., President, Atlantic Realty Company
Jesse **Hill**, Vice-President, Atlantic Realty Company
Daniel B. Hodgson, Alston, Miller & Gaines
Robert M. Holder, Jr., President, Holder Construction Company
A. A. Huber
Samuel E. Hudgins, Arthur Andersen & Company
Joe B. Hutchison, Executive Vice-President, Henry C. Beck Company
Ira Jackson, Jackson Service Station
Dr. Thomas D. Jarrett, President, **Atlanta University**
Boisfeuillet **Jones**
Gordon **Jones**, President, **Fulton National Bank**
Richard L. **Kattel**, President, **Citizens and Southern Bank**
Alvin Felley, Manager, Hyatt-Regency Hotel
Alfred D. Kennedy, President, North Pryor Steel Corporation
J. W. Kercher, Ernest and Ernest
Monroe Kimbrel, President, Federal Reserve Bank
Mills B. **Lane**, Jr., Chairman, Citizens and Southern National Bank
Dr. Noah **Langdale**, Jr., President, Georgia State University
Wallace L. (Bill) Lee, President, Atlanta Gas Light Company
Charles **Massell**, President, The Massell Companies
Rolland A. Maxwell, Chairman, **Davison's**
William P. Maynard
Arthur L. Montgomery, Chairman, Atlanta Coca-Cola Bottling Company
Brannon Morris, President, **Muse's**
Dr. William R. Nash, Office of Planning and Budget, State of Georgia
James Paschal, Paschals
Dr. Joseph M. Pettit, President, Georgia Institute of Technology
Claude H. Poindexter, President, **Coastal States Insurance Company**
John C. **Portman**, Jr., John Portman Associates
L. E. **Rast**, President, **Southern Bell Telephone and Telegraph Company**
Charles **Reynolds**, President, **Citizens Trust Company**
Richard H. **Rich**, Chairman, Executive Committee, Rich's
Hugh I. **Richardson**, Sr., President, Richardson Properties
Herman J. Russell, President, Russell Plastering Company
Simon S. **Selig**, Jr., President, Selig Enterprises, Inc.
Jesse Shelton, President, Robert and Company
James M. **Sibley**, King and Spalding
Alex W. Smith, Smith, Cohen, Ringel, Kohler, Martin and Lowe
Edward D. **Smith**, Chairman, **First National Bank**
A. H. **Sterne**, President, **Trust Company of Georgia**
Joe S. Stone
A. Dean Swift, President-Elect, Sears, Roebuck and Company
Jack Tarver, President, Atlanta Newspapers
Allen J. Terrill, Manager, Marriott Motor Hotel

Table 2. Central Atlanta Progress, Inc., 1973 (*cont.*)

Pollard Turman, Chairman, J. M. Tull and Company
Bill C. Wainwright, President, Atlanta Federal Savings and Loan Association
Milton Weinstein, Chairman, National Service Industries
Lloyd Tait Whitaker, President, Downtown Development Corporation
Norman H. White, Peat, Marwick, Mitchell & Company
Q. V. Williamson, President, Z. V. Williamson Company
John Wilson, President, Horne-Wilson, Inc.
Dr. Prince Wilson, Executive Secretary, Atlanta University Center
Robert M. Wood, General Counsel, Sears, Roebuck and Company
Alexander M. Yearley IV, Robinson-Humphrey Company, Inc.
Dr. Harding B. Young, Professor of Management, Georgia State University

Past Presidents of Central Atlanta Improvement Association

Robert E. **Maddox**	1941–43	John O. **Chiles**	1952–53
James D. **Robinson**, Jr.	1944–45	Ben J. **Massell**	1954–56
Jesse **Draper**	1946–47	Fred J. Turner	1957–59
Fred B. Moore	1948–49	Jack **Adair**	1960–62
Hugh I. **Richardson**	1950	Alfred D. Kennedy, Jr.	1963–65
Ivan **Allen**, Jr.	1951	Alex W. **Smith**, Jr.	1966

Past Presidents of Uptown Association

N. Baxter **Maddox**	1960–62	Virgil W. Milton	1965–66
Hix H. Green	1963–64		

Past Presidents of Central Atlanta Progress, Inc.

Alex W. **Smith**, Jr.	1967	John C. **Portman**, Jr.	1970
Robert M. Wood	1968–69		

---

*Among the organizers of this association were Robert F. **Maddox**, banker, former mayor, and father of N. Baxter **Maddox**, first president of the Uptown Association, which was merged with the Central Atlanta Improvement Association to form Central Atlanta Progress; Ivan **Allen**, Sr., father of Atlanta's dynamic mayor of the sixties, and grandfather of Ivan **Allen** III, who is now on the board of Central Atlanta Progress; A. B. **Cates**, father of CAP director Alvin **Cates**, Jr.; L. L. **Gellerstedt**, father of Larry **Gellerstedt**, past president of the Chamber and a director of CAP; Clarence **Haverty**, father of Rawson **Haverty**, a director of CAP; Ben J. **Massell**, prominent developer and uncle of Mayor Sam **Massell**; Alex **Smith**, father of CAP past president Alex **Smith**, Jr.; and Hugh **Richardson**, who is currently a director of CAP, having maintained active participation in this organization for 32 years. The late James D. **Robinson**, Jr., was very active in all three organizations. Again, the historical continuity of power structures is clear.

inner core of such organizations as those developing the extended state university system, the rapid transit system, or the continued downtown renovation inevitably contained an overlapping, hard core of the membership (approximately 40 percent) of the power structure of the moment.

It is assumed to be redundant to outline the purpose and to illustrate the carry-through among all of them by citing power names which for two or three decades have guided the destiny of downtown rebuilding. The membership lists are studded with power names considered by the community at large to be a select group indeed.

Central Atlanta Progress represented to the power structure much more than a new organization with prestige built into it. It was a new statement about building beyond the borders of downtown. Dick Rich and John Portman, prominent among others, represented those who were partisans of downtown development before "outside-of-town" development. Those who wished to border the great freeways with commercial enterprises represented major forces of development within the city, and they covertly and often actively opposed the traditional commitment to exclusive downtown capitalization. One sees in the new association names of many of these earlier opponents. Portman is in the chair with Rich close beside him, but others are present—the "outsiders"—who are now joined with the "insiders" for a concerted assault on the great potential of the immediate hinterland of the metropolis. A new policy era is in its infancy. Dreams of the wall-to-wall city of the future abound. The expansionists of the city could go ahead without conflict. (They were going ahead anyway, but with certain feelings that they were not at one with the downtown builders.) Peace and harmony again reigned in continuity, at least among those who were capital builders. Accommodation had been achieved.

As one observes the Atlanta power structure as it proceeds in continuity, one decade and one generation after another, it becomes clear that it, like any other social structure, is a phenomenon made visible mainly in the roles people play in it and by the objective consequences of their individual and collective behavior.

The Power Structure
of the Black Community

Although a few members of the black power structure of Atlanta are recognized by the white one, the general outline of that structure is not generally well known. By 1970, most white leaders understood that there was a power structure in the black community, but if they knew three or four of its members and were assured that they indeed were super-powerful among their people, this was enough for them. They relied upon this handful for information, occasionally asking those they knew to recruit a few more members of their kind for settling school problems or any other project concerning the two major races of the city. It was well known that many political offices had fallen to blacks and that political appointments had been awarded the few now patronized by the white structure. Only two whites among those I interviewed openly and spontaneously expressed hostility regarding gains made socially and politically by blacks.

In Study I, considerable space was given to explaining a number of intricate ways in which black citizens approached the upper reaches of power with problems that concerned them. These included ways of working through long-established civic welfare and betterment agencies with white professional workers as intermediaries between blacks and top power leaders; prominent blacks working directly with a few prominent whites in sub-rosa relationships; a very few blacks working directly with white politicians in efforts to influence them regarding the many issues and problems confronting black individuals and groups; and blacks participating in "back-seats" in community-wide fund-raising ventures and other ad hoc betterment efforts. A chart "routing" citizen participation was drawn in Study I to show how blacks were able to gain admittance to policy-making structures on various projects, economic, governmental, religious, educational, professional, civic, and cultural. In each of these pyramids of community power, blacks could enter at the lower levels of power but were screened drastically from direct participation in top policy-making levels. The situation pointed out a grave structural fault in community affairs. The circuitous routes of information tended to distort it, and the structures themselves were an ever-present affront to the black participants in civic affairs.

Happily, today such charting is unnecessary. With the exception of the "cultural" pyramid of status, blacks enter—a select few, selected by themselves, as whites select their own elites—into the very top of policy-making groups in business, government, education, religion, the professions, and civic affairs. Some segregational restrictions remain, but a number are pragmatically self-imposed. Even some social barriers are slowly crumbling, e.g., ceremonial eating together. The mass of blacks, however, remain, de facto, segregated.

New relationships still do not include any substantial breaching of the walls of Buckhead's (north Atlanta) exclusive living space, nor do any top-level black businessmen occupy main offices in the central business district of Atlanta, but solutions to such matters seemingly are but a matter of time and timing on both sides. Nor would it seem that a very long time in either case is involved.

No better illustration of evolving relationships between blacks and whites in terms of power wielded by the ownership segments of power can be given than that of the case of Herman J. Russell. His rise to riches and community-wide honor is one that would have been impossible but a few years earlier. It is my view that Mr. Russell's success has come from, first, perhaps, his own drive for it, but very importantly from the fact that a goodly portion of "political" power has been wrested from the larger structures of the power of the community and the nation by the massive movement toward civil rights of his people in the 1960s and 1970s. Whatever Russell's individual contributions may have been in the open political struggle, the results of that struggle opened the way for greater social and economic successes than any man of his background may have hoped for but a decade or two ago. He and the political officeholders of the community have taken, as predicted correctly in Study I, the traditional route to power in the republic: open political movement followed by the rewards such movement inevitably entails for a few and in lesser degree for the many.

However Alex Poinsett may have viewed Russell's rise, in an enthusiastic article by him written for Ebony magazine in 1972,[1] the elements of political and economic recognition eddying around the man are impressive. One sees Russell, who got his start by graduation from a great black university, Tuskeegee, and later following his father's footsteps as a plasterer, depicted as a rising capitalist in the city of Atlanta. Skyscrapers cannot be built without plaster and its allied materials. The time had come for a black plasterer to be picked up by the skyscraper builders. Not only has Russell achieved economic success, estimated by Poinsett in the tens of millions, but he was enjoying the friendship of the then governor of the state of Georgia, Jimmy Carter, with whom he had flown to St. Louis, along with nine other owners and wives of Atlanta's professional basketball and hockey teams, Russell being the only black in the nation endowed with such ownership.

Russell's promotions of a chain of subsequent successful business ventures, his struggle to achieve his present place in Atlanta and national affairs (in 1978 he was nominated by President Carter to an important federal policy post), his friendship with Jesse Hill, Jr., of the prestigious Atlanta Life Insurance Company, his membership in the Atlanta Chamber of Commerce board, the Boy Scouts, United Fund, and so on, all point to the American dream again coming true for one of Atlanta's own—this time around a black. He is said to have expressed hope that he may serve as a model for youthful strivers in the hard-core area, and one cannot doubt that for some he will.[2]

The next step for him as a business leader of his race, well recognized by the local white power structure, may be to go public in his financial ventures, and he then may well be on the road to the greatest prize in American endeavor and ownership, the status of owning a billion-dollar enterprise. This, however, is a long way off and a speculative question at this juncture. At this time, it must be stated, Russell and a half dozen others of his race stand almost alone, a token group in the mass of black strivers for power and position in the southeastern metropolis, Atlanta.

There is no turning back the clock. The policy, long pursued by Atlanta blacks, full economic integration, has forged far ahead of its rival black policy, separation. Only a few may continue to snipe at the gains of Russell and those like him, who seem to be garnering some of the larger rewards of the so-called black revolution and, by all measures, now a middle-class black-and-white-dominated one.

That the Atlanta black community was generally ready to welcome Russell's current success stems from policy considerations long held by black business leaders. In Study I this observation was made: Some of the business leaders of the ethnic community expressed the idea that progress in race relations can come for the minority group only through integration into the economic spheres of community activity. They point out that trade knows no barriers, and they feel that they are making substantial progress in building potent economic enterprises. Looking at their business establishments from the point of view of size and comparing them with some of the business establishments of the larger community, one can safely say that the ethnic community businessmen have a long way to go to catch up with the giant neighbors. Power is a relative matter, of course, and the men in secure economic positions in the community feel their influence and prestige mount as they are successful within their own community.

Black businesses still have a long way to go to catch up, but most, like many successful small white businesses, may not even try and will welcome the opportunity of financial integration with the billionaire corporations. It is, we are assured on every hand, the American way.

While Russell's rise has been very rapid and in the pace and tradition of the American tradition, it must be remembered that a handful of power structure persons predating the present era had worked hard and long to make such a rise possible. The pressures applied to those in the larger system by such as lawyer A. T. Walden, banker L. D. Milton, and insurance man Norris Herndon are a few cases in point. The added force of the whole civil rights movement alerted the white power structure to the problems of black exclusion, and its essential answer has been to open the gates a trifle and encourage just such activities as those of Russell. In that whole process, aided in a large measure by a perennial core of white liberals (those who sound "left," but are willing to trade), blacks got the right to vote and hold office.

The price paid by the white financial community has thus been minimal. Faced with demands for a greater equality in incomes, housing facilities, neighborhood amenities, schools, the white reply has been to open the channels to essentially professional opportunities, jobs that otherwise might have been filled by immigrants, and pick up a few black entrepreneurs as showpieces of progress.

Both blacks and whites who fought for fundamental change in the relations between ordinary citizens and the corporate/governmental juggernaut now face the indifference and counterforce of salt-and-pepper power structures that are now part of the framework set for black participation at all levels of American life. The reformers find very slight change, if any, from what has been their powerless lot for as long as living men can remember. Those who make black decisions for black people are quite in accord with the current stream of affairs. Contrary to general opinion, black leadership remains quite conservative.

Let us look more closely at the composition and positions of the black power structure, with particular reference to differences between the present arrangements and those of 1950.

Those who formed the center of power in Atlanta black affairs in the early 1970s included at least the following:

Ralph David Abernathy, Julian Bond, William Holmes Borders, Ben Brown, John Calhoun, Robert Cannon, Warren Cochrane, Fletcher Coombs, John Cox, Grace T. Hamilton, Vivian Henderson, Jesse Hill, Maynard Jackson, Leroy Johnson, Coretta King, John Middleton, L. D. Milton, James Paschal, Charles Reynolds, Herman J. Russell, C. A. Scott, Lyndon Wade, Hosea Williams, Q. V. Williamson, C. R. Yates.

Black policy leaders turned up in Study I were found to hold, in order of rank, the following positions: publisher, banker, minister, educator, politician, social worker(s), insurance executive, civic worker, and lawyer. Other ministers (including two bishops), the educators, and the undertaker were subordinate to the persons holding the positions in this primary list.

By 1973 those ranking in the top ten were: one insurance executive, one construction enterpriser, two politicians, two businessmen, one professional educator, one civic worker, one minister, and one publisher.

In Study I inquiry was made about the matter of the influence of ministers. The answers may be summed up in the words of Morris Elam, civic worker, who said, "The ministers and the undertakers are mostly selfish in their approach to most community situations. They either want to get more for themselves or to increase the size of their own organizations. People catch on to that sort of thing and when they are asked to choose leaders, they think of people that are not so much out for their own benefit. The doctors here are in the same category. They are interested in making money, but they are withdrawn from community life. They could not lead anyone."

A notable exception to these statements occurred with the rise of the dynamic political leader and minister, Dr. Martin Luther King, Jr. King was never considered a powerful local leader in Atlanta, but rather was looked upon as a very famous national leader. As indicated elsewhere in this writing, King's father and his wife have assumed greater Atlanta prominence since his death, but their influence in Atlanta affairs remains minimal. Both have fame, but there is considerable difference between celebrity and power. Dr. King, Sr.'s having been picked up by Carter during his campaign gave the old gentleman great national publicity, but he visibly has shared little if any power with him.

Also, the presence of black political officeholders tends to institutionalize political protest and political action generally. Preachers again preach.

None of this diminishes the historical role of the black preachers who at one time may have been the only politicians the black community had. Both the minister and the professional social worker by 1970 had given ground to the politician, who now had the responsibility, as the ministers once had, of assuring the leadership of the majority community that they can keep order in the ethnic quarter.

Such role changes within the black power structure do not perceptibly shift the industrial and technological hold on power by the larger Atlanta power structure. The policy goals of the black power structure coincides with that of the white: the general maintenance of the larger American system. The black role changes merely bring the black power structure closer to its parent model, even though many underlying policy differences between the two groups of populations they dominate remain.

The major occupational differences between top leaders in black power structures of Study I and Study II may be noted in the summary of power in table 3. The decline of professionals and the rise of political figures is evident. However, even though the figures show the business and financial leaders about equal in both eras, conversations with both black and white power structure personnel made it evident that three or four persons in these categories carry more weight in influence than had been true previously.

The professional groups in 1973, including a lawyer, three civic workers, three religious leaders, and two educators, were but half the

Table 3. Numerical Changes in Leadership-Generating Categories, Atlanta Black Power Structures, 1950 and 1973

Power-Generating Categories	1950	1973
Banking and insurance	3	4
Business enterprises	8	8
Politics	1	6
Professions	19	9

number nominated in our 1950 poll of top black leaders. The occupational listing of black professionals in lesser numbers is now more comparable to the traditional relationship of white professionals to the overall structure of power in the larger community.

The leaders of the black community, like those of the larger community, still live apart from their followers. The trends of settlement have remained relatively stable from 1950 to 1970, although there are many hundreds of excellent new homes in the old areas; they are priced between $40,000 and $60,000 (inflated more each year) and located in developments in southwest Atlanta that are named, among a growing number of such bucolic names, Cascade and Peyton Forest. It has been estimated that more than half of Atlanta's black population could be classified as belonging to the middle class in 1970. In other words, roughly 20 percent of all families had succeeded in bringing family income above the poverty level within less than two decades. Such progress cannot be denied. It is visible in the homes mentioned, in jobs, in autos driven, and in a relaxation of segregation in commercial facilities.

Those occupying dwellings in the northeast section of the larger community represent families who have lived in the area for many years. This area is now increasingly catering to residents who cannot afford the luxury homes of the southwestern portion of the city.

There is tacit agreement in the community as a whole that the westward and northeast movement of black dwellers shall proceed unabated. The northeast movement now falls into a renters' category. The Buckhead area and other northern portions of the city remain white in ethnic composition. This movement still represents a black-belt development, but to the black community it also represents, through the better homes offered them, a way of breaking the bonds of a ghetto-like existence that has plagued the area for many years. Withal, however, the ghettos remain intact for the majority of the unskilled workers and the poor. It remains the greatest visible "uncracked nut" among all the indications of progress.

In defining power in terms of action, we have said that it is not so much what men say that counts, but rather what they do. In regard to the "doing," for the next few pages three or four syndromes of action related to policies of major concern to both white and black top leadership, and their interactions with each other, will be discussed. It will be noted that, in each instance, blacks called upon whites to aid in the solution of a particular problem. The black power structure is still powerful, in a real sense, only so far as its members are granted power, credit, and social recognition by the white overlords of urban power in Atlanta. Black power figures are now joining them at their sufferance. Thus the caution put into the next few sentences.

In order to put the black business sector into clearer, present perspective, one must not overdramatize the black businessman's growing role in policy-making affairs in the community. That role, in the black community, has always been there in proportion to business size and success. In earlier days, such roles were not well recognized as important by the white power structure. Whites believed that the black preachers and undertakers were the powers in the black community. Activist pressure, growth of two or three businesses, plus better sociological data and reporting on these subjects helped change the views of those businessmen in the majority community, who began to judge black power more accurately during the 1960s.

Only four or five business operations in the Atlanta black community are relatively large. The largest local black insurance company, the local bank, a savings and loan company, and one of the major construction outfits nearly exhausts the list. There is considerable drop-off to the next echelon of business enterprise, occupied by a motel operation, the owner of which is named over and over by blacks as a prominent power figure. The next businessman is an operator of a small cosmetics firm. Neither of these two could qualify for a place in the dominant white community power structure. Significantly, those "picked up" by the white power structure are from the larger black enterprises. These, of course, in contrast to liaison leaders of an earlier day, are picked up as relative equals, with respect for their relative financial achievements. No Uncle Tomism is visible; no back seats at the banquets provided; no remarks of patronage intended—although the attentive eye and ear might catch a little of each on occasion. One must recall occasionally Frazier's *Black Bourgeoisie*.[3]

As we shall see, when the Reverend William Holmes Borders is quoted presently, the black community as a whole may not be as much in accord with the narrowing of the "bridging leader" groups as are the present top black leaders, those, at heart if not in rhetoric, in accord with the same principles of systematic exclusion in policy-making as their white counterparts. As the top leaders have prospered, their values resemble more and more the prevailing values of the city and the nation. They feel that it has been their duty to achieve financial and corporate success in order to be a part of the larger system. Their policy has been systematic integration, not separatism, the conservative black policy since at least the time of Booker T. Washington. Both black leaders and followers, contrary to their image among many white liberals, have always been conservative.

It came as a surprise to most liberals that, as the blacks gained power, they dropped alliances with liberal groups. The problem here was the whites' lack of perceptiveness. The struggle of both white liberals (the majority of whom were educated, professionals or scientists) and blacks has been for political recognition by the ruling local or national power structures. The higher recognition of black professionals in their own communities was a factor sought by whites in theirs. Within the black community, however, the black professional represented an educated, talented individual capable of earning respect in the white community, of furthering the black cause there. Blacks saw white, liberal professionals as they were, relatively powerless, but educated and sympathetic, persons who could, on occasion, voice for them to whites the worst of the blacks' frustrations. However, as the black mass began to express its own frustrations indelibly in fire and storm, few if any middleman whites were necessary. Nor were professional blacks interested in having any whites ride their train to power.

The relative powerlessness of white liberals, except as a small voting bloc, was never lost on black politicians. Astutely, as only black men could, blacks saw their white helpers as hired hands in the white community, hired for their brains and talents but generally denied positions of great power. Black politicians, public or private, have left the liberals to fend for themselves as they have moved toward the greater prizes of the system. They not only reached for the prizes of power, they demonstrated how well they had learned the more basic strategies of personal and group survival. With the exception of perhaps one or two, one finds few, but very few, liberal thinkers in the board rooms of power; indeed, continued associations with such liberals could be a distinct liability. Such are some of the calculations of the power equation.

To be sure, black professionals (now losing out in the local power brokerage scheme) and white professionals interested in civic betterment work together toward exemplary goals, but they remain cogs, wittingly or unwittingly, of the system. They help to keep the poor and dispossessed quiet, black and white. They furnish data on tensions and distress useful to those who make the larger decisions. Some of the data is filtered up the capillaries of power for consideration in decisions, but much of it is sidetracked en route, the principle being, "tell your patrons what they like to hear. They'll like you better if you say, 'All is well,' or at worst, 'Pretty good!'"

The little publications of some of the dissident, liberal organizations are filled with articles describing the incredible apathy of

John Q. Public, or they may highlight the fact of poor health among the poor along with demographic data on their prodigious reproductive powers, all of which is designed to shock social and economic dominants. But such information is either brushed aside by policymakers or taken into account as items to be blandly denied—or tactically admitted then belittled as being unimportant. Black leaders as well as white leaders read the same reports with, apparently, much the same reactions. Such has been the drift of affairs in recent years.

By 1970, Norris Herndon, a prime mover in 1950, had become, for personal and health reasons, a historical figure in his own community. (He died in 1977.) While the majority of people there may remember him and his father, those now knowledgeable about the situation recognize that for all practical purposes the original business has been for some time operated by Jesse Hill, who, unlike Herndon, has become a part of the major power structure of Atlanta while also being recognized as a prime mover in the black power structure.

Illustrative of this new and important role in black community affairs, by the early 1970s Hill primarily, along with Herman Russell and four or five other black leaders secondarily, was being recognized by whites in the white power structure as *the* black community leader, a fact which could not have been reported in Study I. He was also a member of the new board of the Metropolitan Atlanta Rapid Transit Authority (MARTA), and was made a member of the prestigious board of Rich's department store. These two facts coincide as power facts.

Richard Rich, whose downtown department store in 1970 bordered the black community on one side, was greatly dependent upon black trade. Also, as the International Omni project had grown, a corridor had been made possible by urban redevelopment that wiped out a substantial number of black living areas and connected it with Rich's entrance. The corridor provided a greater buffer area between a large number of black residents and white shoppers, which had eased the fears of some of the Rich's management that the downtown store might have catered, at last, primarily to blacks. Finally, Rich, as chairman of the MARTA board in its early stages, wanted black as well as other support for providing a MARTA stop at or near his store entrance; this is why Hill was appointed to both positions cited above. The move was made both for economic reasons as well as to keep the support of black residents. If all of this seems complicated it is so because of the ever-present black-white pull-and-tug in any matter of policy that concerns both groups.

The analysis just made is one that does not get very much open publicity in the local media. Blacks are pleased to see Hill's successes; that is, most of them are. One important exception was noted.

During one of my last visits to the city, Mr. Borders, who himself used to be a very prominent liaison person between the black community and the larger city's power structure, had grumbled publicly about Hill's domination of the bridging role, which at an earlier time might have been open to him or any of two dozen professional members of his community. Meeting Hill recently, Mr. Borders was quoted as saying, "Jesse, what you're doing is fine, but I want you to know, and I want the white folks to know, that Jesse Hill is not the only black man with brains and ability."[4]

This, of course, is an open criticism that reveals the subsurface struggle for power roiling continually in the black community. The chips are down for real, for public power with its enormous potential. The shift, as shown, is from professionals, who historically held center stage in the days of a certain amount of "make believe" power, to men who are more like the leaders of the dominant white power structure.

In the minor-league arena of public politics, Jesse Hill was denounced by former Senator Leroy Johnson for his support of Johnson's opponent in the mayoral race (Maynard Jackson won that 1973 election). The struggle split traditional forces in three or four ways in newer alignments of power.[5] Hill came out a winner.

Soothing Borders' wounded feelings, Hill addressed himself to his constituency in the larger community by saying,

> Reverend Borders wasn't kidding [about other able community leaders]. . . . too often there appears to be a trend for white leadership to identify a single black and to call upon him to fill every spot.
> That's unfair to him, and it's unfair to the entire black community. Certainly, my abilities and skills are greatly exaggerated. And I think that, here in Atlanta, there is great need for us to create opportunities for leadership for blacks.[6]

In the same newspaper interview, however, Hill gave the back of his hand to two leaders who had defied one of his principal white power structure supporters at the time, Mr. Rich. Ralph Abernathy and Hosea Williams, in action reminiscent of earlier days of protest, summoned a substantial number of their constituents to stage a buyers' strike against Rich's department store (May 1973), protesting against their laggard policies in hiring blacks and upgrading those already in employment. The strikers had even run a tingle of fear down the spines of residents in the white neighborhoods of Buckhead by picketing Rich's home during the struggle, a tactic which once again, as expected, landed Abernathy in jail.[7]

Hill contended that he had already been negotiating with Rich's on the whole matter and that his quieter tactics may have won much more than the public protest at last achieved. He said,

If Hosea Williams and the strikers [as a politician of the private sector, refusing to name the more popular leader of the strike, Mr. Abernathy] knew the full implications of the discussions I have had with Mr. Rich and Rich's president, Mr. Harold Brockey, it wouldn't have been necessary for them to strike at all. . . . Some of the commitments these men have made regarding fair play and the upgrading of blacks go beyond anything Hosea Williams and the strikers can ever imagine.[8]

Such remarks certainly ingratiated Rich's board member, Hill, with his white constituency in the overall power structure. Even the reporter of the metropolitan press felt obliged to conclude in his story that "With remarks like these, Hill could be taken to be a black businessman reacting very, very much like a businessman, period."

Indeed! And this is the new political (policy-making) face of Atlanta's black and its white-black power structure. It is a face carefully watched, according to one of my West Coast informants, Ivy Lewis, by blacks throughout the nation. The black power brokers of Atlanta, including Hill and others, were responsible for a school busing settlement that has been debated for the past two or three years in black communities around the nation. The gist of an agreement reached between white and black leaders in which segregation would continue among three-fourths of Atlanta's school population, according to *New Yorker* reporter Calvin Trillin, boils down to the fact that the black community leaders agreed to call off action against recalcitrant whites *if* the whites would agree to upgrading blacks' jobs within the whole school system; special attention would be paid to administrative positions, in total some "five hundred thousand dollars worth of jobs." The whole agreement, with its power-structure implications, was summed up by Trillin as follows:

The moderate, middle-class Black leaders—sick of arguing about school integration, sharing some of the fears of white businessmen about the social and economic effect of white flight to the suburbs, feeling some pressure from their own constituents against busing, accustomed to negotiating for jobs and power—were amenable to a deal.

The white businessmen who usually make the important civic decisions in Atlanta seem to have reacted to the possibility of splitting the local N.A.A.C.P. away from the Inc. Fund more or less the way the management of a furniture plant might react to the possibility of persuading its most skilled and experienced craftsmen that the union had not been acting in the true interests of the workers—particularly the true interests of the workers who happened to be skilled and experienced craftsmen. The school strategy of influential whites in Atlanta over the past fifteen years appears to have been based on protecting the schools of the white Northside and providing stability for business development—both of which seemed threatened by the possibility of a drastic integration order. Whites have been talking to promi-nent black spokesmen for a long time about the advantages of pressing for administrative participation rather than classroom integration. At a meeting last fall of a biracial business group called the Atlanta Action Forum, a Fifth Circuit Judge who lives in Atlanta suggested to Lonnie King and the white businessmen present that the whole matter could probably be settled if intelligent folks just sat around and thrashed it out without being smothered by a lot of lawyer talk.

The settlement was reached after a few days of closed discussions in a room at the Trust Company of Georgia. It was handled in the way such matters have been handled in Atlanta over the years—trade-off and compromise and congratulations all around at the end.[9]

The *New York Times* analyst B. Drummond Ayres, Jr., wrote a story in depth on the Atlanta plan, which brought out, among other relevant facts of the case, the concern of the NAACP that the Atlanta solution might set a pattern for other cities in the nation. He spoke at length of the struggle of the national NAACP with a local recalcitrant chairman, Lonnie King, who was at last deposed by them.

The final portions of Ayres's analysis indicates what some of the real reasons were for the move of Atlanta's leadership to close the door on further desegregation of public schools, and hindsight seems to confirm his reasoning.[10] Leading blacks were fearful that a massive fight might lead only to further defeats. In the latter days of massive protests, Atlanta had a brief night or two of fire and scuffle which was put down, in part, by the leaders in question. Many had begun to see that further escalation of struggle would not only wipe out many gains blacks had made during the sixties, but might also lead to genocidal countermeasures nationally by political administrations that had not been loath to loose heavy fire and destruction on any abroad who thwarted their will. Television wisps of bloody forays by heavily armed police against unarmed populations, city by city, had not been reassuring. The violent protests had been beaten back with massed violence. The voices of moderation in the black communities began to be heard above the tumult.

In Atlanta, the voice of Dr. Benjamin E. Mays, a black educator (and the minister chosen to eulogize King), said,

But 20 years ago, when school desegregation was just starting in the South, Atlanta schools were 70 percent white and 30 percent black. Now they're 80 percent black and 20 percent white.

It's a matter of white flight and private schools, the old story. Massive busing would be counterproductive at this point. We'd end up with no whites to bus.[11]

Dr. Mays was then speaking as a respected elder statesman, a black man who had achieved, by election, the presidency of the Atlanta Board of Education. He long has been an educational policymaker. Many were ready to hear him.

Aside from a few mumbled protests of poor, unpublished blacks regarding "trading off quality education for a few big jobs for a few big Negroes," the program has been adopted with a minimum of negative legal or political aftermath. As many other cities have continued to debate this whole question, Atlanta has used its energies, for better or worse, otherwise.

As indicated in the passage from Trillin, the formulation of policy behind the pacific agreement was largely the result of white-black power structure talks in a private, informal group, Action Forum.

Raleigh Bryans, in an analytical interview with Jesse Hill in the Atlanta *Journal and Constitution*, describes publicly for the first time the fundamentally changing state of white-black power-structure relations.

Right now, he [Jesse Hill] and some peers in the black community are sitting down regularly with a similar peer group of white businessmen in what may be a unique experiment in white-black relations in the entire nation.

In fact, the experiment is two years old, though it has been so hush-hush that little has been known of it, much less printed about it.

For reasons known only to him, Hill now finds it possible to talk with candor about the experiment, though he does not call it that.

What is called the Action Forum was, according to Hill, formed primarily through the efforts of white banker Mills B. Lane Jr. On the white side, besides Lane, it includes such men as J. Paul Austin, chairman of the board of the Coca-Cola Co.; Lee Burge, president of Retail Credit Co.; Tom Cousins, president and chairman of Cousins Properties, Inc.; John Portman, architect; Tom Beebe, chairman of the board of Delta Air Lines, Inc.; and the "chief officers of all of the major banks." [One observes that action, black and white, in Atlanta's power structure moves easily from one major policy issue or project to another.]

On the black side, in what came to be called the "Atlanta Consortium," taking over from the older "Syndicate" were men like Hill, who happens to be vice president and actuary of The Atlanta Life Insurance Co., a $32 million

Black-owned institution. Herman Russell, president of the H. J. Russell Plastering Co. and other enterprises; John Cox, executive director of the Butler Street YMCA; Lyndon Wade, executive director of the Atlanta Urban League; James Paschal, co-owner of Paschal's Motor Hotel; Fletcher Coombs, president of the Mutual Savings and Loan Association; and Charles Reynolds, president of Citizens Trust Co. [i.e., the central core of the black power structure].[12]

One is loath to throw a wet blanket on any euphoric glow of progress, but a word of caution and advice may be in order. One is bound to say from the evidence obtainable that those chosen by the white power structure to be their companions in policy-making are indeed few in number—suggesting hard-bitten tokenism—and they seem to be echoes of the choosers. If this study or its predecessor has any messages, they concern the extension of democratic processes.

On the other side of the power coin in Atlanta, the short side to be sure, are the elected officeholders, the majority of whom at this writing are black, two of them having succeeded to office since my last visit there. I have kept some track of these latter individuals, Maynard Jackson, mayor, and (certainly with little difficulty, because of his national press) Andrew Young, then a new congressman of the Fifth Congressional District of Georgia.

One of my first calls upon Atlanta politicians, after a courtesy conversation with Mayor Massell, was upon the well-known state senator, Julian Bond. He had invited me to an afternoon meeting at his home.

Upon entering Senator Bond's home, I was met by him and introduced to about a dozen people he had summoned to help me sort out some of the power-structure elements during my return visit. One of those present, I am gratified to say, was William Miller, who remapped the physical locations of the power and professional leaders for me and took me around to view the new housing developments for blacks and to revisit the whole area occupied by the current white power structure. Of those in attendance at the meeting, I would judge twelve out of fifteen were white. A number were in street dress of the period, others in conservative outfits. They were the editors of the liberal and more advanced little publications and members of the advance guard, evidently, for helping Bond get the votes he needs in the remaining white sections of central Atlanta to keep him in office. The afternoon did not bring any startling facts to the fore. I went over my list of nominees for top billing at that time in the overall power structure and met nodding agreement and a few further suggestions from those present. Bond, whose wife had excused herself for the afternoon, had to jump up now and then to care for one or another of his children. He waited all afternoon for a plumber to come and do some work for him, a worker who had not yet appeared when I left about four-thirty.

I met a pleasant couple who were about to let go of trying to "remake political Atlanta" through publishing a "liberal journal" in favor of making a living at recording oral history for the University of North Carolina. Later I had dinner with them, and over good lasagna and jug wine we argued the size, shape, and health of the Atlanta power structure; their position, contrary to mine, was that the local power structure had lost its grip when its leader Ivan Allen, Jr., had come out on election eve against the then-incumbent Sam Massell. I came to see, however, that the power structure was interested in a great many activities besides City Hall—for example, in building sky-scrapers.

I kept waiting for someone, including myself, to come up with a new idea during my visit with Bond and his friends, but to no avail. Bond said little, but he did admit that the executive suites downtown still contained power to be reckoned with. I could not help thinking that the company as a whole seemed, with the possible exception of Bond, defeated. The bloody put-down of the sit-ins and march-ins would seem to have taken a toll among them and their friends. I felt also that they were waiting for me to tell them something new and mind-boggling, but I had just arrived seeking information. I had no rousing tales to tell. I felt that I was not living up to advance billing.

My reading of Bond in retrospect runs something like this: as a black, he has a substantial following at home, and he has been able to raise money in other parts of the country. He keeps fairly quiet in his legislative spot. It is comfortable living for him. He is now stacking up seniority points in the Georgia Senate, and such a position has always held good potential at least for modest success. His loyalty to the Democratic party in the A. T. Walden tradition has helped him. Bond, I believe, will succeed by staying power, and importantly upon the staying power guaranteed by an early reputation as an active leader in the 1960s civil rights movement, now a coveted badge of honor in both liberal white communities and in black ones of any political persuasion.

I believe that but for minor details, the same story also might be told of Maynard Jackson, the mayor. Both Bond and Jackson appear to know where the power is located. They keep a low profile. In a recent time of upsurge, following a march upon City Hall of several thousand unemployed blacks led by Mrs. King, Jackson made an impassioned speech to the marchers, but the next day he assured a television audience that the situation was well in hand, that both sides of such questions remain "good old boys." Andrew Young came out as the only man in America to whom President-elect Carter acknowledged any political campaign debt. Bond, I understand, supported primary loser Udall, a liberal Democrat, thus giving Bond consistent integrity.

As for former Congressman Andrew Young, little needs to be said, except that he was President Carter's man at the United Nations and a recognized loyal follower of Martin Luther King, Jr.

Such are some of the personnel changes in the Atlanta power structure, profound changes in the light of even recent history, but changes that seem easily cooptable by the larger structure of power of the system.

Without disparaging the magnificent displays of personal courage and dedication of those struggling for the actual operation of civil rights—many of the rights already written into law, long inoperative—one must measure the subsequent achievements of those wielding the powers of public office with others in the network of community power. While many Atlantans and thousands of others from all cities of the nation were marching on Montgomery, the major powers of Atlanta were extremely busy extending their own and the national juggernaut's private power, the largest in human history to that date.

The power spoken of could be evaluated only in its own terms, merely in capital terms, but it is better evaluated in its total social terms. In its own terms, one must speak of capital gains; in social terms, one must speak of the considerable social loss that may have accompanied them. These latter terms are related to widespread social disparity and dispossession, reaching not only poverty sectors of the society but the middle-class and upper-middle-class sectors as well. One only need examine the real estate prices of this period to know, for example, that those included in these latter classes (classifications) of population could not afford to buy homes for cash in most instances, but were forced into debt and at last into mere life tenure of the properties then occupied. I cite below the capital growth, between 1949 and 1976, of some of the central organizations of the Atlanta community, which traditionally have been considered by their peers to be major power-generating ones: Genuine Parts, $5 million to $305 million; Coastal State Life Insurance, $2 million to $103 million; Life Insurance Company of Georgia, $47 million to $859 milllion; Trust Company of Georgia, $118 million to $1,824 million; Georgia Power Company, $293 million to $4,078 million; Atlanta Gas Light Company,

$32 million to $379 million; Citizens and Southern Bank, $307 million to $3,159 million; Coca-Cola, $204 million to $1,700 million; and Fulton National Bank, $122 million to $722 million.[13] In terms of percentage of increase, these figures range approximately from a high of 6,000 percent to a low of 500 percent; the mean average of them all is 1500 percent.

To contrast such figures with those obtained by the ordinary citizen was impossible for me to accomplish, but I did consult with middle-range-income professionals, Thaddeus Brown and his wife of Study I, for example. Brown had been ousted from his job in Atlanta for being critical of the processes of community power at the time. I wished to learn how he had fared in the matter of capital accumulation during the interval in question. One cannot claim statistical comparability of Brown's case with that of the corporations, but my own observations of events would seem to lend credulity to his typicality with others of his class.

Brown, reinforced by views expressed by his wife, contended that losing friends in the power structure of Atlanta is certainly no way to participate in the processes of great capital gain. As a matter of fact, Brown lost all of his capital following his ouster, i.e., his equity in a home and his savings, and by 1950 he had recouped only a few hundred dollars. By 1976 his capital amounted to a gain of about 5 percent more than his 1950 savings, and even that figure had to be discounted by the fact that the modest home in which he and his wife lived in 1976 carried a mortgage that was deemed by them to be manageable, if, to them, socially inexcusable, and which would apparently outlast his lifetime. The couple had indeed sent four children to college, three of them through it, and, like Willie Loman before them, they had at last paid off the mortgage on their last automobile. His balance sheet was not impressive in comparison with the mean gain of 1500 percent racked up by the corporate conglomerates of Atlanta, but even so, it is being argued, the Browns' circumstances, ouster or no ouster, are not much different from those who were less inclined to demur and who are swamped in the great pool of individual debt—an accounts receivable item adding to the capital-gain accounts of the great corporations—that afflicts every community in the nation.

A "normal" historical rule of thumb in measuring capital return is a decade, i.e., if one puts his whole capital to work, he might reasonably expect to have it returned to him with interest within a decade. To have it returned to him a hundredfold or a thousandfold in two decades, as in the cases cited, represents new rules of accumulation in our society, rules made possible by courts and public administrative agencies which either cannot keep up with the vast and intricate technological organizing activities of corporate and conglomerate monopolies, or who wish to look the other way and pretend that it is just good business to earn between 100 percent and as much as 1000 percent on invested capital. Or, it might mean that gargantuan combinations are an inevitable evolution of the whole process of capital decision-making. In any case, the whole process is called, by some, progress.

Whether more honest, or restricted for lack of opportunity, black capital's increases are more modest; the comparable figure in the black sector is provided by one of the largest financial organizations of the black community, the Citizens Trust Bank: from approximately $20 million in 1950 to $32 million in 1970. However, it has nearly doubled its size in a decade, whereas it had taken nearly thirty years, from 1921 to 1950, for it to achieve its first $20 million. Its accelerated rate of capital expansion during the last decade indicates, undoubtedly, that it has joined the system.

However one may look at the picture, the fact remains that the preponderance of community power in Atlanta remains downtown. Most Atlantans, including those in elective offices at every level, are well aware of this fact, a fact which a few die-hard critics of power-structure theory fail to see, or refuse to admit. Such are some of the strange ways of the professional analysts among us, who for whatever reasons continue to believe in the existence of a democratic equality in a pluralism of general power—which may have never existed in the history of our nation.

Power Succession:
Old Leaders and New

Most informants, when asked about succession in the power structure and offered categories in which to place names in nomination for top leadership in power, 1970, could readily do so. It quickly became apparent that the same businesses and associations were generating the leaders, both old names or new, in industry, finance, retail trade, and so on. Furthermore, sons in many instances followed illustrious fathers, and historical names, as we have noted in our chapter on families, some twenty of them, apparently reappear generation after generation. New power-generating organizations, that is, those not appearing in the 1950 listing, included more banks (many having grown large in the period of prosperity preceding 1970), insurance companies, and real estate and development companies important in the building boom; for the first time, blacks were put in nomination by whites. A closer examination of the dynamics of the building boom revealed that the younger, up-and-coming developers of properties of all sorts, and high-rises in particular, without exception got their start by being backed by older investors such as Ben Massell (in John Portman's case) and Richard Courts, with others (in the case of Tom Cousins). Those active in the money gerontocracy were important in the 1970 scene in Atlanta, more so than in 1950.

The shift in the black/white picture of overall power, it has been noted, was not due to any generosity on the part of traditional white power wielders. The blacks had won their place in the scheme of things. In terms of actual wealth and power, the ratios still overwhelmingly favor the white capital structures, but wisdom has bidden the whites to accommodate the blacks in their drive for public office, where some may ultimately parlay that good fortune into bigger stakes, the money stakes of great power. The three or four black capitalists of the structure still have a long way to go to emulate those at the top in industry and finance, the difference being that they control only a few million and are not in the billionaire class. The people in the latter category are not at all threatened by the takeover of City Hall, nor by the rise of a small millionaire group in the black community. In general, the few blacks who are recognized as rising are being coopted into the capital system of the nation, and the blacks of great means have become a part of the general system in which the little fellows, black or white, do not have much to say about the development and direction of overall policy. The technological system thus becomes no respecter of color. The top black leaders are sounding very much like their white counterparts in the business realm.

While all of this suggests profound structural change, in a sense it is merely personnel change within a system of technology that remains relatively unchanged. The problems of power, the disparities of it, the bureaucratic mindlessness, the isolation of the individual from policy-making structures, the feelings of personal defeat and meaninglessness remain.

The labor nominee was not a unanimous choice. Businessmen knew him from his long residence in the city. "If you must have a labor man, he's probably as good as any." The labor people said, "We really do not know too many of those people downtown. . . ." And thus he received more power-nomination votes than did other labor leaders.

I found that at least one assessment, in the traditional power-structure sense, had been made by an insider.

Ivan Allen, Jr., writes very convincingly about the transfer of power among the local business owners. Writing of the time in the mid-1950s when he began to take over the powers transferred by those older around him, he indicates that at the time of the 1954 Supreme Court decision on segregation, there was a changing of the guard and that the old-time leaders were passing the mantle on to a whole new generation, with a leadership that was not yet mature or solidified.[1]

Never shy about citing the attributes that made him successful, Allen is widely quoted by his contemporaries as having said that he had inherited money, made money, and married money. He conceded that that was a winning combination. He had indeed married Louise Richardson, of one of the most prominent families of Atlanta. Hugh Inman, Mrs. Allen's maternal grandfather, was probably the wealthiest man in Atlanta, the foremost dealer in real estate, with a great deal of property on Northside Drive.[2]

Continuing his discussion of power succession, Allen says that at the time [the mid-fifties] the older white leaders of the city—men like Robert W. Woodruff, developer of the Coca-Cola Company and possessor of the largest personal fortune in the South—were in the process of turning over the leadership to a younger group, of which Allen was a part.[3]

In Study I, a half-dozen years before, I had received complaints from some of the younger "comers," Allen included as I recall, that the oldsters were stubbornly holding on, a fact that a few of them resented. However, rapidly changing times apparently made some of the oldsters more rapidly change their minds regarding giving up their power.

The older group which had dominated the city for four decades with R. W. Woodruff in the lead as community patron, had given a great deal to the city and had witnessed its growth from an overgrown country town to a metropolis of some one million persons. Allen's implication is that they now deserved retirement.[4] (One may be reminded of similar family behavior in other parts of the nation: the Balls of Muncie; Dodges, Detroit; Fords, Detroit; Mellons, Pittsburgh; Rockefellers and Whitneys, New York; Hunts, Dallas; Crockers, San Francisco; and so on. It is a pattern not peculiar to Atlanta.)

Woodruff, unofficial advisor to the city's Mayor Hartsfield for many years, was in the process of turning over the management of Coca-Cola to younger men, and the affairs of city management and direction were also being turned over to younger men—their successors—whom Allen describes as "successors to the throne." He felt that the "throne" would be in good hands, well sat upon. Atlanta, he felt, would be cherished and guided well by those who "inherited" her. The situation was not unlike the takeover of the business establishments the younger men were inheriting from their fathers. Certainly, the takeover of business direction and community direction were, according to Allen, concurrent.[5]

Two items above may be underscored for those who continue to cherish the myth of the separations and differences between business and political power. Allen is saying clearly and forcefully, as a man of knowledge and experience, that the management of Coca-Cola and the direction of Atlanta were to a degree synonymous, and not only was Woodruff passing on this kind of power, but his peers were doing the same.[6] The transfer of such powers coincided with the relinquishment of power in the individual businesses of the older men. Their sons are successors to the throne of power.[7]

Giving emphasis to the sociological factors present in such power arrangements and transfers, Allen concluded that the transferral of power took about ten years, from the early to the late 1950s. As he looked around from his new seat of power, he found himself surrounded by lifelong friends—all born, educated, and living within a mile or two of one another in one of the better neighborhoods of the city. They went to the same schools, dated the same class of girls, and married them. They settled down to work and play in the same neighborhood in which they had grown up.[8] This portion of Allen's statement is a confirmation of the contentions of such writers as William Domhoff and Digby Baltzell, whose theses concerned the transformation of social self-consciousness of class into class power. It does, of course, for some. The transformation, however, is not universal, not uniform. Some in Mayor Allen's circumstances just do not want to be bothered by wielding public power, by the sweaty struggle over it. Many of means prefer to think of themselves as "establishment," which translated means "ownership establishment," plus their courtiers and retainers. Most are willing to let retainers administer their affairs. A power structure contains members who are strivers like Allen, who by his qualifications may have easily entered the establishment of Atlanta, even though his fortune does not equal the great billionaire fortunes of the day. In this regard, Allen relatively remains a little fellow among the giants. Yet, he chose, perhaps for the reason of smaller fortune, to struggle in the field of politics, local politics, and business.

It must also be noted that the possession of money, social position, and the will to power is a combination of factors that certainly gives a leg up to any who may wish to contend in the arena of power.

As it is by so many in capitalistic society, hard work is extolled by Allen, and I must say that many powerful men work harder and longer in life than they actually need to.[9] There is, in our society, a broad spectrum of working rich as well as camouflaged, idle rich (all make some pretense at being useful at something, even if it might be growing prize orchids).

In a time when men might work considerably less, the piling up of more and more wealth, whether personally needed or not, holds a fascination for them as does no other activity.

Pleading the cause of work for himself and his co-powers in the community, Allen states that most of them had been taught the virtues of hard work by their fathers and had grown up in the depression of the thirties when such work was needed to hold together faltering businesses. The work paid off well in succeeding years. He describes in colorful language the virtues as well as the idiosyncrasies of the new leaders around him who had experienced few divorces, were business-oriented, WASPs, nonpolitical, pragmatic, well-educated, and dedicated to bettering Atlanta, to doing something for the people, as one might say, as well as helping themselves. They have been called a *"power structure"* he says, italicizing the term without reference to the source of his pejorative quote.

He goes on to relate that when one spoke of the "power structure," one meant the presidents of major banks, the Atlanta-based industries, like Coca-Cola, the heads of the larger utilities, a triad of retail establishments, a few leading regional branches of national firms, the head of transit operations—whoever that might be at the moment—and one or two larger realtors and merchants, including himself and the Haverty business interests. These numbered around fifty persons, he said.[10] He speaks, of course, of the nucleus of the historical structure of power without reference to its greater periphery. That nucleus accords with today's figure rather than with that of an earlier day. His order of reference—starting with the banks and industries and descending to the utility managers and those of relatively small businesses—is approximately correct. If he does not actually know the source of his quote for the power-structure term, one can see that he has reached his conclusions by an insider's route, while the conclusions of Study I and Study II have been reached from the outside. That fact is noteworthy.

Besides being businessmen for the most part, how did the power-structure nominees train for the tasks of power? Allen suggests that they warmed up for a few years on projects of community uplift to get ready to take over the more awesome tasks of power. Living within a stone's throw of one another, in the Habersham and West Paces Ferry Road region, they shared problems, interests, and ambitions. These included mostly executive problems within a community context, problems of management of business personnel, the larger community projects, and taxes. Their common bond and common goals evolved into a business-civic leadership of the city, generally, and, finally, into the "power structure."[11]

It is tempting to say, in relation to this inclusiveness, "No others need apply!" but I shall reserve judgment on that question for discussion at a later point. Allen has written eloquently and well in behalf of the dynamics and characteristics of Atlanta's power structure of the years between 1950 and 1970.

While the "inheritors" represent a large portion of power leaders, others came to power by other means. Many achieved power rather than inheriting it, and these persons divided into several categories of accession, namely, corporate, professional, and political.

Some of them deserve mention as a part of a new band of leadership in the power structure: the builders, two or three of whom were taking over power where Ivan Allen, Jr., is now in the process of leaving off.

John Portman, of the newer Atlanta forces, is now rather widely publicized for his grandiose ideas of building open-spaced hotels in major centers in Atlanta and other large American cities. He was often mentioned as a member of Atlanta's power structure by informants, who liked his success if not his "adult Disneyland" style of architecture. He is said to be aloof from others and sometimes imperious in his dealings with subordinates, but his story as told by his public relations firm is strictly Horatio Alger.

As a member of the power structure, he is of a new breed. He did not have the cozy, clubby upbringing of which Allen spoke. He is self-made. That is, he was backed early by Ben Massell, large tract owner of downtown properties, in building a trade mart that was an immediate success and that led to the development of Portman's Peachtree Center, a complex including a hotel, office space, and variety stores. Rather than the usual list of civic accolades, reports of Portman's community memberships read more like a curriculum vitae of a successful architect. He is apparently trade-association minded, and his documented civic life carries none of the usual leader-building activities—Scouts, United Fund, and cultural board-tending—which characterized the earlier leaders' dossiers. Portman was apparently too busy to indulge in time-consuming civic activities. He lists no local clubs. His empire, some say, is built on credit, as any self-made man's would have to be in this day of the superconglomerates, and many have watched to see whether or not Portman can last the course. To date, he appears to have done very well.

Regarding the development of policy in Atlanta, however, Portman had always pleased one bloc of the power structure, that occupied by men like Ben Massell or Richard Rich who believed fervently in building downtown first and foremost. These men were joined by the Central Atlanta Improvement Association's leaders (later the Central Atlanta Progress, Inc.), which always included many of those prominent in any power structure. Because of the struggle by those who want neighborhood developments and rehabilitation of housing stocks rather than so much downtown building, the point remains a viable political question, but one in which the Portman, Massell, Rich forces have had the upper hand. As a result Atlanta has one of the most enviable downtown developments and some of the most dismal slums as well as arid middle-class living areas in the nation.

The achievements of John Portman have importance beyond their money terms. Portman, as merely a professional architect, could never have hoped to achieve his present success. Within the system, success is measured by one's ability to control a considerable portion of the land, the money supply, and the technology (buildings, machines, and labor forces, including professionals and their ideas). The architect, usually bound by the principles of his profession, cannot be both idea man and entrepreneur. Portman violated this principle by demanding a piece of any action in which he engaged; he combined abilities in controlling a money supply plus an "idea factory" plus a sector of the technology related to building construction and property management. In this breakthrough he gave the hitherto striving and failing professionals of the community and nation a tingle of hope. Perhaps, in some way, they too might have a chance to grasp the brass ring of their particular merry-go-round. Such dreams are counter to the strictures of most power-structure values, which require that teachers teach, preachers preach, architects imagine and draw, and so on, while bankers, business, and industrial executives plan and deploy financial and labor forces. Portman's independence of spirit manifested itself early. He had not waited for his school to find a slot for him in his profession, but set up shop on his own, then moved step by step to building his dream, a downtown complex, with the support of "maverick money" from the upstart west, Texan Trammell Crowe, and from Ben Massell, a local big real estate dealer but a man held at arm's length by many members of the power structure of which he was a part. He was not considered to be a popular leader, even if respected for his shrewd buying habits in downtown real estate. In short, Portman, relatively speaking, was backed by outsiders and has himself remained an outsider, respected but suspect. It is whispered that only time will tell how the coalition he has built will survive in somewhat jealous, hostile surroundings. But survive he may, for his dreams include larger and larger displays of the might and power of urban capital expressed in long urban malls fringed with greenery, the air filled with electronic bird songs, ripplingbrook sounds interspersed with traffic directions from the hidden loudspeakers.

Portman's struggle for personal independence remains a political struggle, a struggle between segments of the ruling groups within the city, a struggle between centralized and dispersed growth, and between the leaders and a large portion of the population who feel discarded because of the continued demand by both power factions for great capital outlays unrelated to the economic basics of their lives: food, clothing, shelter, recreation, and clean and adequate space. Portman did not beat the local power system to gain his position. He got a local boost, then went outside the local structure to restive new capital, and finally has been welcomed into the older system of monopoly capital as a worthy newcomer.

Tom Cousins, a conventional real estate developer and another newly arrived success in Atlanta of the sixties and seventies, unlike Portman, is possessed of an ebullient personality and openly speaks of his struggle along the way. His first building project in Atlanta, he told me in an interview, involved a piece of property he had readied for subdivision. J. H. Calhoun had been instrumental, he affirmed, in helping him gain the property. He had put most of his cash and a few thousand of borrowed cash into the venture and had advertised an opening day with all the resources he could muster—about five thousand dollars. When that day arrived, a Sunday, he got out of bed and looked out the window at sheets of rain. He went back to the bedroom and said to his wife, "Well here we go again! Over the hill . . . !" Then he had an inspired idea. He ran to the phone and called one of the popular radio stations and asked that they put spot announcements on the air every fifteen minutes stating that the Cousins properties invited one and all to visit the site, where they would be furnished an umbrella along with drinks and other refreshments. Many people came, and he signed up enough housing starts to put him firmly on the road to a brilliant career. In his middle forties he had achieved a headquarters building on one of the major highway interchanges, had stocks in the market with good readings, and was in the way of getting a major project underway that would keep him busy for years: Railroad Gulch, an all-but-abandoned but huge area of switching tracks not too far from Grady Square. It had been a developer's dream for years. If one could acquire the air rights over the tracks and build above them, any number of fortunes could be made. A few years ago, Robert Troutman, Jr., an attorney, had acquired such rights from the state legislature, with the provision that within a half-dozen years, which at the time seemed ample, the first structure would have to be built over the tracks. But it was harder to put such a huge project together than Troutman and his colleagues had anticipated, and consequently a few weeks before his option was up, Troutman called Cousins to see if he would be interested in helping to assure the continuance of the property option. Cousins would be interested indeed, and he had an idea, which he would not reveal until he was assured of being given a major position in the development of the property. Satisfied with an agreement, he said he would build a parking lot over a portion of the area, one big enough to satisfy the monetary requirements of the state in regard to the option. The parking structure was completed in time, in a matter of a few weeks. The whole venture, now called Omni-International, at last includes hotel facilities, an international trade center, an indoor sports arena, and many other major projected edifices, which will be connected by rapid transit and a corridor to downtown. One entrance, not altogether accidentally, said Mr. Rich, is near Rich's department store.

One of Cousins's first backers, an industrial developer, was and remains one of the senior members of the power structure, one of Ivan Allen's neighbors and also a self-made man. Arriving in Atlanta many years ago from a neighboring state and working briefly for one or two of the city's banks, he finally struck out for himself and established, among many other ventures, a very successful local investment company. After a few years his firm was serving the region. Our model developer is a friendly, gregarious gentleman with a genius for making money for others while enriching himself. He has known a series of United States presidents and their top officials intimately. One of his closest friends was one of our secretaries of defense, who often had visited his island estate. He has long been able to spot potential industrial successes and shepherd them along the path to success. One of his greatest accomplishments has been in transport developments. Another, he told me, was the development of a chemical process that put air and carbon together, but the main ingredient of which was air. He learned from his friend James V. Forrestal, secretary of defense, that the product was indeed useful to the military and realized that, with the principle ingredient being air, one could probably lose very little. The inventor of the process was kept in the company for a time but was forced out when it was apparent that his skills did not include a very firm grasp of corporate management. He was adequately compensated for his contribution to the company but could be tolerated on no other grounds.

The principal methods in his operations were to find a man with a good idea and to help him along as much as possible. One finds, he believes, that one will help oneself in that way as well. One of the other major developers of the recent building boom was one of those helped.

His sense of Southern dry humor comes out in his conversation from time to time. I had asked him to illustrate how some of the local leaders had managed to put up one of the many skyscrapers. He outlined the process of financing and mentioned his going to New

York to get the assistance of one of the Rockefellers on one project. While there he mentioned his interest in helping the United Negro College Fund drive, and his Rockefeller contact told him that he was just in time to have lunch with the education foundation board and speak to them about his ideas along that line. During the luncheon, Rockefeller prodded him to go back to Atlanta and get some of his colleagues to raise a sum that the foundation would then match. He was told that he would have to learn to give money away in order to get money.

He went home and called one of his friends, a well-known agribusiness man, and asked him to get together some select people for a dinner. At the dinner, he spoke of his meeting with the Rockefeller group. He later related that when he got to the part about having to spend money in order to get more, he saw one of them drop his chin and yell, "Spend it, hell! We've just got it!"

Fond of such money stories, he recalled that he had gone one time to see Sid Richardson, the Texas oil man, about a money matter. It was at about the time that the "Murchison boys" were trying to buy the New York Central Railroad. The Murchison boys, of whom Richardson was very fond, called him "Uncle" Sid. They had a standing agreement with him that if they found any deal which particularly appealed to them, Richardson would go in half with them on it. One day he got a call from one of them who said that they were trying to get hold of the New York Central Railroad properties and hoped that Uncle Sid would put ten million into the venture. Richardson immediately sent them a check for five million, thinking that it would be his half share. The next morning he got a call from one of the boys, who said, "I believe you misunderstood the amount we need, Uncle Sid. Ten million was the amount of your half share." "Oh," replied Richardson, "just tear up the check and I'll send you another one. And by the way, what did you say was the name of that railroad?"

All of these persons who have been used as illustrations of power relationships have one element of power in common, that is, each had a financial patron who helped him in achieving a particular goal or goals. The patrons in each case were functionaries in various urban power structures. The giving and receiving of patronage money in each instance accords with two Introduction hypotheses:

Power functionaries are those who, in addition to their other societal roles, with formal or informal sanctions, carry specific roles related to the maintenance of any prescribed, differentiated social order.

The means of power are modes of material, money, and symbolic patronage which, at root, are processes in inclusion/exclusion.

Economic patrons are often besieged by many petitioners for grants of money and recognition. Few are chosen. The many are excluded.

The hierarchical nature of patronage is illustrated by the developer's membership on a national board. So far as I know, the national board in the illustration to follow did not directly patronize him with money, but his inclusion on such a prestigious board awarded him symbolic patronage.

He told me that he had enjoyed greatly the opportunity of being on the national IBM board. That corporation reaches so many facets of American business that its problems are common to all, and the information that one may absorb during a term of membership helps one's own business. As he reached what he considered to be retirement age, he submitted a letter of resignation to the IBM board. The other members asked him generously and apparently sincerely to reconsider his decision. He responded with a story that Dick Rich was supposed to have related about Hughes Spalding, Sr. "We'll tell you," they had said, "if you begin to become senile." "Sure, you'd tell me," he had replied, "but by then, I'd refuse to believe you!" The developer is a charming teacher. He, like other people in any power structure, can and does tell stories that illustrate the close relations between the Atlanta, the national, and the international power structures.

As I took notes on the developer's stories, I realized that his were not isolated anecdotes. Certainly, his manifest purpose was to share a number of humorous stories, but more deeply, he meant to tell me in various ways that he is a man who moves on the national scene (mostly toward New York and Texas capital) to pick up money for Atlanta uses. He is able to move easily among the super-rich, who control so much of the nation's capital, and, importantly, he works with others in the community, both inside and outside the power structure, on a personal, first-name basis. His interest in the Railroad Gulch project fits into a long-settled policy in the community, fostered earlier by his friend R. W. Woodruff, particularly the project's World Congress Center.

Not being an economist, I must admit that I could not be sure how well I followed two or three of his discussions. He went into considerable detail, describing how he had guided a number of companies financially through their formative to mature stages of operation. Those most pertinent to the present study were the Cousins Company, a national transportation company, and an "air" chemical company. Each of these revelations concerned the amounts of money needed and raised, and the way a conservative financier keeps a vigilant oversight over fledgling operations and changes corporate management when necessary. His anecdotes frequently revealed how a venture relates the community with its national bases. Far-reaching powers are involved in these activities.

In 1970 during our first visit, I was surprised to learn that he had sold his investment business. Cannily, he had anticipated a downturn in business and in the 1960s had sold his interests to a New York firm. His capital gains were considerable. During my first visit, federal auditors were taking up a good bit of room in and around his relatively modest but comfortably appointed offices. He had decided to invest a portion of his money in a high-rise building, as so many of his peers had, but in his case, he thriftily bought an older building, one of the high-rises in the 1930s, long an Atlanta prestige building which for decades, because of its occupants, was a symbol of business success. It has remained fully occupied, in spite of the plethora of new space on every side of it. It is kept in immaculate condition, is easy of access from any direction in the center of the city, and has an aura of slightly faded gentility about it, a nostalgia, that is still valued by many Atlantans.

Also, in his mature years, long unmarried, he had married one of the women nominated as a "social prestige leader" in Study I. (Like all such "society prestige" nominations, she did not finally make "top billing" in *power* votes). She is the daughter of a man who made good in a prosperous coal business, then invested a large sum of his fortune in Coca-Cola. He assured her and her mother of a life of choosing their own pace and interests. Both lived graciously in the manner of the traditional South and were very charitable to worthy educational causes. The union of these two family fortunes about doubled the assets of either singly. Their marriage thus, in terms of power succession, became an amalgamation of capital, an element of growth and centralization in the whole system.

He indicated proudly that for years everyone but he had been pursuing the young woman who finally became his wife. He had just waited around and at last she chose him. She chose to live in his relatively modest but well-located home, abandoning her ancestral Georgian home nearby. That home is empty now, a little tattered at the edges, seeming to echo, forlornly, happier times of family living a generation ago. I toured the place one Saturday and also visited a property in the vicinity that had belonged to a good friend, whom Coca-Cola had made wealthy. He had died recently and had left the large acreage to his developer friend along with a machined-modern villa deep in its woods. The worth of the property alone was well into the seven-figures bracket. The developer was undecided what to do with both properties. His wife's family home is not antebellum, although it sits along the route that Sherman rode as he entered Atlanta and an important battle was evidently fought in and around what is now the front lawn of the place. The other home is a trifle too modern to be a historical showplace. What to do? To build tract homes in that place was unthinkable to the developer. His wife also deplores the massive buildings along downtown and beyond downtown along Peachtree Road.

I wondered why he had not thought to build parks on that land. The reply indicated that parks would draw too many people, a prospect undesirable to many of the older inhabitants of the area. And, of course, there is no money to be made in parks.

One must say, however, that these people seem to view the area somewhat through the lenses of a previous era. The area's business district is overcrowded, and on its periphery condominiums are rising daily. The traditional area with vast rolling estates has heavy winds of change blowing around it. Aware of this from the point of view of personal safety, the couple have long promised themselves a new home but are quite undecided where it could be built. Such are some of the dilemmas of the seemingly well-established.

As we walked toward the villa the developer had inherited, he told me that he had just changed caretakers. He had hired a professional company to care for the place, but one weekend the men had staged an all-out party, had ripped hangings from walls, thrown catsup on the ceilings, burned a couple of tables in the fireplace, broken lights, and wreaked general ruin on a large portion of the house. An old man, alone, now guards the place. We entered it through one of the garage doors. A Cadillac of late model coated heavily with dust stood in one of the stalls. We came out a door toward the house facing a vast reflecting swimming pool. It was undrained, partially filled with autumn leaves. The white, straight-line silhouette of the villa contrasted strangely with the huge trees of the forest around it. A huge piece of Burmese statuary stood near the entrance door. Our footfalls echoed emptily against it as we approached. I kept feeling as I had when I had visited the famed ceremonial center of power display, the Hearst castle in California. Vanity of vanities. Where has all the rest of it, the life it once had, where has all of that gone?

We entered a hallway, itself wide open to a huge living room still replete with its scars of fire and catsup. Much of the furniture had evidently been removed. The fireplaces were high and deep. The place was very light. At one end of the room a door led into a bar area where a replica of an old soft-drink stand stood, complete with an old-fashioned Coca-Cola dispenser. We walked wordlessly through the great kitchen with its heavy cauldrons and fixtures still in place, as if ready for another huge party. At length we entered the library, now denuded of all books except a telephone directory. One chair and a sidetable remained, the chair facing a panel of picture windows facing the heavy forest beyond. A television set was in place between the chair and the windows. The last occupant of the house had died there, looking either at the television or the woods. None could be sure which.

By the way he talked and wondered aloud it was clear that my guide was troubled about these personal properties—more than he ever would be by the more impersonal central city "property game." Without either—after all his experiences with so many properties— he would probably be at a loss in this late stage of life to know what to do. Without their care he might soon become an old, uninterested man. Troublesome, perhaps, but he would not let them go. Although I had known him many years, I did not know him intimately enough to even try to help him, to say, for example, that there are many things of interest besides real estate.

Leaving this property we went to another location near central downtown where the developer had quietly bought up a large area for a commercial development.

He revealed that he had used seven different real estate firms in order not to drive the price up on properties if it became known that one purchaser was buying heavily in these blocks. He was in the process of explaining to me how one went about building a sky-scraper, a process I shall explain in some detail at the appropriate point. My question has been, "How is this kind of community power wielded?" The power to build large buildings is just as binding upon the citizenry of Atlanta as building the streets and laying the sewers around them—the tasks of public power. The citizens of Atlanta, whether they are aware of it or not, now carry a huge debt load, untold billions, for its policy-makers' building schemes of the 1960s, debts principally made in New York and Texas, I was told. No other projects of the community could equal the vast program of building that seized the powers of the community during that era. Nor were there any viable structures of power outside the central framework that could even question the process or modify its headlong drive.

Before ending our day together, I looked over the Railroad Gulch area in which this industrial developer also has an interest and had lunch with him at the new club center, the Commerce Club, where one of the recently retired utility executives joined us to help me with the second study of Atlanta power. The discussion was frank and open, even though some of the information regarding who was who in power in Atlanta was not by then altogether new to me. If anything, I believe most of the men told me that power is not an unusual thing. Power is the making of the larger decisions concerning policy; the men making those policies are rather ordinary individuals who happen to have roles in these larger arenas. The process fascinates them, and they spend many, many waking hours pursuing its course. Of course, they differentiate themselves by exclusiveness from the powerless, the mass which does not have enough information and is not allowed the roles to make the larger decisions. Of course, power is related, pragmatically, to making money. That is a part of the system. They hate inflation while never daring to note that the very inflation they despise is being created in large part by the building spree they have indulged, building buildings that serve only administrative and ceremonial functions of power when so many need personal shelter and have continued for forty years to demand it. They have erected elaborate blinders that prevent their seeing the sea of human problems lying just beyond their boundaries and around the world. The system, with Atlanta leaders helping it with might and main, produces castles at a very great price, when the ordinary citizen needs bread and housing at a modest price, when world citizens, some of them our own, go to bed each night hungry for bread, or work, or recognition of individual worth.

A part of the drive to succeed within power structures is the determination not to have one's children or any descendants go to bed hungry. Families thus are not only a part of the processes of succession but are important to the basic motivation behind the power structure. Like the older men spoken of by Ivan Allen, Jr., our developer is grooming a younger man within his family to succeed him in his business affairs.

In contrast to this leader and some of his friends are a number of black men who have achieved considerably more power in the past few years than they had possessed earlier. Here, I wish to confine my remarks to the topic of succession. All the black men whom I called upon succeeded their white political opponents by acquiring political power, not by either sweet persuasion or logical argument. They succeeded by power generated within the civil rights movement and with the help of white, liberal lawyers (some of the principal ones from out of state) in getting restrictive laws changed at all levels of government, particularly the harsh county-unit laws of Georgia. Their very presence in great numbers in the central city has helped defeat political attempts at comprehensive metropolitan government. Whites, fleeing to the suburbs for more than two decades, have made blacks a majority in Atlanta proper.

In Study I, the Syndicate, as the blacks then called their power structure, consisted of the leaders of the three largest businesses along Auburn Avenue: the Atlanta Life Insurance Company, the Citizens Trust Bank, and the *Atlanta World*, a newspaper, along with a sprinkling of professional people in education at Atlanta University, and civic and civil-rights workers in quasi-welfare organizations. There were no members of the community in elective public office, although some of the more prominent members of the community had begun to move into positions of the larger community trust, on the hospital authority board and the United Fund board in particular.

With the elevation to public office of some of the younger and more aggressive members of the black community, the influence of the professional black people, a part of which lay in assuring the white community that they could keep down racial tensions and strife, has diminished. The black capitalists and public officeholders now manage peace-keeping in an openly recognized relationship with the power structure of the community at large.

Also, as previously pointed out, the years of prosperity and the demands of blacks for greater shares of capital has made a small number of the black middle class relatively well-to-do. The prime example is Herman Russell, a self-made man in construction and plastering; he has joined one or two other earlier builders in his community in acquiring a privileged position in his trade and, according to a profile in *Ebony*, possesses some forty million dollars.[12] This kind of achievement is appreciated by the white counterstructure of power in the community. The heads of the successful black insurance business and the bank also receive this approval; Jesse Hill, chief executive of the successful Atlanta Life Insurance Company, has sat on the University of Georgia board of governors. Ironically, but as a footnote on change and poetic justice, he also sat there with the traditionalist, a former maker of conservative governors of the state, Roy Harris!

Of the black holders of public office, two things must be emphasized. They got there mainly by the weight of their numbers in Atlanta proper and also because of the power of their people's protest over historical injustices. The white power structure never wavered in its behind-the-scenes opposition to their obtaining office. They remained publicly quiet and put off the day as long as possible, supporting first one white hope and then another. At last, however, they accepted the inevitable, and black men moved into offices at all levels of political life, Julian Bond among the first of them. He early had to hold on to his seat through court action, but however he obtained his position, he had maintained a quiet level of activity in the legislature (according to some whites, "as a good man of his race should") and a liberal stance with his constituents and a number of liberal white followers.

With all of this he has piled up considerable legislative seniority. This accomplishment cannot be denied by the diehards, nor should it be discounted by any. It is a way to power and, ultimately, further capital aggrandizement, if not for him, for members of his race.

The same can be said for former congressman Andrew Young (now [former] United Nations ambassador from the United States). When running for election to Congress, Young also had a coalition of white liberals and blacks behind him in both his bids for his congressional seat, the last successful. In spite of his long association with Martin Luther King, Jr., he is now considered a moderate man by the whites. They have begun to appreciate the fact that King himself was quite moderate. Much of King's early financing came from the same sources that had long supported black education in the area, Rockefeller money. It was only when Dr. King began to question the economic base of social injustice in the nation that whites became really nervous. Many say that the time of prejudice is past, that a new group of men in public office has changed all of that, but I could not detect this trend in Atlanta. It seemed to me that the institutional values long held sacred there are in very conservative hands even when the hands are black. As with the Boston Irish and the so-called Brahmins there, the white majority in Atlanta and its power structure are accommodating themselves to the fact of the ascendancy of blacks to political office. Like the Boston Brahmins of yesteryear, the Atlanta economic dominants exclusively still held the major bank board memberships, the social club memberships, their neighborhood enclaves, and, in the main, their schools inviolate. They could afford to lose a little in Atlanta, City Hall, and a few legislative seats. Again, not that they relished this, but "so the ball bounces," "so the cookie crumbles," "so the world moves"!

For a time the blacks were not convinced that they could capture City Hall. In the election of Sam Massell in 1970 they had been persuaded by the argument of some liberals that a minority candidate, Jewish, now would be acceptable to a majority of whites, and that such a candidate would be more amenable to black interests. The wheel-horses of the conservative black political forces swung behind Massell and put him in office—over the objection of the conservative wing of Atlanta's power structure. Jubilant with that success, a number of white liberals told me that the Atlanta power structure was a thing of the past. They were caught, of course, in the syndrome of thinking that public office is the major criterion of power. Their new theme: "Build neighborhood power!" Out of what? one may ask. I found no answer to this important question in Atlanta during my 1970 visits there; that is, I found no data related to any ongoing, effective modus operandi for the accession of power by the mass of people.

By my second trip into the city in 1973, Massell was in political trouble, and blacks were no longer buying the notion that they had to have other minority intermediaries. They had begun to boost Vice Mayor Maynard Jackson for mayor with the notion that he could pick up the few white votes outside the central city needed to put him in office. Even though many of the conservative blacks still did not like him personally, they were right at last. The power struggle in the black community is now for real, and it takes more than it used to take to make a "leader" a front-runner. This is a political change in the facts of life in the black community.

Within the white community, I inquired regarding this drastic realignment of forces. In summing up the position of his business colleagues, one of the major real estate operators said that they will still give their financial support to any candidate who is sympathetic to business. Real estate relations with City Hall may not be as close as they have been in the past, he indicated, but both the leaders in City Hall and outside of it realize that they cannot live without one another. The speaker had tried hard to defeat the Jackson bid for office. Such men know confidently that the bulk of social power, the power to direct the industry of society and its labor forces, is still with them. They are in a position to deal with City Hall yet on their own terms, not the other way around. They are representatives of the system. They keep it on course, and deviations from that course by City Hall will be little tolerated. They will in many ways make it very uncomfortable for any dissident there. They have had "one or two little unpleasantnesses to date," but none that could not be lived through and lived down. The mayor of Atlanta has been learning the lessons earlier learned by the black mayors of at least Gary, Indiana, and Newark, New Jersey: the powers of government are limited in their ability to deflect or change the system. Some of them, like Ron Dellums, elected to office in California and committed to "turning the system around," have found that within the diversionary maze of government they can only tinker with parts of it. Like their counterpart white officeholders of so many past generations, they find public officeholding comfortable and profitable for themselves and at heart perhaps they never intended to do more than tinker. At any rate, public officeholders have done little since 1776 to change the system. It endures while the names of officeholders and political parties change from time to time.

In contrast to the relatively successful newcomers and older, established power-wielders in Atlanta, another group excluded by both, in one way or another, must be mentioned: those who lost out in the power struggle. In total, such a group may outnumber the successful, but only two or three illustrations will have to suffice here. I did hear of a great power struggle going on in one of the major banks during my visit to the city, but with no more data than I was able to obtain about it, all I can report is that I did hear the current cliché, "Plenty of blood is being mopped up from the floors of the executive suite over there!" Corporate struggles for power, inside struggles and outside assaults related to their control, are commonplace and natural. Much, very much is often at stake in this arena of national power.

In order to check a few figures on succession in the ownership of farm properties under the control of Atlanta's power structure, I visited the Federal Reserve Bank's statistics department. Upon observing the huge downtown building development and perplexed by its enormity, I had examined some of the 1970 census figures. I was trying to see why so many buildings were needed, especially bank and insurance buildings. As I went through a block of the census figures, I noted that between 1960 and 1970 family farms in Georgia had decreased from about 150,000 to under 50,000, or nearly a two-thirds drop in numbers. I also noted that the prices of farmland had increased greatly, nearly doubled. And finally, indebtedness for farm machinery and equipment had shot up in an almost vertical direction on any graph one might draw.

Not being a demographer, I doubted that my figures could possibly be right, but if they were, I was on the track of one good reason for the increased building of central Atlanta. When I visited one of the statistical offices in the Federal Reserve Bank, I was met by Gene D. Sullivan, who assured me that indeed my figures squared with the general trend of rural land ownership in Georgia, and that Georgia was not altogether unique in this sudden shift in ownership. He gave me an article written by him which corroborates my figures.[13] A later examination of the growth of "land departments" or "real estate departments" in the banks had grown from a very few personnel in 1960 to very sizable organizations in 1970. I became and continue to be convinced that one of the greatest land takeovers since Genghis Khan, the English land enclosures, or the Stalin liquidation of the peasantry had silently occurred in our nation, with Atlanta, Georgia, being one of the administrative centers of this vast dispossession.

I learned upon further inquiry that the vast move toward agribusiness, modeled apparently on the California corporate land companies–Bank of America partnerships, had been carried through relatively painlessly. The financial institutions had paid small farmers, in many instances, more than they had ever hoped to get for their properties, and many had happily moved to Atlanta, where they immediately found in many cases that the money they had received for their family farms would not cover the full cost of a single house on a fifty-foot lot in that city. They may have paid what they had in hand as a house down payment (a latter-day form of rent), gotten a job, and become one of the vast majority of Americans who through landlessness and buy-now-pay-later indebtedness are effectively dispossessed of property and many of the traditional rights that go with it.

The pattern of land management under the new corporate owners quickly changed, I was told, from direct management to indirect. The new urban owners rather quickly found they were not very good "desk farmers." They sought out some of the remaining larger landholders, those with a thousand acres or more, and asked them if they would like to add to their operations (either on a corporate or outright management basis) an additional amount of land; of course, the financial giants would bankroll additional capital required. This arrangement of massive land transfers was in full swing in the early 1970s and accounted for the vertically upward spurt in the capital indebtedness chart of remaining farm operators.

It has been said that more than three-fourths of the nation's population now lives on somewhat less than 1½ percent of its land area. That three-fourths figure continues to expand. The goal of paramount possession by a few in the nation is either in sight or has been reached with the energetic help of the U.S. Department of Agriculture, with welcome pressure from the city-desk farmers of the American Farm Bureau, each ever ready to help the big get bigger.

Out of genuine, long-term respect, I wish to speak of one more man in the kaleidoscope of events: a local, successful civic leader who is denied an upper seat of power; he must be content with a life of

dutiful performance and finally succeeds to little more than the testimonial dinner and gold watch award. I have in mind a friend, and an
exemplary character, J. H. Calhoun, black.

Calhoun had fought the good fight for civil rights for many
years. In the 1940s through the 1960s he had served on any number
of civic boards, many of them in later years biracial. He has been a
liaison between the black and white communities, confidant of civic
leaders and mayors alike. A crowning achievement was being elected
local chairman of the NAACP. He has written for the newer of the
black community's newspapers, the Atlanta *Inquirer*, his outstanding
contribution being a series of articles on black community leadership
in which he "told it like it was." With all of this, he has eked out a
living on the fringes of any of the big deals. I recall that when I first
knew him he was selling used furniture and insurance in a narrow,
dimly lit, sparsely furnished store on Auburn Avenue. In the best
sense of the term he might have been called a low-key entrepreneur.
He has some of the genial characteristics of a promoter but without
the bluster and with much more honesty and integrity than most
promoters. He represents so many people, black and white, in
America who have tried first this seeming opportunity and then that
in order first to survive and always to hope that some big
thing—which never actually arrives—will break in their favor. In
many ways, the system programs their dead-end track from the
beginning. This would appear to be the economic side of Calhoun's
life. His civic services, where he seemed most happy, have at last
been recognized, and when I last saw him he had a foundation grant
that allowed him a room on the campus at Atlanta University and
time to write a history of the Atlanta black community—the "gold
watch" of his life. It may provide any number of insights into black
life in Atlanta. If Mr. Calhoun writes the history, it assuredly will
be true.

Near the doorway leading to his offices, a marble plaque on the
wall, a precious heritage, bore the names of persons who had first
contributed to the founding of Atlanta University with amounts they
had given, the highest amounts in the tens of dollars, the majority
being one-dollar gifts. Plaster had fallen from the walls of the stairway
leading to his suite of two rooms. Above a tumble of papers and periodicals on his desk rose Calhoun's shaved, polished, large, magnificent black head with his face in a broad, genuine smile of welcome.
We spent a few hours reminiscing about the old days, about changes
and the lack of change. Calhoun has told the white leadership of Atlanta, including John Portman, he said, that the need in the city is not

for more skyscrapers, but for more modest-priced housing in the city, for more jobs for young blacks, and so on down the usual list of pressing needs in a large portion of the community. No one yet seems to have acted upon his suggestions. He tried in vain to reach one of the black leaders who had not answered my calls asking for an interview.

During the early portion of our talk, I mentioned to Calhoun that it had been more difficult for me to get interviews with some of the blacks, particularly the black capitalists—still but a handful in number—and he surmised that they were too busy making money to want to take time out to give an interview and guessed that some of them might not wish to have their activities in relation to the white community "overpublicized." I said that I had not quite caught the full gist of what he had meant by "overpublicized." He fished out a news clipping in which Reverend William Holmes Borders had taken Jesse Hill, insurance executive, to task for "monopolizing" major posts of interracial activities, posts which, I could not help recall, had earlier been monopolized by Borders, Calhoun, and two or three others in their community. The shift has been from the impecunious professionals to the affluent blacks.

Having illustrated the identity of various figures in the Atlanta power structure for nearly three decades, having illustrated by case example how some of them carry their individual roles with special differentiations made between white and black roles, and having shown how both newcomers to the general structure and those who fail to enter the circle are included or excluded, I now turn to an analysis of the ways that most of the people of the 1970 power structure came to their positions.

Inquiries were made concerning fifty-six leaders, black and white, in the 1970 power structure. It was revealed that five out of the ten of those deemed by their peers to be most powerful had succeeded a member of their own family in acquiring their present position. Among the top ten also were two men who had no immediate family member who could succeed them, one because he had no issue, the other because his only son had suffered debilitating birth injuries. A favored employee of the banking corporation had already begun to assume the duties of his predecessor and had already begun to be named (by others in the city) as a top power leader, moving to the spot among the top ten being vacated by his superior. (By the end of this study, the bank was again looking for a new president. Such are the vagaries of power.)

Of twenty-six persons in the next lower ranking of power persons, seven or nearly one-fourth held power as an "inheritance." Among the yet lower-rated remainder, twenty-one persons had gained power by achievement as a corporate executive in one or another of the older, power-generating corporations of the city. Six in the next lower category of community powers had achieved their status by founding and operating a successful business.

Political achievement accounted for seven of the total, two of them black (this figure had changed to a majority of blacks by 1973); four men had achieved success and power by their skills as professionals and three as leaders of major associations. Among the whole number, fifty-six, six persons had also had an upper-bracket power rating in the study of 1950, i.e., roughly 10 percent of the total.

On the whole these figures say that, as Study I showed, a high proportion of the very top power figures inherit their bases of power, with a fifty-fifty ratio of status ascription and achievement among the top ten. Among all contenders in the power race, however, the achievers in corporate, personal business, political, association, and professional roles outnumber the inheritors better than three to one, forty-four to twelve. The ratio is in accord with the American dream of achievement, even though the figure narrows to an even ratio among the top power influentials.

In terms of interlocking activities among the whole number, twenty-seven of the fifty-six had received published civic honors; twenty-three held overlapping corporate board memberships. Only fourteen of the number, however, held overlapping community club memberships in the status clubs of the community. Among political, association, and professional achievers absences from both corporate boards and status clubs were notable.

Because of the high number of inheritors of power positions (as it has been in other cities studied by the author) the role of families in history becomes important in the Atlanta scheme of affairs. In previous studies by the author and associates in Salem, Massachusetts, and in Savannah, Georgia, it was evident that the sociological function of power, that of inclusion and exclusion, related to historical as well as to current assumptions of priority among a few families, especially among those who had acquired wealth and/or fame.[14] Such is also the case in Atlanta.

Atlanta in Political Perspective

No community is an isolated power entity—particularly when it is as large and complex as Atlanta. The policies of Atlanta are inextricably bound up with state and national policies and, to some extent, with international policies. They thus are inextricably bound up with partisan politics. We will first, therefore, concern ourselves with politics in Georgia, and, as we shall see, politics in Georgia, especially because of its long history of concern over the "Negro Problem," has changed considerably. The voice of "'gallus snappin' Ol' Gene Talmadge" (called in Study I Traverse Simpkins), has long been stilled, and even echoes of his sentiments, often voiced immediately following his death, have been hushed to indistinct whispers by a number of court rulings against segregation by both federal and district courts of the region. The most sweeping change by political court ruling was that which swept away the county-unit law, which had given undue voting influence to rural counties. The repeal of that law put blacks into every level of elective office from the urban districts where they had concentrated in growing numbers for two or three generations.

It would be a great pleasure to say that such a drastic change in political affairs has wiped out the black problem that has so long dominated the state, but a large residue of the problem, unfortunately, remains. It remains a hard, undigested lump, especially in the urban bodies politic of the state—this in spite of all the gloss and glitter of urban redevelopment going on everywhere in the state, and one may add, in the nation. The problem is based, of course, on the syndrome of poverty, which our leaders at all levels of government, public and private, and the general public, one must add, have so far steadfastly refused to solve. Much of the description of this political malaise in Study I is therefore still valid. As can be seen in the next few paragraphs, a few were becoming conscious that changes must come in black/white relationships, but when it became possible for the new broom to sweep clean, it merely dabbed about the edges of the problem with a show of exaggerated busyness. The changes applied to the upper-income blacks and barely touched those who need rather ordinary things like jobs and income comparable to their more fortunate neighbors.

Gradually the state's urban areas, through the dominance of various corporate groupings, have gained power, de facto. To retain and legitimize this power, "urbanized" candidates are sought who can command a large following in the rural areas while at the same time be sympathetic to the urban and corporate interests. (The situation is clearly exemplified by the corporate support for such candidates as Jimmy Carter who can appeal to both rural and urban voters.) Few of the rural areas in an older sense of the term remain rural. The survival of corporate interests is of paramount importance to the leaders in Atlanta. At midyear 1979, Charles Kirbo of the prestigious Spalding law firm was still a Carter confidant. Because of the dominance of Atlanta in the state, no other community group of leaders, corporate lawyers included, is quite as interested as the corporations in the outcome of state and national elections.

In large measure the corporations have been able to exercise control over state politics by holding key posts in one or another of the factions in the major political party of the state and from these positions using influence to name gubernatorial candidates. All candidates are financed largely by the big business interests, who control the elected governors. These facts of political life in the state are an ill-kept secret among both rural and urban voters. Some of the few remaining rural people are under the impression that they still have a potent voice in state politics, and by political seniority in many cases they still do. At least an appeal must be made periodically to the rural electorate for their support of chosen candidates. The old tried-and-true formula for a successful campaign that used to appeal to the rural voters, the race issue, is no longer openly used.

The race issue had been a convenient one. It appealed to the rural people, and it detracted from many of the real issues that beset the larger cities. As an issue, race always had far less appeal in Atlanta than it had in the rural communities. There was, consequently, difficulty in choosing candidates who could appeal to both the urban and the rural electorate. Some of this difficulty still remains.

The manipulation of the voters of Georgia is still carried on to some extent by the ability of candidates to speak to voters in "folksy" terms. To elect state officials, the people must be appealed to in fast-disappearing folk language and music, partly religious, which now is appreciated nostalgically in the cities. A part of the Carter appeal to them lay in this ability to invoke an image with folk overtones.

One of the difficulties in choosing a man who is in sympathy with the goals of the larger interests in Georgia, and who can also appeal to the people of the state, is that most corporation executives and attorneys are city-bred men who may not speak the language of the people.

Of course, a part of the folksiness of many candidates in the past was to appeal mainly to rural voters and, in their appeal, make explicit their racist demands. Neither of these "folkways" is any longer needed, and in some districts they would certainly not be tolerated.

During my 1970 return visit to Atlanta, I was invited to a black luncheon forum of candidates held in the Butler Street (black) YMCA. My host, a former director of the Butler "Y," Warren Cochrane, had for many years been one of the more influential professionals in his community, and one who knew his way around in black politics. He had been funded, at the time of our reunion, by a few white donors for the purpose of organizing a black foundation to aid in housing the poor of the community. Cochrane had always been eager to maintain good white-black relationships, and his stance appealed to a hard core of moderate whites and blacks, a hundred or so dedicated people who had bridged the race barriers by lunching together at a monthly meeting of the Hungry Club (opportunistically hungry for power) long before that kind of behavior was fashionable. The crowd of whites was an assortment of well-intentioned people ranging from old bolsheviks to jacketed, bearded labor types to the slightly pink social changers. The blacks were a well-groomed, easy-mannered group who purposefully sought out old friends among the whites, or newcomers, to sit with them and exchange pleasantries and views. Society at its best. All hostilities repressed behind many friendly smiles; all dedicated to change, but not too rapid change!

The sight of a few dozen alternating blacks and whites at the head table would not have been an uncommon sight in this club group, but to have a candidate for the governorship, Jimmy Carter, among them was a sight to cause a second take. It could not have been true, Cochrane and I assured each other, twenty years ago. The meeting was tediously long, as I remember it. Each of several state and local candidates was speaking in his own behalf and indulging all of the usual platitudes of concern over the particular plight in which each in the audience might find himself. I did, however, listen with a little more attention to Carter, billed in his introduction as a "peanut farmer." However he may have managed it, he came through as a low-key, friendly kind of fellow who seemed to mean what he was saying: "more blacks ought to be in positions of influence in order to be able to do more *with* their people"; many problems might not disappear in a day, but "the time is *now* for an honest try," and so on. (All this is now elevated to international "human rights.") The impression he made was indelible enough that I certainly was not surprised to see him showing up well among blacks in his later try in the national primaries and even later in his race for the presidency. He certainly fit in well with the Hungry Club group that day in 1970 in Atlanta. During his governorship, he further ingratiated himself with blacks by doing what he said he was going to do, that is, he elevated a few to good positions and, in a meaningful gesture, as so many now know, he hung a portrait of Dr. Martin Luther King, Jr., among the gallery of Georgia greats in the State Capitol building, and, as one wag put it, among the "dead great, and over the 'dead bodies' of any number of his fellow Georgians." (Like "Jack" Kennedy, insisting on being called John, Cochrane and I later wondered, "Will 'Jimmy' become James, if elected?" Answer, of course: No!)

Jimmy Carter's ride with Herman Russell, described in *Ebony* and referred to previously, was not lost on the large, middle-class readership of that publication. As one TV pundit put it, he seemed not so much a Southern "good old boy," but a Southern "good new boy." At any rate, he cannot be tarred with racism. He is too deft a politician (and just probably too religious a man—the news pundits cannot understand it!) for that. But his state administration did not solve the major problems of Georgia's poor blacks. To be fair, however, that may be asking more of a state administration than it could possibly deliver. The problem is a part of a national problem that *could* be solved by so affluent a nation as ours. We shall speak of this again at more length. The immediate concern here is the state setting of politics.

It was apparent to me in interviewing for Study II that relations between the corporate groups of Atlanta and those involved in the general legislative process had not basically changed. Some of the larger companies, because of their statewide operations, still retain local legal counsel (retainers) and exercise their influence in traditional ways. I saw corporate lobbyists loitering around the halls of the legislature in 1978, most of them representing the same interests that they had represented in the "Third House" in 1950, all ready for a quick handshake, a joke, or a few earnest words as the representatives moved to and from roll calls or committee meetings. They remind one of Willie Loman, the salesman, always ready, standing around "with a shoe shine and a smile." A dreary spectacle, indeed, no matter how "educational" lobbyists may call their missions.

Concerning corporate domination of the state legislature, several sources indicated that the "X" Company of Atlanta still holds a great deal of power within that organ of government. An earlier president of the "X" Company had been asked if this were true. His answers still apply in the 1970s.

Inquiry (1973 and 1978): "Can 'third house' corporate representatives (lobbyists) operate as effectively with new black legislators as they have with whites?"

Answer: "Yes."

The domination of Georgia politics by the men of power in Atlanta is a functional necessity so far as these men are concerned.

For nearly two generations Atlanta's power structure has been active in attempting to extend the legal boundaries of the city so that they might coincide with the actual geographical size and shape of the population. Like other metropolitan areas, the central city with small incorporated areas at all its borders is strangled by them. With population moving to the suburbs, the familiar problems of central core blight set in. The poor concentrate in the low-rent areas with their escalating problems. The negative processes, so well recognized, require financial and technical assistance in their solution, ultimately, probably federal. But to many leading Atlantans a step in the direction of progress in this area would be total metropolitan government, a step now largely opposed by blacks who have a voting majority at the city's core.

In Study I, it was pointed out (pp. 210–215) that the leaders were then engaged in an effort, the Plan of Improvement, to extend city boundaries, and subsequently, in 1952, they succeeded in taking 118 additional square miles into the then 34-square-mile area of Atlanta. The areas annexed represent those more easily persuaded by the power structure than other areas. They were upper-class and middle-class neighborhoods on a north-south axis along Peachtree and Peachtree Road including Buckhead. Neighborhoods to the east already well organized in the large city of Decatur steadfastly refused to go along with Atlanta's expansion plans, as well as the south and west working-class areas now joined by the central city's black citizens.

An unpublished analysis was furnished to me for use in this study by William Miller, a student of Atlanta power. Of a number of annexation attempts, the 1952 effort remains the most successful. In 1972 another major effort involving the local power structure and members of the state power apparatus was attempted, only finally to fail because of the opposition of Lieutenant Governor Lester Maddox.[1] The whole process is of interest, partly because it illustrated that the power structure cannot dictate policy (as some have alleged) to public representatives, but even in failure it can powerfully shape future policy. Richard Rich, in commenting to me about the last failure, amended the cliché, "You win one, you lose one, then you try again!" The staying power of the power structure would indicate that, in spite of its recent defeat over annexation, in a year or two it will be back with more data, more money, more suggestions, more lawyers helping, more publicity, and more tempting promises to any who might still stand in its way. The men at the top are used to winning. Defeat is loathesome to them.

Miller's account shows that even though Mayor Samuel Massell had been opposed by a faction of the local power structure, he worked hand in hand with those interested in the latest bid for annexation, this time called the Program for Progress. Of the whole process, Miller indicated that the city's power structure in 1972 was a motivating force behind the actions of the Georgia House Delegation. It played a major role in developing the Program for Progress and then worked behind the scenes to get it through the General Assembly. The power structure managed to overcome effective opposition from black and suburban representatives in the Georgia legislature.[2]

Table 4, compiled by Miller, lists the members of the power structure in 1972 interested in annexation. Many of the heavyweights are together in this one.

It is of interest, in terms of power succession, that on this major project approximately half of the power-generating organizations of 1952 were active on a similar project in 1972. However, only three of the persons involved in the 1952 power structure were holdovers in 1973: Mills B. Lane, Ivan Allen, Jr., and Richard Rich. Of the remainder, new members in the 1973 power structure alignments, according to Miller, were then Tom Cousins, John Wilson, and George Simpson, Cousins's and Simpson's organizations appearing also in our earlier listing of the whole 1973 power structure. Wilson and Simpson were not nominated for power structure inclusion in the Hunter polls. These facts, independently arrived at, show the stability of the Atlanta power structure. Power persons shift on and off various such long-term, major policy committees.

Some of the power structure openly worked for the annexation program: banker A. H. Sterne, Chamber of Commerce president Larry Gellerstedt, architect John Portman, developer Tom Cousins, and attorney Elliott Goldstein were among the white civic leaders

Table 4. Atlanta's Top Power-Structure Personnel*
Supporting the Program for Progress, 1972

Mills B. Lane, Jr.	Chairman, C&S National Bank
Ivan Allen, Jr.	Past Mayor, Chairman, Ivan Allen Company
Jack Tarver	President, Atlanta Newspapers, Inc.
A. H. Sterne	President, Trust Company of Georgia
Ed Smith	President, First National Bank
Pollard Turman	President, J. M. Tull Industries
Rolland Maxwell	President, Davison's
Tom Cousins	Cousins Properties
Edwin Hatch	Georgia Power Company
Richard Rich	Rich's
Ed Rast	Southern Bell
John Wilson	Horne-Wilson, Inc.
Rawson Haverty	Haverty's Furniture Store
George Simpson	Chancellor of the University System of Georgia
Opie Shelton	Executive Director, Atlanta Chamber of Commerce

*These men heavily represent the directors of the Atlanta Commerce Club, which Ivan Allen described as the strength of the Atlanta business community (Miller's footnote). These men do not represent the entire power structure but they are among the top level of the power structure (my addition; see general power structure listing, 1973, pp. 50–51).

working for the Program for Progress. Although apparently the whole private power structure was behind the plan, the most vocal and energetic supporter of the Program for Progress was Mayor Sam Massell. From the day that Massell took office he knew that it was essential for him to work with the "establishment" (power structure) if he had any hopes of being an effective mayor. According to Miller, the Program for Progress was simply the culmination of a mutual compatibility between City Hall and the business leaders regarding the enlargement of city boundary lines.

When asked who was most responsible for the success of the annexation bill, Representative William M. Alexander replied, "The Mayor. He's the one who did the arm-twisting."[3] Alexander said that the mayor called up the representatives, especially the black representatives, in an attempt to drum up support for his bill. He had become an obedient soldier for the powers that be; he himself, as mayor, had become a vital cog in the local wheel of power.

In comparing the successful Plan of Improvement with the unsuccessful Program for Progress, we can see some distinct similarities and differences. Under both plans, the city's power structure was working with the legislature for the successful passage of the plans. The primary basis for both plans was economic revitalization of the central city. This revitalization was to be accomplished by annexing high-income areas into the city. Finally both plans were approved through legislative action (although the Program for Progress was doomed to failure in the Senate).

Although there were similarities between both plans, the differences are more numerous. In 1952, the city of Atlanta was only one-third black and of that number only a small percentage voted. But in 1972, blacks constituted a majority of the city's population and formed a powerful voting force. Yet, in spite of a refusal to vote on the question by all of but two of the Fulton County (Atlanta) delegation, the proponents of the legislation did get their bill through the Georgia House.

Even after pooling the formidable efforts of the Atlanta leaders and the Georgia House delegation from Fulton County, proponents were unexpectedly thwarted by Lester Maddox.

The Atlanta power structure with all of its mighty clout finally could not control Lieutenant Governor Lester Maddox, a man whose popular support still came largely from rural areas. Unfortunately, the expansion issue had gotten tangled up in a personal feud between Maddox and Governor Carter, and Maddox in a petulant, angry exercise of power, as lieutenant governor killed the legislation by refusing to call the legislation up for a vote in the Senate. Some felt he hoped to gain black praise which, however, never surfaced publicly. (It now may be noted that he also, by alienating himself from the Atlanta power structure, effectively signed his own political death warrant. His later third- or fourth-party run for the presidency became a pathetic last gasp of a once-powerful jingoist.)

One may only speculate over the voting behavior of the blacks in this legislative situation. Had they voted against the proposal they would have shown an independence of influence by the power structure. By merely abstaining from voting, they showed opposition. The posture is one of accommodation—to a point. What the political trade-offs in the future may be will depend of course on what price the Atlanta structure of power will be willing to pay. Of course, it will be back ready to pay.

In order to illustrate the fact that the Atlanta power structure occasionally separates along factional lines on policy questions or merely along rather subtle lines of personal preference (and this contrary to some who have called power structures "monolithic" structures), I wish to repeat an incident reported by newly elected

Governor Jimmy Carter, who seemed at times quixotic to some. His protagonist in the tale was the leader of a great portion of Atlanta's top leadership groups during the 1960s, but he was of a banker crowd, one not always admired by the Trust Company of Georgia and some of the Coca-Cola crowd, although some of both groups were admirers and supporters of "new politics" Jimmy Carter.

Governor Carter had just been introduced by Coca-Cola president J. Paul Austin as a speaker at a meeting of the Central Atlanta Progress Association. He began his address with Carter-style "nothing-but-the-truth forthrightness" to the delight of many present, as follows:

I never thought I'd be introduced by the President of the Coca-Cola Company.

Just a while ago I was sitting over here trying to decide what I would talk about. And I was interrupted in my thoughts by Mr. Lane [Citizens and Southern Bank], who leaned over and pointed out to me that he had a boat —a ship—in Savannah and had been accustomed to flying an admiral's flag on the stern and that as Governor I had the authority to give out admiral's commissions in the Georgia Navy. He asked me if I would give him the authorization for continuing this practice. I told him that I was thoroughly familiar with Maritime Law and the penalties for flying a flag when it wasn't properly authorized. I also reminded him that several times during the last four years I came to his office to seek his political help. But, although he was always courteous I very quickly found myself on the way out the door. The only thing that was ringing in my ears, was his favorite phrase [one used when Lane would dismiss many from audiences with him and with whom he might be in disagreement], "It's a *wonderful* world!"

So, my reply to him was, "Mr. Lane, it's a wonderful world!"[4]

Some thought that the public gaffing of Lane by Carter was an unpardonable breach of political manners; others were delighted with his "new politics"; still others felt that he had gone too far even with honesty that actually showed veiled hostility; yet others merely said "Quirky!"

"The Coca-Cola people," said one, "are still bigger than the Lane C&S Bank!"

This statement contains a misconception on the part of many in Atlanta, one that also may have misled Carter. For many years, as far back as the 1920s, it was conceded by most Atlantans that Coca-Cola was indeed the biggest thing that had ever happened in the town. By the 1950s, however, if one looks at statements of worth (see pp. 82–83), neither Coca-Cola nor any other perennial runner-up was at the top of the heap. Both Georgia Power Company and the Citizens and Southern Bank had edged them out with some $4 billion and $3 billion, respectively, nearly $2-to-3 billion ahead of everyone else in town. Such facts are rarely lost by dedicated power-structure watchers. Of course, Coca-Cola and the Trust Company of Georgia (where Coca-Cola money had historically resided) remained well within the upper brackets of any power structure of the period, ending the latter phase of it with nearly $2 billion in hand apiece. One may well speculate that the upper rating of Georgia Power has helped Carter firm up the vigorous support he has consistently given to the energy-producing forces of the nation, but the main influence on Carter, apparently, is still those prominently related to Coca-Cola.

A charming account of Governor Carter's paddling a canoe down the Chattahoochee River with one of the Candler heirs (Coca-Cola) was reported in an issue of the *New Yorker* as a rather apparent presidential timber production.[5] During the ensuing presidential campaign, J. Paul Austin made another introductory speech for Carter, this time with some thirty people at the 21 Club in New York, the purpose of which was to sell his presidential candidacy to a select company of top business executives, prominent among them, Henry Ford II. I was reminded of Woodruff's having told me during my study of national power of how he and "young Henry" helped to groom and make General Eisenhower president, Coca-Cola and Ford being in the forefront of that successful effort.[6]

Atlanta does not rate extremely high with large numbers of private-power status-bearers who function on the national scene. Coca-Cola and a few textile manufacturers with offices in Atlanta, plus the financial go-betweens like Richard Courts and one or two others, would nearly exhaust the list. The public lines are kept open to Atlanta through Carter appointees Griffin and Kirbo, among others, one presumes, since President Carter does not appear to be a favorite with many of the power structure there. His grave fault: he keeps spending!

The policy-making group in Atlanta is primarily interested in how power, both public and private (one and the same to them), shall be exercised, and consequently, it is interested in who shall be in governmental positions in the exercise of public power. Public power has the sanction, often in their behalf, of "legitimate force." There are many direct or indirect methods by which the men of power in Atlanta may intimidate or coerce the understructure personnel to do their bidding, yet once in a while force becomes necessary. It is used in Atlanta when, in the opinion of the men we have been talking about, it seems necessary. One need only refer to the advice to Mayor

Allen during his administration concerning black rioters. The only later criticism he received for a heavy use of force (much more than was reported in the press, according to black informants) was from whites in the power structure who felt Allen should have moved up tanks and artillery! Disobedience to the orders of the powerful cannot be tolerated in the public arena of power. Disobedience to private power also involves many sanctions: drying up of credit sources, job dismissals, blacklisting, ostracism, hassling and harassments by private thugs, private investigations, whispering campaigns, and finally in some instances by shadowy groups, "quiet" murder. The average citizen has become more aware of some of these methods in recent years, but he has been able to do little more about them than he has excesses in the public sector where he is presumed to have a voice.

Many of the private power decisions that rule the lives of private citizens quite as much as public decisions seem obscure to the public. Inflation caused very largely by private manipulations of pricing, wasted expenditures in military building heavily aided and abetted by the private sector, expenditures of corporate funds for national and international bribery, plant closures (which are tantamount to strikes by capital), expenditures of corporate funds to convince voters to repudiate legislation that may actually be in the public interest, these are among the many "symptoms" of policy decisions by the private sector that may appear briefly in the news and then as quickly disappear in a swamp of trivia. All people are vaguely aware of these problems and their effects on their lives, but they seem to have no redress for any grievances. The private sector is nearly immune to citizen pressure except through little-used and very expensive court processes; such measures have made a middle-class folk hero of Ralph Nader, but they are actually available to very few.

Of all policy decisions, none has more influence on the pocketbooks of average citizens than decisions about capital expenditures made by the dominant corporations, many of which have little actual need for further expansion. Such decisions, however, are rarely considered by those who may be paying more for them than they may be paying in public taxes. Whether or not a company should be capitalized involves any number of policy decisions. Ultimately capital decisions actually affect how very large numbers of people may spend the next few years, if not all the years, of their lives. Many vaguely know this but have not formulated any political opinions on the questions involved.

With some of these thoughts in mind, I decided that during the second Atlanta study I would inquire a bit more deeply into the processes of capitalization, which are of such a commanding concern to the city's power structure, in order to outline, if only tentatively, a few of the processes involved in policy decisions. I believe they are of importance to all of us since I also believe they govern so large a portion of our lives and individual welfare. They are yet another facet of Atlanta power that reaches out to the nation and world.

We have seen that Atlanta's power structures, present and past, have been preoccupied with getting and *keeping* money. It is the general preoccupation of the upper strata of the business leadership everywhere in the nation. It may be noted that I have stressed the idea of *keeping* money as a major preoccupation of the top strata. People in the lower strata do well to *get* enough money to keep their heads above water. Keeping money for the great majority of Americans is almost an impossibility. Getting out of hock may well be their second preoccupation. Their lot, as repeatedly suggested, has been systematic dispossession. Most people, up to their eyes in debt for inferior homes and shoddy autos, are essentially dispossessed.

With our spiraling technology, the obsession of a few to pile up nearly all the wealth is becoming more and more absurd with each succeeding year. Yet, few are ready to admit the inherent absurdity of the whole matter. This, within itself, becomes another, if negative, dimension of Atlanta power. Let me be more specific.

During World War II and through ensuing wars and military forays, the nation moved technologically from its mechanical age to the present spiraling age of electronics, miniaturization, chemicalization, and computer controls of processes involving the use of machines, factories, and lands. The ability to make national inventories, to audit gross national production, and to accomplish other refinements of macro-data began to make older methods of market forecasting through stock and bond sales obsolete. Computerization of accounting and inventory functions also began to make obsolescent large entourages of clerical and management forces, which have historically filled skyscraper after skyscraper. Management of untended multi-operation machines through electronic devices made it no longer necessary to locate all mechanical processes within the confines of the already bursting metropolises and megalopolises. The decentralization of myriads of routine tasks would have seemed a logical imperative in the whole situation, an imperative espoused by city specialists for at least two generations. Yet it must be noted that old habits of decision have kept the majority of tasks firmly in place. Some migrate while others take their places in megalopolis.

Economists, the modern-day counterparts of the augurers of

ancient Rome, those who read the future by stirring the entrails of slain animals, keep making their predictions as if we still lived in the agrarian age. "More capital is needed!" they cry from time to time, or "Stop the government spending, or we will all end up in the poorhouse due to its inflationary effect!" The real villains of the piece, of course, are two factors in the private sector, (1) all those twinkling computer lights representing supermoney and superanimated, superinterest-bearing investments and (2) the slowdown of the machines (through computer analyses of markets and subsequent adjustments of those operating the producing machines). During many of the so-called peace years (but years of feeding the inflationary military machine), the production of goods for consumers often ran at 60 to 70 percent of capacity, and sometimes at even lower rates, depending upon the product. Price management had doubled and tripled costs of goods for family use. Little junky autos now sell at prices only a short time ago reserved for the chrome-laden superwagons. Middle-class people can no longer afford homes. They sign papers of condominium tenure at high interest rates, which their great-grandchildren may finally pay off. The correct name for this medieval condition is debt peonage or, at worst, debt slavery.

I am often asked why such major topics are by-passed in sociological study. The only answer I can give is fear. The fear of job loss if one rocks the boat in the corporate-dominated universities, Ivy League and all the rest; fear that one may not advance up the academic ladder with any rapidity (the powers of academia kept C. Wright Mills on the lower rungs of professorship for a number of years because they disagreed with his ideas); fear of federal or state investigations of one's attitudes, and so on. All of this is accompanied by elaborate pretenses of a speaking of minds on matters of absolutely no importance or consequence.

Those fearful of an awful retribution from unseen powers may have a very fogged notion of what the system really is. They do not want to know. They cozy up to ghosts of the dead past for favors, much as many fervently pray to an amorphous concept of God—just in case.

One should not ask for martyrs. It can be said, however, that outright and complete dispossession may seem difficult if one experiences it because of political views, but in America one can yet survive it, and sleep well with his conscience. This may not always remain true.

The mainspring of our chronic, frenetic activity is the obsolete notion that capital is needed, money capital in reinvestment, to keep the show on the road. The reality is the fact that capital accumulation as well as capital dispersal involves a series of decisions by a very few policy-makers in the nation who are already overcapitalized. Some two or three hundred of them, including policy-makers of upper government, deploy the major labor forces and money expenditures of the nation with an eye to aggrandizing that which they already possess. Much of the deployment has become routinized, automatic. Some of it still requires a human yes or no. Lundberg has charted the larger routes of this process in his last two well-documented, major works. I also witnessed some of the processes involved and have written about them in previous publications. William Domhoff has provided a half-dozen works of merit along these lines. While there is an elaborate pretense on the part of many scholars that none of these works exist, or if acknowledged they are pooh-poohed as wrong, the facts remain that they do exist, and none yet have proved them wrong. Also happily, many of the lay public have read them, claiming that these works merely confirm what these astute readers knew all along, augurers to the contrary.

However they may have individually come to it, the president and his advisors would seem to have a rather firm grasp of the concept of power structures, particularly the private-sector connection to government. Although the president would appear to wish, from time to time, to refresh himself in selected households of the people in overnight visits to them, and although the image of him during his campaign and in the early days of his administration was projected as one of a peanut farmer, a Sunday school teacher, and a genial, smiling good fellow all around, his company and his actions within the main purposes to which the White House is disposed has seemed to favor the interests of the big fellows, that is, as of 1979.[7] Big energy, big oil, big real estate, big money, in general, seem to have had an inside edge on the policy concerns of the president. His aides, it has been said, seemed to devote as much time to their own businesses as they did to helping the president with the nation's business.

Although all of these conditions may have been inevitable no matter who became president, because of the very nature of the system of private and public trading for privilege in the halls of Congress and around it, the president seemed to have been losing control, or at least perspective, in relation to such events by late 1979. His remedy, in the best tradition of symbology in American political life, was to call an assembly—not an assembly of the people, but an assembly of top people in the power structure with slight, if any, very real connections to the mass of the people. He called for a domestic summit.

Support for him had been falling to new lows in the polls. I could not help noting that his policies had been following quite well the advice that I recognized as coming from at least some of his backers in Atlanta, those who supported low welfare expenditures coupled with high military ones, a balanced budget regardless of social side effects, anti-inflation measures, unless they affected a particular business or informant, and a quiet setting aside of major campaign goals like a substantial reduction of the many government bureaus, a general tax overhaul, and so on. Carter had seemed preoccupied with any number of image problems that he worked at correcting. He smiled less when things were serious, and he traveled to China to show a firm grasp of foreign affairs when the Middle East situation crumbled month by month. These efforts, it seemed, came through to the people as cosmetic, as a manipulation of symbols rather than a grasp of the reality of the situation, *their* situation. When this message got through, a well-publicized conference, a domestic summit, was called at the presidential retreat at Camp David, where leaders of Congress, senior members in both houses, and groups of businessmen were followed at last, at the tail end, by a spate of ministers who came to talk to the president who in his turn mostly listened.[8] "It wasn't a goddam bit different than their regular Tuesday (leadership) meetings," said one congressional source. "They talked. He listened." "This has been a trademark of the president," the authors of the report concluded. "Congressional leaders have been unable to tell whether their advice was being heeded."[9] I was also interested in noting that others among those mentioned in attendance at this meeting included Clark Clifford, an attorney who had been an insider in former administrations as well as a trusted lawyer, a friend and advisor to one of the top Atlanta leaders, and Charles Kirbo, both of whom were on hand, I would say, as monitors for the private interests of power through most of the proceedings. The report of the meeting made a point of stating that when staff advisors, the paid help, were asked to excuse themselves during particularly delicate discussions, Charles Kirbo remained. Clark Clifford acted as the spokesman to the press at this meeting.[10] These tactics all represented good power-structure, community-organization proceedings.

It had come to my attention through one of the senators I had interviewed many years ago that a great number of presidential confidants among the various local power structures move in and out of the doors of the White House, just as they did on the occasion just described. Most of them receive no publicity at all. This procedure is considered to be a normal routine in running the nation, especially when a president is badly in need of advice.

I have traced ties of confidence between leaders of at least six of the larger companies in Atlanta (companies identified during Study II) and the lawyers who were on call to advise them or the president —whoever needed their advice more—on national policy matters.

The grave difficulty here is that these ties of confidence create bonds with various power groups, but they would seem to do little, if anything, about the real problems of the people. Taxes will remain high, oil prices will continue to rise, and unemployment figures will continue to rise, as we have been told. Therefore, many people have asked, "So what was the meeting all about?"

Such meetings do not reach the people. They are not intended to do that. They are a symbolic reference for the people. The people are given a news story, which implies that they are being talked about seriously. Policies may even be talked about at meetings such as these, but the results of these talks remain to be announced.

If one were to trace the policy connections to the local power structure in Atlanta, one need only begin with the names already mentioned. They will lead to interests related to finance, energy production, steel production, soft drink production, apparel distribution, real estate development, and so on, each with a power apparatus of its own reaching to national and international spheres of influence. The trail ends there, so far as participation of the people is concerned. The people at this point are not participants in policy-making, but they become part of a huge set of polar relationships that include those of buyer-consumer, tenant-landlord, creditor-debtor, lawyer-client, and administrator-citizen. One is told what he may pay for land tenure, automobile manufacture, and insurance rates through policies made without his real participation. The symbology of democracy that hangs over such proceedings has little to do with democracy itself.

The aftermath of the domestic summit was President Carter's speech to the people outlining the malaise as he saw it, and he saw it, indeed, in the terms of his earlier popularity with the people. He spoke quite precisely of the imbalance between the economic and spiritual forces within people as defined in their body politic. He saw Washington as a paralyzed system and "Congress [as] twisted and pulled in every direction by hundreds of well-financed and powerful special interests."[11] He tried hard to erase the distance between him and the people he served with outstanding rhetoric and seemingly humble and forthright statements about his own shortcomings.

Yet beneath the words a stubborn clinging to policies already well in place was also voiced, policies relating to coal as fuel—a policy that has troubled so many environmentalists—billions for development of organic gasoline on our precious agricultural lands, and pipelines and cracking plants of one sort or another near cities where people are now forced by the circumstances of their existence to live. Contradictorily, he did state that he would not accept energy solutions that would harm our environment. Yet he did not mention whether or not he would abandon nuclear energy plant production, a position Governor Jerry Brown of California had been pressing on him. These and other topical issues of the hour remained obscure or untouched. In the latter quarter of 1979 one could only await further announcements in regard to them.

The other Laocoön serpent with which Mr. Carter wrestled in the night related to democracy. He had fine words for it, but, in summary, it appeared that democracy, in his opinion, is best served by the people's picking up the results of the domestic summit meeting as interpreted by him and shouldering the immense burdens of the cost of the programs he had in mind.[12] Even with minor differences in settings, this seemed to be politics as usual.

In spite of such a pessimistic assessment of the power apparatus in its general operations and within its present terms, Atlanta's position generally and that of the state of Georgia in the total national power arena may have improved slightly with Carter's ascendancy to the presidency, but earlier indicators tended to classify it as a minor power in national and international terms. Alas, there are those who keep wishing that it might be more than it is, and they cite statistics on such matters as urban growth and the like, but all other cities do the same. Meanwhile, Atlanta, as do its ordinary citizens, remains relatively where it had been before. It remains a regional shipping and financial center holding its proportional place in the national scheme of things. In the opinion of top leaders across the nation, the big "T" of power still extends across the upper industrial portion of the nation east to west, with its head in the northeast, Boston-to-Washington sector.

Since the Civil War, Atlanta leadership has dreamed of being a base for generating capital so that it might be relatively free of the Northern centers of capital. Unfortunately, it is now up to its ears in debt to both New York and Texas for its skyscraper splurge.

To be sure, because of the muscle of its internal structure, the city is a good credit risk to those lenders who have so recently patronized it, but when the tab falls due, interest, carrying charges, and bankruptcy costs included, the people will pay—and pay. This is but one more dimension of power and policy-making put into its proper perspective.

Three of the Introduction hypotheses may now be summed up with regard to the perspective stated above:

The historic, now cumbersome, function of money as a medium of exchange in production and distribution and ultimately as an expression of corporate book-capital is being superseded in practice in technological society (as electronically distinct from agrarian and mechanistic societies) by computer functions, which supply instant control mechanisms in systematic capital accumulation, retention, and dispersal of goods and services among the population.

Monetary policy control is centered on monopolistic price management (including inflation management controls), which in either so-called private or publicly controlled societies results in overcapitalization of production centers (corporations or politbureaus) and in chronic undercapitalization of the vast majority of the world's population.

Institutionally reinforced, systematic biases favor centralized monetary controls which, because of a preoccupation with building capital structures dysfunctional to human life and well-being, transform the social functions of production for consumer uses into capital aggrandizement, thus creating an imbalance among institutional values, which at last is detrimental to the full realization of life-enhancing activities of every individual in the world.

8

Private Power: Building Skyscrapers

I decided to investigate how one actually goes about building a skyscraper because the building of skyscrapers has become such a preoccupation in Atlanta. A second reason was that the buildings were built upon credit secured, in part, because individual leaders in the private sector have power to commit a portion of all workers' future wages and salaries in the community to repaying the vast accumulation of debt without even a murmur of say-so from them.

To get information on how I might best go about obtaining such a skyscraper recipe, I called upon a friend, Lou Niggeman, then chairman of the San Francisco–based Fireman's Fund Insurance Companies, and board member of many other major national corporations, including American Express. He also worked closely with Lloyds of London.[1] Lou was one of any number of criss-crossers of the nation and world in the quest for money and power. I also had called upon him to retest the notion (which I first tested in *Top Leadership, U.S.A.*) that men well placed in the San Francisco power structure would have access to the network of people, knowledge, money, and power that could deal back and forth between that Western city and places like Atlanta.

Lou immediately knew four or five people to send me to in Atlanta to get information on how they might have produced a skyscraper or two. Among them was John Portman, already engaged in helping build Rockefeller West on San Francisco's Embarcadero redevelopment land plus a Hyatt House Hotel just a stone's throw away.

"But," Lou said, "when one thinks of building, he usually is either from an outfit which has outgrown older space and can afford a new building, or he may be someone who needs only half a building and figures if he builds double he'll be able to rent space and pay for some of his own space, or finally, he may be a pure speculator who watches buildings go up and operates on the rule of thumb, if two go up, a third one stands a good chance of paying off."

"A lot of building in Atlanta has been built with outside money," he continued, "and to get a line on that, let me give you some names in insurance who have an interest in this and you can see if they can be helpful. I'll tell them about you with a couple of letters." His introductions were extremely helpful.

Thus, in order to understand how money is gotten by outside borrowers, like those in Atlanta who wish to build skyscrapers, I interviewed a number of executives in charge of such operations in two Eastern companies and asked for point-by-point description of what ordinarily happens in such cases. How can one finance a skyscraper? Does he need the usual 10 percent down like any shopper? I was passed from public relations to groups of mortgage analysts. A summary of transcribed notes taken from several experts' analyses follows:

First of all, I was told, it is the individual or company representative with whom we are concerned, the man with the idea, who is most often an experienced developer. His track record of successes is important.

If he is a real pro, he starts and finances: (1) a site location with analysis, of course, and (2) a feasibility study (the 10 percent down). If big, he may do it himself; if not, he may hire it done by a research outfit. Depending upon the type of proposal, one may look for two base points in the study: (1) large regional or national stores or offices involved, and (2) how many other small stores or tenants they can pull in their train. Next, preliminary drawings of concepts and ideas are made. At this point our skyscraper builder may come to an insurance company, particularly if he is big. Under most circumstances, however, an intermediary mortgage banker is contacted and he will bring the proposal to us, the insurance company, with his own preliminary evaluation.

The contract with a correspondent may be based on his place of origin. (One example—E. S. Merriman & Sons in San Francisco with Atlanta, Cauble and Company.) Our correspondent gets with the development to be with it, to grow with it, as it matures. In most cases the mortgage broker polishes and refines the project proposal with input from everybody along the line.

Some financiers divide the labor in their own shops. Our financing operations are first of all geographical, but unlike some, we do not have specialists according to loan types or classification of mortgage brokers. Our financial people are general by geography. They get on-the-job training and formal schooling as necessary in any individual case while engaging actively in "appraisal" seminars.

Any correspondence on a particular project comes to the geographical analyst. He makes an initial analysis, asking the obvious question, "What is the deal?" Then if it makes sense to him, "Location? Good, bad, indifferent? What is to be accomplished?" He thinks to himself, "It might work in Atlanta, but not in Sioux City!"

If the idea looks promising to the analyst, he will kick it around a circle of other analysts, but only if it looks pretty good. He doesn't want to waste their time or his with questionable projects. There are a lot more "nos" this way than "yeses." The team leader of analyst groups says "yes" tentatively, that is, he says, "come up with a case write-up on it." If that proves satisfactory, it then goes to the Eastern or Western U.S. boss. The individual analyst has to "sell" the project to him. If he is sold, the analyst prepares a "found brief" for departmental committee—like the mortgage department. If the project passes there—the departmental committee being the bloodiest of all—it moves on to one of two places. If it is over a million dollars, it goes to the board of directors; if under that amount, it is processed within the department.

The analyst then writes a "commitment." The legal department is of course involved and the commitment is made binding. A commitment is made to the *borrower*. Actual money payments may thereafter go two routes. (1) A services fee (for the 10 percenter) is passed on to the mortgage banker, in which case the broker probably gets the actual cash in the pay-off. However, (2) in the case of a very large developer, the check may go directly to him.

"Clear?," I was asked, or words to that effect in each instance. I answered, "Yes, I think so, but let me quickly repeat the process to you if you have time."

"By all means," were the courteous replies.

Some outfits, one of the insurance lenders told me, break all the rules. They may even "develop new developers." One of the billion-dollar club's favorite investments in recent years, as in Atlanta, has been urban renewal and redevelopment. Job creation and buildup of services are usually big arguing points. He cited an example of "a real lummox" in one city who started as a financial counselor to a group of laundries. He then began working directly with banks when a business needed expanded space. He learned the money route and is now a "real swinger, up in the chips."

Or in Atlanta, Richard Courts (or a half-dozen others of his status) might have gone directly to the Rockefellers or to Texas oil-mining people with a sketch of plans in his pocket notebook.

Such are some of the circuits of decision related to Atlanta's policy of building downtown's scores of new buildings.

Viewing the process of building a skyscraper from another point of view, that of the developer, Thomas Walker, writing in a special edition of the Atlanta *Journal and Constitution* devoted to a decade of change, analyzes the case very well. Walker describes the task of the real estate developer as a very complex one. The details that must be coordinated in any development of magnitude, whether it be an industrial warehouse, apartment complex, or office skyscraper are formidable. The larger the project, the more numerous are the details to be attended to: working out arrangements for land occupancy; working with a host of specialists—planners, lawyers, architects, economists, market forecasters, and income analysts; assessing and securing financing of both short-term and long-term character in relation to the project; working with and getting approval from a host of government planners, code enforcement officers, and licensing agents; and, finally, assembling the work force—concrete workers, plumbers, carpenters, and supervisors—to contract the whole thing. Concurrent with these difficulties, one must meet the objections of citizens or neighbors who might resist the development. Weather might be a factor that could put the project behind schedule or end it altogether. Inflation might make it unfeasible in the long run. Cost may outrun any possible gains. Borrowing money may become impossible.[2] Atlanta met for a decade all of these obstacles.

Whereas many cities were building in the suburbs as fast as moves could possibly be made there, in Atlanta one of the local aristocratic corporations, the Georgia Power Company, decided to stay downtown and consequently built an imposing, modern high-rise building at Peachtree and Baker streets, on the same side of the famous street as the carriage-trade department store Davison-Paxon and the politically famous old Henry Grady Hotel (now demolished to make way for the tallest hotel structure in the world).

Having given at least moral support to this move on the part of Georgia Power (the power structure having quietly argued the outlying vs. downtown developments for a decade), Ben Massell (owner of "half of downtown property," according to hearsay) decided to pick up the proposition of an imaginative young architect who had tired of trying to make architecture pay by just drawing building plans and not participating in the ultimate profits of the structures built. While the code of ethics of the profession of architecture prohibits an architect from engaging in both planning and construction of buildings, there is no law that prohibits an architect's becoming a developer who can hire and supervise any architect or set of architects he might choose. This is what Atlanta architect John Portman did. Portman dreamed big dreams of not merely building single buildings, but building total downtown complexes that would guide other builders toward rethinking and rebuilding vast areas of the central city. One of the first buildings to be put up, a giant merchandise mart, was backed by real estater Ben Massell (1950 power structure).

All questions of the legality of the ownership of the parcel of land were solved, a parcel that had for years been a downtown eyesore of deteriorated buildings shrewdly held, one is told, for speculative purposes by Massell. There was no problem of rezoning or of neighbors who would complain of the upcoming development—conditions that occur often in building developments. Everyone seemed delighted that one more large construction would join the new Georgia Power building to "anchor" the upper end of town.

The speculative nature of the Merchandise Mart development revolved around its proposed purpose, that of providing large areas of covered space where manufacturers could display their wares to wholesale buyers from the region and beyond. There were initially no tenants, no income, but history reveals that tenants flocked in. The Atlanta building boom was underway.

Studies were made of possible income and outgo, such as mortgage payments, taxes, maintenance, and other expenses. The general market conditions were assessed and predictions made. All signals said go, and go they did, "they" being the Merchandise Mart Corporation composed of Massell, Portman, and the Dallas entrepreneuring firm Trammell Crowe. Portman at one time was president of the latter concern. He also has between fifteen and twenty skyscrapers to his credit scattered across the country, notable among them the gargantuan Rockefeller West, the Embarcadero Center in San Francisco, and a downtown hotel in New York.

Walker concludes his article with an account that essentially agrees with the formula laid down by the insurance lenders I had interviewed. Walker had gained his information from an interview with James Caswell, Jr., manager of the Peachtree Center complex put together by John Portman. Caswell had made a distinction between long-term financing and short-term construction loans. Perhaps Walker's main point concerns the permanent long-term lender's ownership stake in the project. He is not unlike the landlord realtor who grants ownership tenancy on very strict conditions, the owner (so-called)-developer having what amounts to possession so long as he keeps up his payments on his loan—a condition familiar to so many automobile owners, so-called, and house owners, so-called, in debt-covered America.

Walker's account summarizes very well what a great majority of power structure members had been doing during the past fifteen years. The summary is of little interest to the little fellows of Atlanta, who intuitively know that none of this high-flying money-making is going to do them any good. Yet for awhile, they had to admit, for many there were more jobs.

Also, questioned in regard to the chronic inflation and money supply from long-term lenders, Caswell admitted that many institutions now not only ask for substantial interest rates but also require some form of equity participation in the project, a share in its income. This protects the lender against inflation so long as the owner-developer can pass on increased costs of maintenance and taxes to his tenants.[3]

When I presented Tom Cousins, another developer, with a list of power-structure names to see whether interaction among members of the power structure occurs in relation to the vast building events of the decade, he wrote the following by the side of each of five names: Ivan Allen, Jr., mayor, "indirectly, as Mayor"; Richard Courts, realtor and financier, "Stock underwriting" (confirming Courts's description of their relationship); Mills B. Lane, Jr., "Gave us first bank credit"; Edward D. Smith, "First National Bank was first large creditor"; and Q. V. Williamson, city councilman, "Broker on early minority housing projects."[4] One sees a repetition of such names, one project after another, and by such actions large buildings are built and gigantic enterprises erected. This is the heartbeat of Atlanta power. The power of its City Hall, in relation to this vast power, fades into insignificance.

One day a few weeks before the end of this study, from one of the taller of Atlanta's new skyscrapers, I gazed out at the mass of green of Georgia's Appalachian highland spring foliage that rims the entire metropolitan area and extends north for hundreds of miles. I searched for a spot north and west of the city, out toward Smyrna along the Chattahoochee River near the Georgia Power Company's Plant Atkinson. During World War II and for a time afterward, I had lived on a farm in the area, where I had come to know some of the north Georgia mountain people of the neighborhood, some of the little people of Georgia, the tobacco road kind—so different in many ways from those I had just been interviewing, but in so many ways the root-stock of these very people. I felt that I needed perspective *on* this height, on the skyscraper in which I was standing, as well as the perspective I had *from* this height.

In my mind's eye, I recalled Granny Tuggle and her family, who had lived at the head of our lane, near where I would pick up mail each day. I would often stop and chat with Granny and the one-eyed man in residence with her, Pinky Leathers. Occasionally, their "roomer," Harley Rainwater, who lived with Granny's daughter, Gertrude, was there to join in the conversations, if they could be called conversations.

"Howdy, Mr. Hunter! Come up and set awhile," one of them would say.

I would go up and sit on the edge of the porch, and likely as not there might be some brief conversation about the weather followed by a long silence. Then Pinky might say in a stream-of-consciousness colloquy, "Harl, you remember when that big car came a toolin' down the road? I believe I was a settin' here in the swing and you was where you are now under the tree . . . ? Or no, I believe I was a set-tin' under the tree and you was here in the swing. Anyways, that car was just a barrelin' it down the road, you remember that, Harl?"

Harley would appear to be thinking hard, then he would reply that he remembered the car, that it seemed to be burning up the road.

After a long silence, Pinky might wonder why they were in such a hurry. (End of story.) Another long silence. I might ask a question or two. Once I asked why Pinky had a sign on his old, beat-up pickup truck advertising a Talmadge political campaign for public office, one that I did not approve of politically. I thought I could get an argument going.

"Hell, Mr. Hunter," I recall Pinky saying, "that don't mean nothin'. A fellow came up to me at Carmichael's store and said he'd give me ten dollars if he could put the sign on my truck, and I just said, 'sure, put 'er on there!' It sure don't mean I'm gonna vote for him. I don't vote noway!"

As I stood at the window in the high-rise years later, gazing at the woods in the distance, I decided that I must revisit these people before concluding Study II. I had a very difficult time locating the Tuggle neighborhood. The new freeways had cut the neighborhood into two parts. On one side, a farm I remembered, the Baker farm, was nowhere to be seen. It had been paved over with tract homes. The James Carmichael store, a country grocery and livestock feed store, was sitting dilapidated on a road that ended abruptly at a high wire fence now bounding the new freeway. Carmichael's son, Jimmy, when I knew him, had become prominent in state politics. Having run unsuccessfully for the governorship of the state before heading up a ballpoint pen business in Atlanta, he was also a part of an earlier power structure there. He was one of the little people who through education and upper-peasant background had made it big. The old store was empty, the old house vacant, and I knew that James, Jr. (Jimmy) had died a few years ago. From their road, I could not see the city. An old "interurban" electric trolley line that had connected the area to the city had been removed and houses had sprung up where its tracks had lain. A narrow road nearby had been thinly paved with asphalt, a fact that indicated some betterment for a black rural neighborhood in the hollow below.

In a very circuitous way, I finally reached the Georgia Power Plant Atkinson site. The plant had grown tremendously. I recalled when my children had played cowboys and Indians in woods nearby. The woods then still had trench depressions the Georgia Confederates had dug to stave off Sherman's advance. On occasion we would find old uniform buttons or pieces of musket lead in walks among the quiet trees. Now the woods were gone. A huge hole yawned across the road from where I stood, beyond which the power plant stood. I later learned that the power company had greatly expanded its production in this area and was building additions to the mammoth electrical plant already in place.

Granny's house was no longer where it should have been. A neighbor up the road told me that they had all died but Buster, Granny's grandson, who, when I last heard of him and according to his mother, had joined the army, as she put it, to work for his pension. The land had been sold to a developer.

A neighbor of the Tuggles, Elbert Smith (a pseudonym), an ex-bookkeeper, whom I also had known, was now a chair-bound paralytic. His wife did the talking for him, mostly asking about my family and telling about theirs. Her son had become a trucker. His son, in time, hoped someday to become one. I had a list of some of the power people in Atlanta with me. I had hoped to get opinions from the Tuggles about it, but used it with the Smiths instead.

Mrs. Smith went over the names and picked out Rich's name as being a familiar one. She then handed it back to me, indicating that if her husband could talk, he would know a lot of those people, but since Atlanta had grown so much, perhaps they didn't know anyone there anymore. Except for their house and small lot, the Smiths had sold off all their fifty acres of farmland. The Smiths and the Tuggles are yet another facet and minor, rarely thought-of, dimension of Georgia power politics.

The Tuggles also took national matters of politics in their stride— at least Granny did. During World War II, along with other citizen participations fostered by the government, scrap-metal drives were among the most important. People spent prodigious amounts of time in cutting tops and bottoms from tin cans and flattening them for efficient transport to and from collecting stations.

Earl Haines, a good friend and the man from whom I leased a part of our farm, thought he might benefit personally from the genuine civic enthusiasm over metal conservation. Earl lived in Washington, D.C., and was employed as a lobbyist to Congress and an educational messenger to many government bureaus for the vegetable-oil interests of the nation and world. He had long been disturbed by the fact that the Tuggles had built a small barn on their place made of flattened pieces of tin from both large and small containers. A poorly constructed and badly built eyesore, it faced the farm entrance road. An old, semi-retired mule, used but once or twice a year for plowing the Tuggle garden, inhabited the barn. Earl had spoken to us several times about his desire to ask the Tuggles to remove the barn, but out of friendly feelings for the Tuggles he could not bring himself to do so. But during the scrap-metal drives he hit upon a plan.

He asked one of his friends on the White House staff to furnish him with a few sheets of official stationery upon which he could write a letter to Granny Tuggle stating that President Roosevelt had asked him to write to her and ask that she patriotically contribute the tin barn to the next scrap drive. He signed a fictitious name to the letter, and soon afterward related to me what he had done.

For several days on brief visits I waited to hear Granny speak of the letter from the White House, but she remained silent on the subject. At last I inquired about the matter, saying that I had heard that she had received an important letter from Washington.

"Yes," I recall Granny saying with visible concern, "I did receive a letter from President Roosevelt about giving our barn to the government, but I've thought and thought about it, and I don't quite see how I can. You see, Mr. Hunter, if I give the barn to Mr. Roosevelt, old mule just wouldn't have any place to sleep and it just don't seem right." She turned to another topic.

Her bright eyes peering out of her old, careworn face looked squarely into mine; her speech impressed me greatly. She had given the matter deep thought, and her old heart felt for old mule more than her head felt for the massive war effort. The fact that the "president had written to her" did not seem to impress her very much. It was kind of him to have her in mind, but she had a mind of her own, high-placed as he may have been in faraway Washington.

In historical hindsight, one may know that the mass of farmers of the nation looked to the cities to manufacture economic basics for them: machines to make it easier to till the soil, pump water, build fences, furnish inexpensive weaving, and get to and from market. It is highly doubtful that they had asked for the avalanche of trivia that now dominates the marketplace, wringing the last few cents of disposable income from Joe Bloke's pocket, Joe being grandfather Bloke's grandson, who now landless, grubs for a living in the city. The cost of mechanization to feed burgeoning city populations earlier had dispossessed Joe's father; the cost of wars and the ensuing electronic revolution had put him in wage peonage. The city has become, in the larger society, a huge sponge absorbing all it may have touched within its borders and beyond at home and abroad. The process is not limited to the United States but extends to nation states around the world. The process is not so much ideologically guided, but rather, it operates in consonance with the day-to-day requirements of technological extension even to its Greek-tragic ends. The cities represent the political failure of land and population policies. Volkswagen comes to two Pennsylvania towns and the media celebrates!

The Baker, Tuggle, Smith, and Haines (the farm upon which I had lived) farms had been absorbed into the mechanics and processes carried on in the downtown complex of skyscrapers, absorbed into the very skyscrapers themselves. The farm upon which I had lived was visibly absorbed into the Atkinson plant and invisibly into the new Georgia Power edifice downtown. The Carmichael store, once an edifice of small proportion but within human scope of local distribution of goods for use, busy and energetic, had been absorbed into downtown road contractors' establishments, material suppliers' headquarters, and into enlarged public and private bureaus devoted to routing money back to the private sector in order to repair and extend the whole vast system of highways. Over a million square miles of arable land of the nation lie under such jurisdictions.

Close by lay a large tract held by one of the larger land speculators of the city whom I had interviewed; farm properties, some five thousand acres, I had been told, were awaiting systematic overbuilding when the price structure is maneuvered into the proper levels for him. This fact was revealed by this man as a passing, illustrative aside. His properties lie directly west of Atlanta's exclusive Buckhead area. He is a member of Atlanta's historical corporate aristocrats.

Parts of the social picture add up ultimately to the greater whole. When I conducted Study I, though alluding to the greater whole, I had only touched upon the relationship between Atlanta and the larger system in which it operates. To have done more then would have been a speculative exercise with an insufficient empirical base, insufficient hypothetical assumptions. Intervening work has provided these.

On my way back to the city, and viewing once again the immense volume of downtown building, it occurred to me that the technology of it marked a distinct epoch in history. The massive building program would not have been possible but for the huge growth of technology during and following World War II. Georgia's agrarian age, marked by plantation cultures on its coastal plain and small farmer's husbandry with episodes of populist unrest and the protection of its mountain acres, had been superseded by a mechanical age that had reached its zenith by 1929 when there was "overproduction," i.e., the machines were making more than could be profitably sold, and the owners of factories and mills had "struck" for higher income. They were waiting for supplies to run out and for demand to pick up, in the classical sense of those terms. It took a war to put everything back on the system's track industrially, a war that ushered in the electronic age in which we now live.

Our present age is characterized by the results of scientific efforts in a number of fields, notably chemistry, miniaturization, computer processes (including the computerization of money), automation, electronics, communications, and macronization (space explorations, tectonic plate analyses). These and allied extensions of technology have made a new world environment for our citizenry, one which we have wonderingly accepted, but which we do not really understand or perhaps altogether need. It is one in which the private sector, unleashed by war deregulations and subsidies, has been able to produce instant skyscrapers along with instant cocoa and breakfast cereal, along with chemical pies (foodstuffs with no foods). We have experienced government by news announcement and recurring depressions, which have been media-managed. We have witnessed the growing concentration of money in fewer and fewer hands, as well as lands and properties concentrated in the same restrictive way. We now have a government presumably devoted to involving the people in its execution, but the best it can come up with is television phone-ins to the president. We still believe that money is real and thus is the answer to any number of ills and world faults, although at base it is but a process of decisions made by a few.

Looking at downtown Atlanta from afar brings such thoughts to mind.

Before a series of interviews to end my study, I went to the new Omni-International complex. It was mid-morning. A huge hotel, an awesome indoor sports arena, a cavernous open area containing an ice-skating rink, were located where only railroad tracks in Railroad Gulch had been before. One of the largest concessions, an adult "Disney-like" playland was closed, bankrupt. (By 1978 the whole Omni project had pleaded bankruptcy.) I had just returned from the north via Peachtree Road, where I had seen a new multistoried building that had been vacant for nearly six months. It was obvious that the 1960s building boom had slowed to a walk by the late 1970s.

As I looked up at the steel structural skylight over a great portion of the roof of the Omni, I could not help thinking about the countryside I had seen a day or two before. Georgia honeysuckle and kudzu vines have a way of slowly creeping over everything in their paths, as yet other tropical vines have covered some of the Aztec and Mayan cities of Latin America, South Asia, and elsewhere. I could not stifle a brief fantasy. I looked at the dome and tried to imagine how it would look when the Georgia honeysuckle will have begun to twine into it; how the ice rink would look to the first deer and rabbits that bound onto its surface after men have abandoned this great city as they have at earlier dates abandoned others all over the world. The fantasy has that shred of reality. Automation, industrial processes, satellite communications, and computerized paperwork and controls make the city an obsolete social form.

When societies in history have abandoned their cities, as huge portions of New York and others of our cities are now being abandoned, the citizenries have invariably melded back into the countryside to repossess the land, their sustenance, there to live in self-contained villages or on the countryside itself. Our people have as yet merely gone to the suburbs to practice land and population controls on a smaller scale, a closer personal scale. Who knows where the American scheme may finally extend or founder?

As every researcher knows, one always gathers more data than will fit into the book one means to write. In this book, the focus, for the most part, is on the succession of power, and yet I picked up along the way many items related to power that do not seem to be directly pertinent to the context of this book. In all, I took some 150 questions along with me on my first revisit to Atlanta. One by one they were all answered; some of them were answered during discussions that wandered far from the topic of the succession of power. Some of the tangential things I learned while looking into the matter of skyscraper building among the powers in Atlanta seemed important, and I shall enter them here because of their relevance to the general topic of social power and not because of their partial relevance to the building of skyscrapers.

When I arrived in 1977 at one man's desk, I found that he had already put upon it three letters and a short piece he had written regarding inflation. He explained that in his estimation inflation was worse for the nation than any foreign invasion could be. One letter had been addressed to Arthur Burns, Federal Reserve Board, applauding his conservative efforts. The second was written to Charles Kirbo requesting that he get these views to President Carter, for whom this man had not voted, but with whom he was well acquainted. Kirbo was the local lawyer who became the confidant of President Carter. The third letter was written to Clark Clifford, who was also presumed to have influence with the president. Clifford had been a client of the man I talked to.

"How did you first know that Clifford had influence?" I wondered.

The answer was that in a visit to Clifford's home during the Johnson administration he had noted that Clifford was called from his dinner by the president to help decide an important issue. The assumption of my informant was that he held the same kind of informal advisory position for this Democratic administration. The popular periodicals also allude to this notion. The thrust of all three letters was that federal spending should be cut by one-third to two-thirds of its present level. Thus the "outs" continue to speak up. I cannot argue that they prevail, but they do not cease speaking.

I checked the fact that attorney Robert Troutman, Jr., had indeed had a hand in getting Omni-International started, and that at last perhaps fortunately he had retained but a minor position in the whole development. As I had read, it was stated that Cousins's company had taken on a partnership with the Florida-based Alpert development firm. A separate corporation had been formed for the venture to protect holdings of both companies. Another source stated that Cousins had been taken to the cleaners, as the phrase goes, but was bearing up bravely and was determined to carry on.

I had wondered how Portman was getting along. One reply

indicated that he was protected by a cushion of multiple corporations and interlocked stocks and bonds issues underwritten by the "bigs" of the building industry.

During another interview I asked, "Why do you always operate under names other than your own?" The reply was that, according to a good rule, one never put one's name on anything whether one believed it would be successful or unsuccessful. If a venture was successful, one reaped a lot of jealousy and ill will, and someone was always trying to get a part of what one made. If the venture failed, everyone remembered it.

I was curious about secrecy in business negotiations. An illustration was offered of a man who had decided to sell a large operation he had managed for several years. The New York buyers were asked to submit a contract of sale to him without his name appearing in it— just a blank space where his name might ultimately appear. He was told that the buyer's lawyers might object to going forward with such an ambiguous contract, but upon the seller's insistence, the buyer did as directed. At the close of a business day on a weekend, the seller inserted his name into the revised document, sent it by courier to New York, where it was signed by the buyer. On Monday morning the sale was publicly announced.

"Why such secrecy?" I asked.

It was further explained that the business in question was an organization with valuable employees under contract to the seller. Some of these, if apprised earlier of the negotiations, might have sued to be relieved of their contracts and gone to other firms or launched their own enterprises, leaving the seller with nothing actually to sell except vacant goodwill. As it was, their contracts had been sold, and on Monday morning they were working for the new owner of the whole business.

My informant was happily showing his business astuteness. He had within the decade purchased a building in the city, and I was interested in getting him to go into the ways in which he had accomplished this sizable feat. Also, I wanted him to talk about the business downturn and how it may have been affected by low occupancy rates in the whole area.

In answer to the first question, he said that the purchase of the building had been the result of gaining money from another set of transactions. A realty promoter in the city had one morning thrown onto his desk a packet of near-bankrupt properties, and asked him whether he would like to purchase them at a bargain price. He had started to say no, but then he noticed that near-bankruptcies had paid some $10,000 the year before, which had put them in the black. However, they would have paid the promoter only about 4 percent on his investment, not enough for him. The promoter depended, it was explained, on rapid appreciation of his investments and could not wait for long-term gains.

The would-be buyer in this case asked for an extension of time to think about the proposition. He had, he said, pretty well made up his mind, or he would not have put down $25,000 as an option fee demanded by the promoter.

The prospective buyer then approached a half-dozen real estate operators to get their opinions. The first five thought the proposition extremely risky. The sixth thought well of it and was thereupon asked by the buyer if he would consent to manage the properties. The answer was yes. The buyer then said that he would impose only two restrictions on the administration of the property trust. First, make few or no repairs on the properties. He said that he had never laid eyes on them, and he was only buying them because he believed their values were going to inflate rapidly in the near future. Second, list all of the fifty properties in order, putting the worst property first and the best property last, and sell them off as rapidly as good profits could be realized.

Within a few weeks the property manager reported that he had sold the first two worst properties to two ethnic minority buyers for a profit of 70 percent over their investment price.

Before he had—or his company had—reached a halfway point in such sales, his company had made enough money to buy the building referred to. Someone had asked him immediately after the building had been purchased whether he had gone into the real estate business. He replied that he merely bought leases. The building he had bought had three major tenants on long enough leases to pay for it. Thus he described it as a business, not as real estate.

He then expressed criticism of those gambling on speculative buildings during the building boom and revealed that the city is thus heavily burdened by a high vacancy rate.

The interrelationships of local and national operations is illustrated by yet another segment of an interview. I asked how another developer was progressing in face of the downturn in building activity. The answer was that the other developer was going in over his head, that he was operating on bad advice. My informant mentioned the name of a principal in one of the major New York banks, one which Ferdinand Lundberg has written about extensively. He then explained that the developer in question had but recently, the previous January, freed himself of debt and was some $18 million in the clear. He had been well-advised by his financial counselors to invest, in the immediate future, no more than one-third of his free money, $5 million, but a call from the New York financier had tempted him to take on a project that the New York bank would finance at between $50 million and $100 million as necessary for the completion of the project.

His local advisors felt that the time was not right for such a venture and advised against it.

It was apparent that the speaker, who knew the banker well, had called him and asked him why he would want to put the local entrepreneur to such risk—five times beyond his free money's worth. The reply was that the banker had not had enough of this man's capability. He had had two loans with him, now paid in record time, both for $15 million each, but in each case he had had only half the contract. He had shared the first contract with Chemical Bank and the second with an Arab friend who wanted to invest some of his money here. Thus he actually had only $15 million riding on this very productive man. He concluded that he wanted some more and he believed that that was understandable.

My informant did understand the desire for more profit and left the matter at that. He concluded by saying that he had hoped he could save his friend from an ulcer, but allowed that his friend was probably so bemused by the name of that banker and the glamor of handling $100 million that he would go along with it despite the risky prospect of putting up buildings in Atlanta.

I asked what the labor situation was like in Atlanta now, how it fitted into the community picture.

The answer was that labor does not fit, that it never had. For a while it had backed off its "southern battle" and that resulted in a few good years. But now labor seemed to be back at the same game, this time sending in organizers from the North, New York, and Washington, and, of all things, it was buying houses to show that it was going to stay a while.

I wondered how the black mayor was doing. The answer was that he was doing as well as could be expected. He listened well sometimes. Recently a "consortium" of New York creditors had come down to look things over—especially the status of rentals in the buildings. Toward the end of their stay, they went to see the mayor and told him that they were extremely worried about the high vacancy rate in the buildings downtown. Three or four good years would eliminate the deficits, they believed. They told the mayor, however, that their creditors could stand no increase in property taxes at that point. They were sure the mayor would understand, and they underscored the point by saying that *if* taxes were to be increased, Atlanta could expect absolutely no credit in the New York area.

This, for those who may not wish to get the point, is the private sector speaking directly to City Hall.

The mayor assured them of his personal good intentions.

Another answer to the same question regarding the mayor was that a new, "business" mayor was needed. "Like Mayor Ivan Allen?" I asked. The answer was that a mayor like Mayor Hartsfield (the "Coca-Cola mayor" of Study I) would be better. "How is Robert Woodruff's health?" I inquired. The reply was that it was poor, but that in a round of golf the other day he had lost $3.00. The implication was that he had minded losing it badly, even with all the money he had.

An interview with *the* leading real estate man, and another arranged by him with his president of operations, produced a good deal of technical detail on how rentals are plotted, and some detail on public-private power relations. Their views have been woven into this narrative.

In another quarter, fear of renewed riots during the summer of 1978 was expressed. I wondered whether the fear was caused by business downturn. The reply was that there are always some people who don't know a good thing when they have it.

I noted in a parting meeting with one of Atlanta's principals as we rode up the elevator to the top floor of the Commerce Club that some are "private power watchers" in the club. My host had said that we would go up to the sixteenth-floor dining room since the fifteenth was the more "popular" (too crowded) place. The sixteenth floor would give us more privacy for talking.

When the elevator stopped at the fifteenth floor, four or five men were waiting in the lobby in front of the elevator. Since I was partly hidden by the door of the elevator, I saw one of the men nearly fall out of his chair trying to get himself into position to see who it was riding up the elevator. It was quite apparent that he wanted information, in order to see what my host was up to. Knowing of such relationships, even if not in this instance but in others, might be valuable in terms of business investment or direction!

"City Hall watching" is much easier. The newspapers may do most of it for one. Not so with the private sector. One has to be "in the know" or must inquire among them about their activities. In such ways, one learns at least how some of the inner groups downtown disport themselves, and what they talk about among themselves.

A well-informed power watcher suggested that I would have to update a recent listing of power figures for the following reasons: Henderson was deceased; Young was no longer a local power; Lane had retired to Savannah; Johnson was put out of commission by Mayor Jackson; and Selig's son, he believed, was now in Washington. When asked to comment on the succession of power, he announced that Robert Strickland had replaced Billy Sterne at the Trust Company of Georgia and Thomas Williams had replaced Ed Smith at the First National. Mills Lane's successor at the Citizens and Southern, Richard Kattel, had already left his new post, but no heir had yet been announced by that board.

With regard to future politics, this power watcher speculated that Maynard Jackson by law could not succeed himself for a third term. Talk had it that Atlanta had elected a Jew, a black, why not now a woman? Prominent names that could be considered included Panke Bradley and Barbara Asher, both of whom were then councilwomen.

Since it had become clear to me that many in the power structure had not been too happy about the last two candidates and their wins in the city, it might just go for a woman. But again, only time would tell. The general feeling about black candidates seemed to be, even among themselves, that for the moment they were in a kind of eclipse. The prolonged recession of 1975 had put the power structure into low profile. The mood of all seemed tentative, murky.

What had the men of Atlanta been doing between 1950 and 1970? They had been busy building skyscrapers and within them were, during the 1970s, carrying on business as usual.

9

Other Projects, Issues, and Policies

Of the hypotheses about power set forth in the Introduction, none may be more important than those concerning the policy-making function performed by the people in community life who are accorded roles in this vital area. These hypotheses state:

Those ascendant in any given power structure assume its policy-making function.

The manifest function of formal American government is that of adjudicating various institutional claims regarding their rights and the rights of their individual members, but because of the ascendancy of the economic institution, a bias at this time exists in its favor.

Economic institutional values are present in both private and public power centers in such degree that they, in effect, form a dual, coordinate system of de facto power, existing constitutional governing theories to the contrary.

In Study I it was suggested that long-settled policies present no challenge to community leaders. Private property, public education, city housekeeping services including law enforcement, voluntary association for civic purposes, and the like are presumed to be guided by settled policies. The term *policy*, by dictionary definition, means "a settled or definite course . . . adopted and followed by a government, institution, body, or individual."

Policies, it was also pointed out in Study I, vary in magnitude and complexity, and could therefore be divided into "big" policies and "lesser" policies.

Examples of big policy consideration in Study I were the adoption and execution of the Plan of Improvement, which largely concerned street and highway improvement and the expansion of city boundaries. This policy formulation then had guided actions of the community for two decades and ultimately had led to a gigantic building program in the city. Certainly the development of the coliseum, the whole unfolding of downtown renewal policies and projects, the development of the Georgia State University complex, the maturing of the Omni-International project, the building of skyscrapers as seats of power, and the initial construction of a rapid transit system were all examples of big policy attended to by a relative handful of men and their immediate successors at the policy-making helm. It is also clear that an interchange of many individuals took place at the central core of the Atlanta power; according to individual interests, they moved from one major project to another during the period between 1950 and 1973. Each project required considerable time in policy development, a decade being the common time span for the big policy matters, certainly for those the size of the Plan of Improvement or rapid transit.

One policy formulation, segregation, long considered by the power structure and the whole community to be a settled matter, became unsettled in the mid-sixties. An illustration of how this question was partially relieved but not altogether settled (although one is led to believe participants thought it would be) by one of the major luncheon clubs is supplied by Ivan Allen, Jr., in his book on his experiences as mayor. Allen had been trying to slightly integrate the Commerce Club with little success. After the many struggles of the fifties and sixties by blacks for recognition, it had become increasingly difficult to explain why some black officeholders and businessmen could not attend policy-making sessions among members of the power structure, held within each club.

Finally, Mills Lane, Jr., a banker-lender, promoter of the Commerce Club, told Allen that the issue of blacks coming into the club had simmered too long. The club needed to face up to the problem, and he suggested that it be brought up at the next board meeting. At the next meeting, attended by a number of the top business leaders, some sixteen of the members heard Lane rather offhandedly mention that Allen had a matter to present to the body. Allen addressed the issue directly. He argued that the Commerce Club should admit blacks as guests of members (not as members yet). He emphasized that the Commerce Club differed from the more cultural clubs (which still banned blacks and Jews) in that the club had always tried to bring the whole business community together, and he implied that black businessmen were an essential part of it. He therefore moved that they accept Negro citizens as guests. There ensued a dead silence. Of those present, Robert Woodruff, then one of the largest (anonymous) patrons of the community and the man in control of its largest industry, leaned over to Allen and said in a stage whisper that he was indeed right. Immediately hands flew up seconding Allen's languishing motion, which then quickly passed unanimously.[1]

It also was eloquent testimony on Allen's part regarding an incident of transition in policy-making in Atlanta. A new policy for many in top leadership positions was born in those brief minutes, even though it only allowed "guests," a category long applied to Jews, who hate the club term. Most would welcome the word "membership." To be sure, only a select few of the black community would immediately benefit from "guest" invitations to that club, but the door had been opened.

In the majority of cases where civic questions arise, the abiding rules of institutional behavior and relatively fixed customs among the citizenry are sufficient to ease the load of the policy-makers, but there are, nevertheless, along with the reaffirmation of the more established rules of social order, a great many new issues that constantly clamor for attention.

Unsettled policies are in a category by themselves. They are the troublesome matters that come before the policy-makers, public and private, and in spite of efforts to solve the questions involved these same matters reappear with perplexing frequency. Most of these problems often are shrugged off initially by the community's top leadership as being unimportant. They are too busy with the big issues—building buildings, building highways, building rail lines—to pay much attention to such things as chronic unemployment among a considerable portion of the able-bodied citizens of the community even in times of unprecedented prosperity. Remaining unattended are: inadequate housing for the general population (because of war shortages, insufficient building in peace times for all segments of the population, and a steady rise of inflation in the general economy), inadequate police protection in many of the poorer areas, the fact of poverty itself, and a host of related questions that greatly trouble the underlying populations of the city; these are matters apparently of little concern to the top leaders. When they are pestered about their failures, they become angry.

While the preceding scene from the Commerce Club illustrates how quickly a private club's policy can be modified and how acutely in tune those who surrounded Woodruff were with him, the action (which occurred in the 1960s) was some ten years late and too little. Had it occurred nearer the time of the Supreme Court's famous decision in 1954, it would have been a phenomenal show of intelligent social action. Instead, following instead of leading, the power structure representatives present at this particular meeting merely showed their indebtedness, not to Woodruff, but to Martin Luther King, Jr., and his host of followers. The whole thing makes one wonder why so many feel that they must follow the cues of any identified or presumed structure of power.

As I examine these policy considerations of Atlanta, actually its recent urban sense of direction, I shall continue to view its whole system of policy decisions critically. While criticisms of its workings have been implied throughout this writing, they have been minimized in order to allow the facts of power controls in Atlanta to speak for themselves. Since I am of the opinion that piecemeal reforms will never be able to change the basic drives of the present capital system for its own aggrandizement at the expense of the general citizen, I should now be more explicit about my judgment and finally offer what I think are the possible ways to make the system more democratic, so that people control their own affairs and capital development. I have determined that in this work at least, social science analyses would be bolstered with suggestions for citizen action.

It can be shown that attention primarily is focused on policies relating to the interests of the power structure, while those relating to the underpopulation of the community remain unsettled. For a moment, I should like to discuss this imbalance through the use of a meticulous piece of work done by Clarence N. Stone, who examined urban renewal policies in Atlanta from 1950 to 1970.[2]

Stone examined in minute detail how a series of decisions about urban renewal in Atlanta were dealt with by the officials of the governmental agencies and private groups involved in housing and neighborhood development during a decade of unprecedented citizen action, sit-ins, run-ins, wade-ins, and pray-ins. The renewal officials were subjected to a full array of citizen protest during a period when there was no citizen apathy. Yet with all of this, Stone at last concluded that urban renewal policy in Atlanta favored the business interests over the activists and vocal minorities with regard to neighborhood and housing improvements. It became clear to him that the leading economic groups were more successful in their attempts to influence policy decisions than any others, even those who were stridently vocal.

It will be recalled that one Introduction hypothesis quoted at the beginning of this chapter suggested that: *The manifest function of formal American government is that of adjudicating various institutional claims regarding their rights and the rights of their individual members, but because of the ascendancy of the economic institution, a bias at this time exists in its favor.*

Stone argues governmental neutrality may break down, first of all because official behavior is only sporadically visible and loosely accountable to the electorate, and secondly because some groups are better positioned than others to further their interests through the political system. In short, a city's governmental machinery may be influenced to operate *consistently* in favor of some interests at the expense of others—even if the other interests are a sizable and active political force.[3] He then proceeded to prove his points by showing the favorable bias toward the business community, a minority force, against all comers.

Stone's conclusion rather sums up my own views in both Study I and II. Some people are indeed better placed in the scale of societal dominance than others. The weight of historical opinion would seem to favor this description of civic judgments. Stone, a political scientist, evidently is trying to turn his so-called pluralist colleagues around, thinkers who argue otherwise. As a matter of fact, his whole work is devoted to theoretical arguments regarding the objective data he has collected, and his empirical data are exceedingly valuable in our discussion of policy-making. We can only summarize a few more of his findings here.

In a most significant statement regarding the primary position of policy in relation to the many decisions that are made in its wake, Stone asserts that the [Atlanta] Housing Authority Board had made a gentleman's agreement to reassure realtors and members of the Chamber of Commerce that public housing would not be built on renewal land and that the Housing Authority itself would initiate no requests for additional units of public housing.[4] This single policy is responsible more than any other for Atlanta's 1960 midtown resurgence.

Mayor Ivan Allen is one "gentleman" referred to in the gentleman's agreement along with other members of Atlanta's business-dominated power structure, especially in this instance to that sector most concerned with downtown development as opposed to building homes and neighborhood facilities. The informal gentleman's agreement with its bias was tacitly and readily accepted at all levels of government, local to national.

Stone suggests that the term "community decision" in both the city administrations that his study covered, those of Hartsfield and Allen, meant, in essence, "a matter to be cleared with the major elements in the city's business leadership,"[5] i.e., its power structure.

The results of such policy direction is perhaps best illustrated by the ratio of business successes to ordinary citizen and neighborhood successes in gaining policy objectives in both the Hartsfield and Allen city administrations. In the Hartsfield era, business was successful in four out of five tries; in the Allen era, business was successful in five out of six tries.[6] Ordinary citizens, extremely concerned about the use of the people's money to subsidize overcapitalized corporations, only won once in either case. Stone's work is replete with graphic accounts of the struggles between those competing for allocation of societal and community resources and bears close reading by any who may be looking for such detail. Our purpose here is merely to highlight Stone's work, which has made our task easier than it otherwise might have been.

In apparent contradiction of Stone's earlier evidence, I was told that in the late 1970s there had been a revival of "neighborhood power," not so much interested in overall economic development of the central city as in neighborhood development. Some victories were said to have occurred, but the specifics, except for voting success in one neighborhood, were somewhat vague.

One does not like to discourage any bettering of the overall Atlanta power imbalance, and I do wish the neighborhood movement well. My observation of such movements, however, does not arouse in me the same amount of enthusiasm as it does in some. As I looked more extensively into the matter, I could see that the new member of the legislature was fairly well enmeshed in the conservative power structure of that body, but only time will tell. True, downtown development was in a lull, but neighborhood building did not appear to be in full flower either. Further, the struggle to keep black voters within the city limits by development of "clean up, paint up" neighborhood campaigns is failing, as black populations spill out into suburban areas, just as do the whites. As these movements continue, more blacks may opt for regional government with no neighborhoods at all. Neighborhood efforts hark back to ward politics, with all the controls their historical ascendancy represented, controls the blacks wish desperately to throw off.

I am convinced that one might take any one of the differences between the Atlanta power structure and the underlying population on any one of the issues that follow and come to the same conclusions regarding systematic bias that Stone has indicated in his work and that I have repeatedly pointed out in mine. Let us turn to some of the tabulations of other long-term differing policy contentions in the Atlanta situation. During the next few pages we shall make some important comparisons and contrasts in policy-making activities of the community's power structures in both the 1950s and the 1970s.

The overview reveals numerous instances where they failed to recognize or meet the expectations of the underlying populations. The fault is a grave one, one that needs to be universally addressed.

All informants in Study I were asked the question, "What are two major issues or projects before the community today?" The answers are indicated in table 5.

When the professional understructure was asked the same question, the answers differed somewhat (table 6). It will be noted that in only two instances did the power leaders in the community choose a matter related to international affairs as a major issue before the community; two men insisted on listing morale-building to prepare the nation for war. None of the professionals, however, mentioned an issue pertaining to the threat of war, and few spoke of the international situation in interviews. "Out of their area of competence" is the phrase most often used by their presumed superiors in this case.

It can be seen that the Plan of Development had high priority both in the top leader group and among the professionals. A total of twenty-three out of twenty-six top leaders chose this problem and four of the fourteen professionals did likewise. Traffic control, the general black question, and the Voter's Plan all received consideration by both the top leaders and the professionals. The sales tax measure mentioned by several of the top leaders stands out as differentiating them from the under-group. Housing and slum clearance had considerably higher priority among the underlying population than with the top leaders.

Table 5. Major Issues or Projects Reported by Twenty-six Top Leaders before the Community of Atlanta, 1950–1951*

Issue or Project	Number of Times Reported
Plan of Development	23
Traffic control	9
Sales tax measure	4
Negro question (general)	4
Medical plan, Negro housing	3
Morale-building for war emergency, general taxation	2 (each)
Education (university project), Negro education, meeting facilities, for luncheon clubs, increased bonded indebtedness	1 (each)

*Table 8 in Study I.

Table 6. Major Issues or Projects Reported by Fourteen
Professionals before the Community of Atlanta, 1950–1951*

Issue or Project	Number of Times Reported
Plan of Development	4
Housing and slum clearance	4
Negro question (general)	3
Voter's plan, segregation, traffic control, black education, political reform	2 (each)
Rent control, safety (fire), increased welfare grants, more adequate financing through Community Chest, police action against Negroes	1 (each)

*Table 9 in Study I.

The top leaders of the power structure do not believe that fully meeting the demands for better housing of the poor, better incomes for the poor, full employment, or full income for those unemployed because of systematic failure is the proper way to manage an economy. There is no profit in it. They hold to centuries-old economic beliefs about capital accumulation and its attendant "trickle down" theories. Build big buildings and employment of many is assured, they say. Yes, one may reply, that may have been true in 1776, but today a lot of building is done with machines, which leaves large reserves of laborers standing on the sidelines. Capital accumulation by those already capitalized and dispossessing and undercapitalizing all others cannot solve the problems of the economy of 1978. It is how capital is distributed among the population and utilized that makes a great difference between what is and what might be.

It becomes evident upon reviewing the efforts made by the men of policy decision in Atlanta today and comparing their efforts with needs, that something is grossly lacking—as it was in 1950.

In order to further compare and contrast the policy priorities of whites and blacks in 1970 with those of 1950, those interviewed in Study II were asked to make their own listing (see table 7). It will be seen that, as in 1950, in 1970 the white and black community priority listings differ markedly. The political directions suggested by whites are diametrically opposed by blacks. The whites wanted more and more building—of huge central city projects, rapid transit, airport improvement, Omni-International development, and expanded higher-

Table 7. Priority Community Issues, by Races, Atlanta, 1950 and 1970

White	Black
1950	
1. Physical improvements	1. School improvement
Airports	2. Housing, slum clearance
Freeways	3. Voting rights
Extension of city boundaries	
2. Sales tax	
3. Black question (general)	
1970	
1. Physical improvements	1. Acute housing shortage
rapid transit	2. High unemployment
new airport	3. Resistance of unions to black
Omni-International	membership, particularly
2. Housing, outlying areas	plumbers, steamfitters, electrical
3. Inflation	4. High incidence of crime
	5. Fragmentation of black leadership;
	emergence of political conflict
	6. Cross-town transportation
	7. High prices (inflation)

income housing in outlying areas. In the interviews, they could speak of nothing else. The blacks were seeking solutions to their housing problems in the city and were concerned with steep unemployment rates. They still are trying to open the labor unions to their people. They are concerned with crime problems, including drug addiction among their young, and they are worried about the political conflict in the new scramble for power among the opportunists in their numbers. Last of all, they were, contrary to the white first priority of mass transit, concerned about *cross-town* transit; fewer blacks have access to autos with which to use the handsome new freeways much used by affluent blacks and most whites. They felt that the substations of rapid transit have been designed to serve suburbia, a notion that may be more felt and believed than actually true.

Inflation, a chronic malady around the world, is also mentioned as a problem by whites and blacks, with whites giving it a higher priority. In our country it is an economic condition primarily caused by price management of big business in the larger system of production, the national system, where major decisions are made in national corporate headquarters. Prices are set to maximize profits in the classical monopolistic sense and to limit production so as to produce chronic scarcity in the market. The machines of the nation, except in war boom times, operate at little better than 50 to 60 percent of capacity. They reflect money-making decisions rather than production for use. Enormous profits are reaped from these kinds of limitations, and the gigantic increases of such capital made available year after year are put into savings certificates or low-risk ventures such as building skyscrapers or palatial factories, monies which therefore do not produce directly consumable goods and yet employ multitudes of people producing nonessentials, which further fires inflation. Add to all of this the insatiable demand for glossy expendable military equipment, military housing, advertising huckstering, and all the etceteras of such unproductive uses of money: yet more inflation. But piously, the producers of these maladies blame it on the other fellows: big government and spending too much for the poor! So many young mothers are on relief! No, the fault must be laid at the proper doors. They are the doors behind which too little that is useful is produced at too high prices.

Inflation in the United States differs from world inflation in that it could be eliminated from our system by slightly upping production of basics: food, clothing, shelter, and lowering the production of nonconsumer items and impounding excess profits. In the world, the remedy might lie in building more capital machines, possibly on a regional basis, and building them only for consumer goods, not war supplies. But our producers, in Atlanta or elsewhere, cannot think in these simple terms.

Most of the white and black leaders alike in Atlanta were unprepared to think about or seemed to wish to discuss these terms, which are not in the lexicon of the local powers of the system. Most of them are ill-informed and intransigent in their accumulated social and economic ignorance. A few, like the industrial developer mentioned above, who once sat on the national board of the IBM corporation and who could personally speak with cabinet members or the president of the United States or the head of the Chase Manhattan bank on monetary policies, is an exceptional citizen in Atlanta. He is a peg in the local, urban anchorpoint of power. He might have spoken more correctly and thus effectively about inflation but he speaks instead of government spending as the bugaboo. Inflation is the consequence of behavior of the national power structure, and, unlike the developer spoken of earlier, most locals have only passive roles in regard to inflation. While top leaders nationally fail to use skills to social advantage, those below this level of power remain silent through suppression, ingrained fear, and learned Uriah Heep postures.

The hypotheses in the Introduction concerning this subject were:

A societal power system, commonly called "the system," represents the sum of all cultural, institutional, and technological policy-making actions within given territorial limits. These elements extend internationally as differentiated power blocs.

Dominant world power structures are at present national, embracing multitudinous, subordinate internal and external systems, communities and cities being their anchor points of power.

Within the total system of power, money credit, production schedules, and yes, shortages are managed by the national powers of the world, who can choose not to listen to any subordinate, local voice, including those of Portman, Lane, or Austin, and certainly Joe Bloke. If shortages occur because of excessive capital retention, Bloke's cries may be heard, but little attention may be paid to his cries alone. Only when he is joined by restive demands of many others will attention be paid to him. To be sure, Bloke's role is to be a spender and a consumer, and as such, his value as a statistic in the whole market process carries a modicum of weight, which finally may become a critical factor in upper-level decisions if he and multitudes like him become too disadvantaged. If his circumstances are a minor factor in the considerations of mass movements of goods and services—let's say he is a relief client, considered to be a negative factor, a low-rated spender and consumer in the national equations —his cries, although monitored by social agencies and university research workers perhaps, will go largely unattended.

The economic sector long has assumed latent governing functions in addition to its primary institutional function of the production of the physical means of life for society. It tends to deny the concomitant role of *"providing a buffer of reason and protection between the individual and society"* (another function of all institutions), and in the case of human distress falls back upon its primal functional prerogative, that of *merely* being responsible for the *"production of the physical means of life."* Our contention is that the private sector of the United States economy has assumed governing roles that the ordinary citizen wrongly believes have been assumed in his interests, but which continually fail him and at last dispossess him rather than fulfill his primary economic needs. The same forces dominate government and bend that institutional segment also to abandon roles of protection of the individual.

Through so-called fair-trade-practice laws and many others, and through the industry- and business-dominated compliant public commissions, the corporations tell consumers with impunity how much almost prohibitive insurance rates will be, how much utilities will cost, and in many cases how much consumer goods and needed drugs will cost. The individual has no real redress to either the corporations or to his government; he can do nothing but talk near any election date. Most are vaguely aware of these conditions but remain silent.

I have alluded to the relation of the housing question to redevelopment in my analysis of Stone's conclusions. Housing generally has been a problem in Atlanta for generations. It has been aggravated because the largest profitable slum areas are filled by both black and white poor housing, which more people want, and few earn high enough wages to afford the high-priced homes being built for more affluent people elsewhere in the city. The passage, year after year, of federal housing legislation presumed to be helpful in the matter has become a huge illusion and joke. Most know that its billions mean little more than pork barrel subsidies for real estate groups interested in high-priced tract developments and more downtown and factory expansion. Everyone with low or even moderate income is caught in this intolerable squeeze.

The housing issue was not one on which the top leadership of the city could present a united front at the time of Study I, but by the time Study II had been initiated they had begun to marvel at the ease with which relatively cheap (subsidized) land could be turned into a seemingly never-ending spiral of profits, a recurring capital dream come true, "Something for nothing!"

Unemployment among the blacks and whites within the unskilled groups also in the 1970s has remained a chronic unsettled issue very little discussed among the leaders, who were convinced that the fault lies with the poor rather than with the technological system. The top powers among the policy-makers consider the issue a lesser one, that is, it is of concern to but a minority of the population. On the other hand, among all blacks it remains an issue that looms large in the burgeoning economy. If one is black, twenty years old, and wishing to marry the girl of his choice, the issue is a burning one, and there are thousands upon thousands of these, not only in Atlanta, but in every major city of the nation. To them it is as though history has played upon them its most cruel jest, to be without money in a nation rolling in it! Everyone else seems to be looking the other way and listening to another piper.

There are many genuine lesser issues in Atlanta: where to put street lights, new paving, play centers, swimming pools, and so on. Some issues considered small today may become big issues tomorrow. The understructure personnel, welfare and civic workers, often play around with the lesser issues, and, thanks to their channels of communication with the power leaders, some of their issues may be picked up for top-level policy consideration. When major policy is to be decided on any issue, the top leaders will be well represented by down-the-line personnel on any boards or committees devoted to the particular matter.

Looking at the problem of policy issues as a whole, we can clearly see that, to put the matter as gently as possible, even with the best of intentions (where there *are* intentions at all), the issues that get top priority among the policy-makers are those that in the long or short run will make money. The others wait in the gloomy outer chamber of charity or, worse, in limbo.

Taking into account the many questions that have been raised by the power structure phenomenon itself, many have asked directly of me the core question: "What can be done to break the hold of this mesmeric belief that only a few should make general policy?" One of the better answers to this vital question relates to a general reluctance to talk very specifically about the control of money, especially the control of ownership of it. Its generation as capital and the processes of its disbursement are clothed in massive secrecy. Yet questions about these processes lie at the root of almost all major community decisions. The system is known as a capitalist system, yet the factors of capital elude general discussion. The reason for this is that systems of power, private or public, are essentially those of patronage. I will address this notion now before moving to a final discussion of what, if anything, may be done about the difficulties presented in this framework of events.

10

Ownership Structure Management: A System of Patronage

By constitutional law and by custom the function of patronage is at the heart of the processes of management of the wealth of American communities, states, regions, and international corporate ventures. Those who control transfers of capital in this society do so, in name, as "representatives of the people," as stewards of the interests of the whole people, as maintenance functionaries of order in the American capitalistic system. Capital is defined here as any article of wealth capable of being transferred, that is, goods, chattels, lands, processes of technology, and money as a variable measure of worth in the whole process.

The managers themselves, by definition, are presumed to be leaders who may move in and out of private roles of institutional life and into governmental roles of management, always as representatives of the people. At least that has been the traditional civics-book definition of role assumption in relation to the managing of the common wealth generated by the people and extracted from them in very large measure by public taxes and private levies. Private systems of levy, which accrue as capital to the leverers, are activated by legal as well as quasi-legal and outright illegal maneuvers. Whatever the processes may be, none of them may be called democratic in any strict sense of the term, the term meaning that the ordinary citizen may have effective and open access to participation in all political decisions, whether public or private, which vitally affect his or her well-being.

In Study I, I assumed more open democratic management of capital than apparently has existed historically and the error must be corrected. Terms of democratic idealism, so far as I have observed, no longer fit the facts in Atlanta or in the nation. The processes of power described in this work and backed by nearly thirty years of work by myself and others, at any number of dimensions of the social processes of power, indicate elite management at all circumferences of policy decision. Power holders at the inner circles of decision making in all institutional frameworks consort with one another in directing community, national, and international policies, none more so than those at the helm of economic and political affairs (in that order), who announce their choices of direction to a seemingly complaisant, if actually restive, population. The assumption of this function of direction by the dominants in these two institutional groups creates the imbalance in society, repeatedly pointed out here, which is the favoring of economic and technological decisions over others. The social glue that holds the scheme together is patronage, which may be generally classified but which must be observed in operation in community contexts and in regard to functional divisions of labor in society. By communities, from small to large, I mean those groups which serve as real anchor points of power within the whole system. The individual in American life, regardless of idealized rhetoric, remains a nonentity in the mass, a symbolic figure in mass communications within this system. The individual's power is practically nil even when his opinions regarding the directions of power are sampled and presented as mass wisdom, usually after the fact.

The speed with which decisions can be made in an advanced technological society gives rise not only to anomie on the part of many but to mass anxiety because of alarmingly accelerated production processes harmful to people and their world environment. Whatever may be happening to the public in Atlanta or elsewhere, the news about the people suggests that decisions being made for them seem to deny not only their welfare but their very lives. Patronage to many seems to be reaching far too few in far too small amounts while it piles up into choking abundance at a rapidly narrowing upper end of the distribution scale. The majority of the people in the circumstances described appear to be yearning for an earlier, less hectic time, one in which the policy-makers may have been slightly more in touch with broad facets of their communities. Community in modern America seems to have become a kind of packaged consumption beneficial mainly to the packagers—the patronizers of all others.

If patronage is an important public and private syndrome of activities in technological society, under what sociological structure is it subsumed? What is the framework of such patronage? How is it classified? How may it be experientially observed? However one might sketch in the general outline of the society in which American power structures operate, it can only be characterized as oligarchical. That is the reality. Oligarchy is the maintenance of order invested in a few, in a dominant class or clique—that seems the most pertinent, the most real, of historical definitions.

The oligarchs in American society, as has been true in all oligarchical societies, are indeed the owners of great wealth, but their modes of operation in regard to that wealth and their relations to the general populace differ markedly from those of other historical societies. The difference may be characterized by the use of vast, interlaced, urban, bureaucratic structures, public and private, which operate between those who own vast amounts and the general population, which owns relatively little. The chief difference between the past use of the term and the present one is that most oligarchies have had rural, feudal origins with formal hereditary functionaries making their system operative, while the current Western system has salaried bureaucratic functionaries, public and private, serving similar purposes.

Most of these bureaucratic structures are production organizations, banking groups, and materials distributors, but many are an unproductive array of service organizations, propaganda bureaus, governmental organizations, political parties, and so on. Within all of these are contained roles of power, which are enacted in behalf of the ownership structures.

Some of the organized groups, particularly the so-called voluntary community and national associations, the lobbies, and the propaganda media may be characterized as "bureaucratic-like." They may not explicitly follow orders from any one superior combination of oligarchs, but in their general direction they perform, nevertheless, for ownership structures and the power system as a whole. Thus, because the chain of command is so constituted, the whole may be called a bureaucratic oligarchy. Its ends relate to the massive task of managing a national and a select world system of patronage.

The general insoluble problems for patronage managers in the present capital system of which I speak are: lower-class poverty, institutional biases favoring the business sector over the general population, profligate spending for headquarter buildings when general housing production for the population has run three or four decades behind social demand, gross practices of inequality of the division of land, capital, and disposable income between all sectors of the population, holding ingrained, if negative, values in regard to individual and collective human worth, widespread dispossession of ownership rights, and accelerated public and private debt.

At least the above items of social failure chronically plague Atlanta; in addition the city suffers problems that affect the society at large: massive and wasteful capital expenditures for past and future wars; excessive overcapitalization and technological development of uneconomical goods, gew-gaws and knick-knacks to amuse and exploit the gullible rather than products to meet people's needs for the economic basics of food, clothing, shelter, transportation, and recreation, and educational and cultural offerings suitable to the needs of people rather than the needs of bureaucrats and profiteers. And by no means the end of such a list must include its most glaring failure: government by announcement. Policies are announced to a complaisant population and not presented to the public for scrutiny, suggestions, debate, and direct political action. This study reveals that a very small number of people assume roles of policy direction in Atlanta life, a pattern that is repeated on the national level. It is a pattern that needs fundamental examination and change. The sticking point for such needed change is ingrained by false education, which results from the very process of policy-making and the notion that only a few are capable of making policy.

Minor adjustments and tokenism that allow for a slight increase in power for a handful of educated blacks and quagmires of indebtedness for the rest are hardly worthy of being called solutions to the massive problems that have chronically beset Atlanta.

Because of manipulative attitudes toward others by those who are high on the social status scale of ownership, all-but-impassable barriers to adequate social change and social elevation are created. The class attitudes carried in varying degrees by each of us become a part of the barrier, and the manipulative forces of the controlling powers add yet to the heaviness of it. Attitudes (values) are firmly rooted in the ego and are based on lessons of the past: habits of obedience and meekness, the level of one's sense of self-worth, one's capacity for self-assertion, learned at mother's knee, from experiences in kindergarten, the workplace, the corner bar, the television set, and the comic book. Social class attitudes are an important behavioral mechanism, through which the rulers of our society sanction patronage.

A hypothesis in the Introduction states: *Variable, learned attitudes concerning personal and collective ownership of property may be classified, thus providing the behavioral basis of that which has become known as class (classifications) structures.*

Fundamental classes in American society are determined by ownership of property. All other considerations are peripheral: manners, years of education, one's occupation, and so on. One may know people with many years of education who may be making leather belts for a living; others may have good manners but live in a slum; still another may do nothing of any consequence each day because he is a recipient of land rents. The latter person would win any poll on social status. What one *owns* determines status.

Ownership status works out according to a descending order of four classifications (classes): (1) the lords of patronage; (2) the managers of patronage; (3) the patronized; and (4) the dispossessed.

Processes of patronage are at the root of status orders everywhere, and the operators of national and international economic systems are the lords or managers. Large masses of the patronized (a fairly satisfied consumer class of skilled workers and professionals) appear in all advanced industrial countries with but rumbles of dissatisfaction expressing its striving, actually capital-less status. The final class—the dispossessed poor—is to be found in vast quantities everywhere.

The lords of patronage ("lords" here is used in a sense similar to land*lords*) are those for whom the computer is used as an address for the larger sums of rents, profits, and other monetary accruals in the whole society. They, or in most instances their managers, distribute funds accruing to them according to the accepted, particular ways of the economic institution and in agreement with notions concerning the eventual return of such funds with interest, plus assurances of respect and security for societies' overlords.

The managers of properties are well-paid corporate and governmental people who have some hope of eventually gaining access to a role as a lord of patronage. Many of these occupy informal positions in various local and national power structures.

The patronized are the mass consumer groups who work each day at the lower-paid professions and trades in order to receive salaries and wages that immediately are almost entirely returned, through credit channels, to the donors. The patronized are almost without hope of saving funds that, in terms of the larger system, can be converted into personal capital accounts.

Finally, there is the group that has lost most rights of income and property and is thus for all practical purposes bereft of any hope of recouping them. Such people occupy the slums of cities and such areas as the Appalachian highlands at Atlanta's backdoor (Granny Tuggle's neighborhood), some of the nation's marginal arable or desert areas, and are dispossessed, yes, into the fourth and fifth generations.

Institutions for the last century and more have opted for syndromes of values operationally skewed toward the dominance of private ownership and attendant dispossession and lifetime indebtedness in Western society. Our schools, market forces, political operators, and other institutionally operative groups laud the notion of fewer owners on an ever-greater scale and defame the rapidly growing number of individuals who are systematically dispossessed. Such a premise, one must insist, offers a poor foundation for any society.

Such is an objective picture of social class relations as they now stand in Atlanta and America. As hard as it may seem, change in these conditions is yet possible—given more constructive and more democratic teaching and some experience with, as we shall see, more appropriate models of behavior.

11

An Assertion Regarding
Effective Community Change

Although I am convinced that a new social structure of policy-making
is needed, I do not believe that mechanically imposed changes in the
existing one will do more than perpetuate it, essentially in its historical formulation of social order. As has been demonstrated, mere
personnel shifts in the structure, regardless of race or previous conditions of subordination of that personnel in the power processes of the
community, has created little change in Atlanta's position toward the
power structure. Faces come and go, a few fortunes are improved,
but the steeply pyramided structure of community decision remains
just as it has been to most of the citizenry for a century or more.
Deeply rooted community change must come from profound change
within the multibases of the whole population pyramid.

One cannot merely whistle change into being nor sit down some
evening and think out a new structure of power and thus bring it into
being, nor is it likely in this time of industrial and military might that
confrontation in revolutionary array will, even if it is successful, do
more than exchange one dominating oligarchy for another.

The real formula for change has to do with recognizing the
people's values first and the power structure's values second. This
formula was the one upon which the civil rights movement was
grounded until it collided with the ascendant powers of the community and state. The economic demands of that movement were
never allowed to stray beyond the prescribed rules of order of the
dominant economic forces of the nation.

Simply because no hypothesis related to fundamental social
change is operative in Atlanta or elsewhere, none is contained in the
listing of power structure hypotheses in the Introduction. A new
hypothesis must therefore be formulated, perhaps as follows:

In order to bring about balanced change in society, the ordinary citizen must have open access to participation in all political decisions, whether public or private, which vitally affect his well-being.

This hypothesis does not deny history; it but adds a new democratic requirement. It parallels one of Lincoln's great phrases and adds a vital component to it when it is rendered as it might be: "Of the people, by the people, for the people, and *with* the people."

The fundamental nexus of change is related to democratic freedom which must, to be meaningful at all, be expressed in more than patriotic or propagandist rhetoric. It must arise from a determination of individuals to act collectively to maintain the fundamental values in their institutional heritage. These values are implicit in social survival. They include preserving biological continuity, providing the physical means of life (food, clothing, housing, etc.), transmitting social values and skills, giving meaning to life, providing aid to the needy and debilitated, and providing a sense of balance and perspective to personal life. Given these values in their variety and comprehensiveness, then, and only then, will the people be able to effectively address the maintenance of order. In the Introduction hypotheses, order does not come first, but it is not isolated from the full array of institutional values considered by the people to be indispensable to their well-being. Putting structure before such values and in place of them, as the people say, puts the cart before the horse and creates a societal imbalance.

In sorting through the several solutions of our time regarding social change, and discarding those which seemed obsolete or harmful to the freedom of man, I came back again and again to the proposition of cooperative endeavor between men themselves through structures forged by them, not for them, newly and democratically formed generation by generation.

If effective changes in social relations are to be made, vertical changes in American society must be made and based on changes between those who own capital and those who are unable to do so. Both the patronized and the dispossessed classes are in need of such change. There is no social advantage in change that works only in favor of existing large-scale owner groups, some 3 percent of which own more than three-quarters of the wealth of the nation. Change in these disparate conditions must come through finding ways of distributing capital, not just by ameliorative shifts of income, to the advantage of the larger underclasses of the nation. Such ways can be found only in exercising broader and deeper rights of direct democracy than have been exercised in the American scheme of capital accumulation and distribution to date. Any question of a distribution of power posed in lesser terms than these would dodge the central problem of property ownership and management. I believe these propositions apply to the so-called socialist countries of the world as well as to the so-called democratic ones.

Models for change—one of which can be found on the northern outskirts of metropolitan Atlanta—will be sketched in the pages to follow. It must be repeated that these models represent but a beginning toward a more adequate management of policy affairs generally in capital arrangements, not an immediate panacea for all urban problems. They do, however, in my judgment, offer one of the most possible directions for profound change in a broad spectrum of community relationships, and they are attended with less pain and disruption than most of the other community contexts in which many disadvantaged people live.

In many places the cooperative movement in America has great strength, especially in several large rural areas. Facts related to the steady growth of the whole movement remain unpublicized largely because it is a people's movement, one that has as its stated aim an alternative to exploitative capital in the generation and distribution of capital.

As a member of a local consumer's cooperative, one becomes cognizant of other branches of the larger movement. Strong producer cooperatives, rural as well as urban worker-owner groups, will be illustrated within the whole range of cooperative endeavor. All offer a yardstick of performance as well as competition to untrammeled capital exploitation. Those who belong to any of these groups are given hope that at last the iron yoke of economic dominance may be successfully challenged and finally broken. The method of achieving that goal is that of cooperative self-help. Nothing is handed to one out of benign patronage. The movement is peaceful and a profound relief to those who may have become discouraged with any preachments of violence at all poles of extremity. A mature cooperative movement is a very real deterrent to dictatorships right or left, a safeguard very much needed in any land of narrowing opportunities and unsolved problems in which massive weapons of repression may come into the hands of frightened or threatened minorities. It is, of course, but one of the safeguards in the democratic way of life, but it is an important one.

Carroll Arnold has written a succinct summary of the cooperative movement in the United States:

> More than 50 million people in the United States belong to cooperatives. They are member-owned-and-controlled organizations belonging to

the people who need and use the services. Members work together to serve themselves and each other, rather than for the purpose of making a profit. There are cooperatives in housing, food, farm supply and marketing, health, rural electric and telephone service, credit, insurance, memorial societies, fishing, nursery schools, auto repair, crafts, pre-school [services], legal services, and other consumer goods and services.

Cooperatives in America are modeled upon the Rochdale (England) Equitable Pioneers' Society, founded in 1844. Started by 28 people, including one woman, who generated a total capital of 28 pounds, the Rochdale Pioneers formed their cooperative store with a pathetically scanty supply of flour, butter, sugar and oatmeal. The co-op began after flannel weavers in Lancashire mills were turned down in their bid for a wage increase. They reasoned that only through lowering the cost of living could they survive on wages often no more than the equivalent of 45 cents a week. So the cooperative store was launched in rented warehouse space by these mostly mill workers. Sales grew from 710 pounds in the first year to more than 4 million pounds in 1968.

Through the Cooperative League of the U.S.A., American cooperatives are joined with those in 63 other countries in the International Cooperative Alliance. ICA serves national cooperative organizations with a total membership around the world exceeding 330 million, joined together in 660,000 cooperative societies.

The Cooperative League, the only U.S. federation embracing co-ops of all kinds, serves its members through programs in the field of government affairs, information and education, public and member relations, cooperative development (through the Cooperative League Fund), international representation and development. [1]

While historically the whole cooperative movement is often related to the guiding hand of the English entrepreneur Robert Owens and to the Rochdale principles enunciated by that movement, its most spectacular successes have occurred in the Scandinavian countries. [2] These countries, largely because of their cooperative movement, have nurtured correspondingly progressive political movements. A small group of Finnish people who migrated to northern California in the first quarter of this century brought this valuable knowledge with them to that area.

A century and a half ago, the English Rochdale Pioneers laid down a few principles that have guided successful operations of cooperative groups everywhere in the world ever since. They are:

1. democratic control: one member, one vote
2. limited interest on vested capital
3. patronage refunds in proportion to purchases
4. open membership: anyone may shop, anyone may join

5. neutrality in religion and politics (generally now interpreted to mean *partisan* politics)
6. constant education and expansion
7. cooperation among cooperatives

During one of our worst recurrent depressions in the late 1920s a group of Finns in Berkeley, California, were joined by many dissident University of California faculty members, who also were frustrated and angry with a system that even then was not serving them well, and together they formed a cooperative "buying club." Their total investment was a few hundred dollars' worth of inventory along with considerable planning and other voluntary effort. Their success in this venture has been progressively phenomenal.

By the end of two years they had tripled their membership to 345 and were doing a business of $75,000 a year. Other co-ops followed their lead in northern California, some surviving and others perishing for a variety of reasons: bad management, insufficient starting capital, or poor educational procedures. The successes, however, have far outweighed the failures of this movement, and by 1977 the whole area had a volume of business of nearly $100 million a year with approximately 90,000 active members. This business included thirteen food stores, Berkeley's and Palo Alto's operations being the largest; a thriving bookstore, Books Unlimited; and consumer financial services including a credit union and savings and loan activities.[3]

Through affiliated organizations in the area, other cooperative services included mutual insurance, legal aid, medical benefits, an art exchange, travel services, a funeral society, garage and service stations, a taxi service, hardware and variety stores, pharmacies, bottle shops, wilderness shops, garden shops, a natural foods store, and home economics services in each center. Indeed, it is an impressive accumulation of services in four California counties within four decades, more impressive still if one knows that every development in this gigantic organization was discussed, planned, brought into being, and kept alive by the active participation and service of the membership and, one must add, fought all the way by giant competitors and political opponents. For any who may feel left out of the decisions that vitally affect his life, and out of the ownership of organizations vital to him, a few weeks of co-op activity is a certain antidote.

Although the organized business activities are extremely impressive, the way in which they came about, the principles of organization, and the philosophy of "people first" are much more impressive.

I believe that co-ops offer a way for people to compete directly with the giants we all know rule our lives. It is the cooperative dynamic, more than any other type of organization, that could turn our seemingly overpowering system of capital levy around and make it serve people rather than selfish, narrow interests.

This glowing account must not leave a false impression that all in the movement always "comes up roses." At the present date, the co-ops are struggling with huge problems resulting mainly from inflation. During recent years of intense competition, rising prices, and operating costs, profit margins often have not allowed very substantial consumer dividends. Many members have tended to become critical of co-op management, and by exerting pressure on the Berkeley board and in membership meetings they have forced two management changes in Berkeley professional leadership in fairly rapid succession. If the experience proved anything at all, it proved that the voices of the membership speaking as a part of direct democracy at work are heard and action inevitably ensues. At any rate, the discussions have been lively and on the whole, I believe, have strengthened the movement. Temporary reversals because of market pressures or even incorrect judgments require a rallying of members to strengthen and sustain the co-op in the interest of the very democratic solutions to problems its organizational structure offers. Its greatest contribution, as a vital social structure, is that "it changes the basis of ownership: it substitutes service for profit incentive."[4]

Although northern California certainly may not be typical of America in its energetic cooperative consumer movement, it shows clearly what can be done in good times and bad when consumers work with each other and for each other. Nor do the members of the northern California co-ops stand alone in their endeavors. They are served by an Associated Cooperatives group, a small professional bureaucracy which, with the advice and consent of community board members and executives of member co-ops of the region, coordinates the whole buying and distribution program.

This group also reaches out to producer co-ops across the nation, the principal coordinator of services at this circumference of affairs being the Cooperative League of the U.S.A., which maintains offices in both Chicago and Washington, D.C. It maintains relations with all types of co-ops, consumer-goods cooperatives, insurance, housing, and supply cooperatives. It publishes a weekly *News Digest* and a reporting service to newspapers and radio stations. It provides information to governmental agencies, especially in encouraging the use of the cooperative method in solutions to problems affecting people overseas. It is an active member of both the Organization of Cooperatives of America, a regional association of the Western hemisphere, and of the wider international organization, the International Cooperative Alliance.[5]

At an operating level, the buying power of consumer co-ops is pooled through National Cooperatives, Inc., with headquarters in Albert Lea, Minnesota. Its membership is drawn from all cooperative regional organizations. It owns the co-op brand, establishes quality standards, monitors labeling practices, and negotiates national purchasing contracts with organizations within and outside the cooperative sphere. Besides groceries, the co-op brand is widely used on tires, automotive accessories, electrical appliances, hardware, and farm supplies. National Cooperatives also produces milking machine equipment in a factory located in Albert Lea.

The cross-country locations of consumer co-ops include Puerto Rico, the Greenbelt Cooperative in the Washington, D.C., area (the largest of all consumer co-ops in the U.S., serving a region including Maryland and the suburbs of Washington in the Virginia area), New York (where a number of cooperative supermarkets are located in cooperative housing complexes), northern New Jersey, eastern Pennsylvania, and Ithaca, New York. Another cooperative distributing center is located in Framingham, Massachusetts, which includes in its territory areas occupied by Finnish settlers as well as other ethnic groups in Connecticut, Vermont, and New Hampshire. As one would suspect, the north-central states with their Nordic settlers in northern Michigan, Wisconsin, Minnesota, and a part of the Dakotas have numerous cooperatives even in the smaller communities, as well as supermarkets in larger cities. The distribution warehouse for a full line of staples and perishables is located in Superior, Wisconsin.

Among other full-fledged co-ops, the farm organizations of the Midwest may be mentioned. They handle hardware, farm supplies, petroleum products, automotive accessories, paint, building materials, fertilizers, and insecticides. They are supplied by private wholesalers.[6]

One may very simply distinguish between the "good guys" and the "bad guys" in the cooperative field. Those who subscribe to the Rochdale principles are considered here to be the "good guys." Often producer co-ops in various endeavors will use the co-op label for purposes known only to themselves. Sometimes these organizations turn out to be small groups of entrepreneurs who enrich themselves without ever consulting with or calling upon their so-called membership. They are like unions that have no democratic principles. They are often raw-materials producers' organizations.

Buying clubs often call themselves co-ops, but most violate the Rochdale principles. Very often these consist of small groups of volunteers who go into the commercial wholesale markets weekly or biweekly and purchase from a shopper's list provided by their memberships. They want an immediate return on savings from frugal purchases. Most of these organizations die out in a year or two from membership fatigue, due to the shopping and distribution exercises they undergo.

The successful co-ops are those which from the beginning become sufficiently educated by successful co-opers, and capitalized so that they may operate in market competition with existing commercial consumer outlets in their communities. They actively educate their members and foster continuing, democratic interest in the organization. In all ways they follow the basic Rochdale principles.

In a very correct sense, the co-ops are capital-generating organizations, but unlike all other capital-generating organizations in the larger system, they are devoted to the good of their membership, good in the sense of maintaining high-quality service and a return on purchases to the membership in proportion to the amount of those purchases. Full, voting membership in the northern California co-ops costs $100, but one may become a participating member for as little as $5, and credits are thereafter given toward full membership according to one's annual purchases. Such a member can participate in the many activities of the organization, but until his full dues are paid, he cannot vote for candidates for cooperative office or act on policy decisions in membership meetings. One may invest any amount of money in co-op certificates, but the investor's vote is still that of one member in this most direct of democratic organizations.

While both France and England, as well as all of the Nordic nations, have common ownership plans that work in behalf of their people, the most dramatic example of common ownership of industrial production (as distinct from consumer cooperation) has occurred in Spain during the past eighteen years in the Basque town of Mondragon. As a part of the broader movement of "industrial common ownership," the Mondragon example is important for both its operation and its success. It prefers to be known officially as a "worker ownership" movement.[7]

In 1943 a Basque Spanish priest (Father Arizmendi) founded

a technical college, specializing in metallurgy, in Mondragon. The purpose of the college was to provide social as well as technical education, but significantly it followed Father Arizmendi's desire to humanize industry, to bring a Christian dimension to industry: not as some "class war" tactic, but as a means of enabling men at work, "firstly to work together in harmony, and secondly to pursue objectives other than mere acquisition of money."[8] In other words, the goal was to adjust many of the institutional imbalances in Spanish society. The founders were dedicated to finding a means of not only working for their mutual benefit, but also a means whereby they might work for community benefit.

To this end, in 1956 five young graduates of the college began to plan a worker-owned enterprise. Local support was at once forthcoming from the community *from workers willing to supply their own capital.* In November of the same year thirteen men started making paraffin cookers. The enterprise was called Ulgor, formed from the initial letters of the names of the five originators of the idea. The enterprise was an immediate success.

By 1959 the Ulgor membership had increased to 170, with an additional product, gas cookers, added to the enterprise. At the same time six other cooperatives had been started, and three of these had joined with a consumer cooperative in setting up a worker's bank.[9]

Widespread goodwill toward the movement resulted in the bank's receiving large numbers of deposits, which provided the funds for an expansion of existing enterprises and the founding of new ones. There has remained a waiting list of workers willing to pay the capital entrance fee required to join a Mondragon enterprise.

At the end of 1972, the Mondragon industrial enterprises numbered 47, with a total of 10,055 worker owners and an annual sale of 168 million pesetas (or $107 million) worth of goods. The sizes of the industries and the products produced by them are indicated in tables 8 and 9.

In addition there are other coordinate cooperatives: two service enterprises, one of which is operated by women, who provide laundry and catering services to the factories. There are also four agricultural and one fishery cooperatives, with a total of 1,719 members, and a combined consumer cooperative with 26,383 members.

At the center of the Mondragon organization is the technical college with a staff of 40, and the Worker's Bank, with 54 branches. These two organizations are controlled by the movement as a whole.[10]

The process of enterprise capitalization rests upon worker participation. It has been estimated that each new job now costs £7,000

Table 8. Sizes of Mondragon Enterprises, 1972

Relative Sizes	Number of Enterprises
Over 400 members	7
Over 100 members	17
Over 50 members	11
Under 50 members	11

Table 9. Functions of Different Mondragon Enterprises, 1972

Enterprise Function	Number of Enterprises	Number of Members
Foundries	4	927
Machine tools	10	1,699
Components	16	2,676
Household durables	8	4,075
Building	5	915
Various	3	140

to create; the worker himself need only subscribe £500–700, with £1,000–3,000 loaned by the government on long-term agreements, and any remainder (where not provided by an existing enterprise) is found by the Worker's Bank. In practice, because of the excellent worker record, expected value of work from each new applicant is set up as a "trust" amount to be repaid by him as he works, and accordingly his initial input of capital now averages around £600 for all enterprises.[11]

Remuneration to workers depends upon the earnings of the enterprise and is divided among the workers on a point system of job ratings, with a maximum differential of 3 to 1. Payment is made partly in cash monthly, and partly in capital credit at the end of the year. On quitting or dismissal the member is paid back his capital entrance fee, as increased (or decreased) by the progress of business during his period of membership.

Under Spanish cooperative law, half of any operating surplus must be applied to reserves. Of the remainder, it is usual to allocate 30 percent to social purposes and 70 percent to member accounts. The practical effect of this return to members is to increase their capital accounts each year by 25 to 35 percent of annual cash drawings. In order to compensate for inflation, it has recently been found necessary to write up members' capital credit by a certain percentage each year. As yet a rare occurrence however, accounts theoretically, and sometimes actually, are written *down*, if the enterprises lose money.

The enormous success of the Mondragon movement is a credit to the fertile ideas of Father Arizmendi and to the fact that the enterprises have adhered to basic social principles laid down by him. Flexibility in adapting the principles to changing conditions (e.g., to problems of inflation) has also helped. The Mondragon principles are as follows:

The controlling body is the General Assembly of the members. This body meets at appropriate intervals and makes decisions by majority vote.

The General Assembly elects a Control Board, which has full authority over the enterprise. Its president serves for four years, and half its members retire every two years in order to provide for an orderly rotation of members and continuity.

The Control Board appoints a business General Manager, who in turn appoints the managerial personnel.

In the larger enterprises there is also an elected Social Council, which advises the Board and the General Manager. The workers are divided into appropriate groups, each of which elects the members of the Council.

It has been the custom of the General Assembly to elect a Vigilance Committee, but it is now thought that effective auditing will fulfill this function. [12]

It does not take a great stretch of the imagination to visualize American corporations' transformation into such democratic control groups—except for the struggle they would put up at the mere suggestion of its real possibility. Yet, it remains a fact that they are creatures of legislative approval in their charters and may ultimately, because of their excesses, be forced to meet at some level the realistic social cost in the production of goods and services for the benefit of the whole people. The people need to demonstrate their awareness of the possibilities in such a suggestion; interesting results could flow from that very fact.

The Mondragon proposition is not altogether a foreign notion on our shores. I am told by Professor Lawrence (Larry) Busch that to his knowledge there are at least four or five worker-owned organizations in the country: one in insurance (the largest, employing some 400 workers), a garbage collection organization in San Francisco, an auto mirror firm in Tennessee, a shoe manufacturing concern, and a plywood manufacturing concern in the West. This viable alternative to the system is a reality, not a mere utopian formulation of a possible alternative, not large, but in being. [13]

In this brief survey of what is being done to build organizations to capitalize those who, to date, have been missed in the process, let us assess an organization that exists in Atlanta's rural Appalachian backyard, Gold Kist, Inc., a truly remarkable organization.

Having searched the telephone directory and the library in Atlanta for possible leads to cooperative endeavor there, I found nothing because I did not recognize Gold Kist as a cooperative. Following a hunch, I called upon William N. Cox III, vice-president and associate director of research in the Federal Reserve Bank of Atlanta—the right man. He not only told me immediately about Gold Kist but called one of the officials there and arranged for my visit the following day. He described the organization in respectful terms, with high praise for its organizer, D. W. Brooks.

The next day I visited a number of officials of Gold Kist, who reviewed with me their organizational chart and methods of operations, cordially answering any questions I could raise. One of my first was, "Are you operating according to Rochdale principles?" Indeed they are, I was assured, and my informant illustrated the point: he explained that as a rural, producers' co-op, they had moved during their 44-year history from merely being a cotton farmers' organization to one of many interests. As cotton phased out of the Deep South because of the boll weevil, the cooperative moved into many other farmer-related activities, one of them being that of encouraging the raising of soybeans, a profitable crop.

Unlike soybean raisers in the exploitative market, the cooperative farmers sell their soybeans to Gold Kist, who pays them the going market price. Gold Kist then processes the beans producing soybean oil, livestock feed from residuals, as well as fertilizer by-products. Profits from this fertilizer operation, less actual operating costs, are shared, according to the original purchases of beans among the member soybean farmers. In the general market, one may add, this latter windfall of capital would not have come to them. They would have sold their soybeans in the market, period!

The divisions of the cooperative partially indicate its outreach. They are in order: Crops, Feed and Farm Supply, Farm Service, Commodity Trading, International Marketing, Oil Products, Peanuts, Soy and Grain Procurement, Poultry and Eggs, Poultry Marketing, Feed Manufacturing Services, Pork Department, Feed Mills; Financial Division: Accounting, Credit, Corporate Audit, Corporate Insurance, Investment Certificates; Corporate Tax Division; Engineering Division; and Human Resources: Benefits, Employment, Personnel, and General Office Services.

One can see at a glance that Gold Kist Cooperative is no fly-by-night operation. Indeed it is not, but let us let their *Annual Report* of 1977 clinch that assertion. Its first page begins with the simple statement headed "Progress Through People":

All members and employees have contributed to the progress reported in the 1976–77 annual report of Gold Kist.

Members through their patronage, have pushed volume to exceed one billion dollars for the first time in the association's 44-year history. Employees, by fully utilizing their talents, have effected savings in operations and introduced ideas that will aid in the growth of Gold Kist in the future. [Estimated, late in report, at $2 billion within five more years]. [14]

Certainly PEOPLE—officers, directors, employees, members, and customers—can move forward together by continuing to cooperate in the future as they have in the past. [15]

The credit line in the statement above is, of course, its punch line, beginning with "PEOPLE." If you will read over other corporate reports of 1977 and look hard for any reference to ordinary people, you will not find them; customers maybe, but not people.

D. W. Brooks, chairman of the board, reporting by letter to the organization, happily reported more exactly the 1976–77 dollar volume as $1,083,678,000, the volume having more than doubled since 1971–72. Brooks did not add an important point about his organization. It sits as an item of financial news about midway in the annual listing of Fortune's 500 list of top-volume industrial organizations in the nation. [16] As a capital-generating organization with regard for the welfare of people, it is not only competitive with the very large exploitive corporations, it has overtaken and passed more than half of the largest! It speaks well for the future of such people's organizations. All that is needed now is for the people to become aware of their opportunities *for themselves and for others* in this regard, and organize, organize.

Certainly Gold Kist did not start forty-four years ago with any pretensions. It started (during the heady period of the early New Deal and TVA when planning with people was a leading concept) with the help and advice of a few committed people and with the Department of Agriculture, which was then concerned; it was greatly helped along the way by the creative imagination of D. W. Brooks, who would be, I am told, quick to protest that any other dedicated co-oper would have done as much. That may be hard to believe. At any rate, all of the co-ops have started with a handful of people, from the English and Danish originators to the most recent.

I shall not, but could, go into descriptions of Latin American, Chinese, African, Israeli, English, and many other national cooperative movements. I have drawn a suggested pattern and perhaps have made the point: there are effective ways besides those of monopoly capital to raise and distribute capital. The alternative ways are demonstrably more democratic and provide means by which the strictures of capital patronage may be largely eliminated. Capital accrued and disbursed under cooperative effort remains with those involved in the process, and all dispersals, it must be emphasized, must be approved by those persons.

It remains for the people of Atlanta to decide when these effective processes of capitalization operating outside its urban borders may be brought inside the city to serve them.

Notes

Introduction

1. In working through the methods of study that I would employ in both Study I and Study II, I must say that I was helpfully guided by the ideas of Robert K. Merton (social structures, functions, latent functions), Ralph Linton (status, roles, role sets), and, among others, Talcott Parsons and Edward A. Shils, Stuart Chapin, Sr., and A. B. Hollingshead (institutional stratification).

I must also say that, contrary to the assertions of some critics, my work is not dependent on that of the Lynds or C. Wright Mills, with whom I sometimes have been equated. To be sure, the Lynds' work (*Middletown*) was empirical (field-oriented), and I share the general admiration for their pioneering effort, but I approached my problems quite differently. The Lynds took an anthropological approach by sampling the whole community of Muncie along institutional lines (how men work, govern themselves, live in families, etc.). My own methods were related to sampling, but sampling of persons of special knowledge—knowledge of those familiar with power figures and power relations—identified leaders (identified by their peers) within central, institutional organizations (men active as exponents of institutional values).

C. Wright Mills, the other contemporary with whom I have been equated, is quite distinct from me in his approach to data. He indicated to me at a meeting we had both addressed in New Orleans that he was never empirical if he could help it. My reply was, "And I am never theoretical and polemical if I can help it." Our differences were remarkable in that he generally was a consumer of empirically derived data, I a producer of it. However, our respect for each other remained firm. As for the use of our works, Mills used all of my published data, while I used his very sparingly. He was a great political philosopher and partisan polemicist with whom I liked to be identified in friendship, but not scientifically.

Chapter 2

1. Figures are for metropolitan Atlanta rather than for the legal boundaries of incorporated Atlanta and are drawn from Atlanta Chamber of Commerce, "Economic Indicators." All figures rounded.

2. Study I: Floyd Hunter, *Community Power Structure*, p. 6, states: "In a given power unit a smaller number of individuals will be found formulating and extending policy than those exercising power."

3. From this point forward each hypothesis, printed in italics, corresponds to one listed in the Introduction.

4. Paraphrase of an interview in 1973 with Judge Elbert Tuttle, United States Court of Appeals, Fifth Judicial District.

5. See Study I, p. 16.

6. G. William Domhoff, *Who Really Rules? New Haven and Community Power Re-examined*, p. 36.

7. Study I, pp. 22–23.

8. Bob Greene, San Francisco *Examiner and Chronicle*, 8 July 1979, ed. section, p. 2.
9. Marshall McLuhan, *Understanding Media*.

Chapter 3

1. Franklin M. Garrett, *Atlanta and Environs*, 3 vols. Biographical materials in Garrett's concerned these families: ADAIR, ALEXANDER, ALLEN, DOBBS, GRANT, HAVERTY, HEALEY, INMAN, MADDOX, HURT, RICH, ROBINSON, SIBLEY, SPALDING, and WOODRUFF.
2. Other works on Atlanta include especially the fine special edition, to be noted as sp. ed., of a decade of Atlanta history published by the Atlanta *Journal and Constitution*, "Amazing Atlanta, 1960 to 1970," 18 January 1970. Special tribute to at least these writers in that edition is here given: Steve Ball, Jr., Paul Beeman, Lorraine M. Bennett, Furman Bisher, Christena Bledsoe, Mike Bowler, Junie Brown, Wilt Browning, Clyde Burnett, Scott Cain, Frances Cawthon, Alex Coffin, Bill Collins, John A. Crown, Lou Erickson, Phil Gailey, Philip Garner, Hal Gulliver, Laurence Kay, Harold Kennedy, Wayne Minshew, Bill Montgomery, Harry Murphy, Reg Murphy, Hugh Nations, John Pennington, Harmon Perry, Charles Morris Shelton, Tom Sherwood, Celestine Sibley, Darrell Simons, George V. Smith, Jack Spalding, Billie Cheney Speed, Diane Stepp, Ron Taylor, Leonard Ray Teel, Gene Tharpe, Tom Walker, William B. Williams, Larry Woods, and Michael V. Wright. Other helpful works include: Ivan Allen, Sr., *Atlanta from the Ashes*; Joel Chandler Harris, *Life of Henry Grady*; B. H. L. Hart, ed., *Memoirs of General William Tecumseh Sherman*; and *City of Atlanta* (Tech High School Press). Because the bulk of this chapter relies on these works and will be extracted from them, I shall not crisscross the writing with footnotes for short references. References of substantive duration or importance for the reader will be given individual notation.
3. Because I am not a historian, undoubtedly I have omitted important names and I must apologize for this. However, I believe that the number of names coming through the pages of history make their point. The current power structure of Atlanta includes historical names. I did ask Garrett about the names used, but omissions, if any, must remain my fault. I have used historical sources to find names of present leaders related to those of the past and to make creditable connections between them, not to rewrite history.
4. Alex Haley, *Roots*.
5. Diane Stepp, Atlanta *Journal and Constitution*, sp. ed., p. 2J.
6. Garrett, *Atlanta and Environs*, 1:225.
7. Ibid., 1:343.
8. *Memoirs of Sherman*, p. 111.
9. Rich's, Inc., "Facts About Rich's," pp. 4, 5.
10. Dwight B. Billings, Jr., *Planters and the Making of a "New South."*

Chapter 4

1. Data from letter of Franklin M. Garrett to author, 15 October 1973, confirming my own findings.
2. Ivan Allen, Jr., *Mayor*, summary on pp. 154–56, 156–57.
3. Study I, pp. 77–83.
4. For a time during World War II, the USO Regional Offices, one of which was mine, were located in the old Ivan Allen-Marshall Building.
5. Raines Howell, Atlanta *Journal and Constitution*, sp. ed., p. 12A. For analysis in more depth, see chapter 6.

Chapter 5

1. Alex Poinsett, "From Plasterer to Plutocrat," pp. 84–96.
2. Ibid.
3. E. Franklin Frazier, *Black Bourgeoisie*.
4. Raleigh Bryans, "Jesse Hill . . . ," Atlanta *Journal and Constitution*, 13 May 1973.

5. Howell Raines, Atlanta *Journal and Constitution*, sp. ed., p. 12A.

6. Bryans, "Jesse Hill . . . ," Atlanta *Journal and Constitution*, 13 May 1973.

7. Ibid.

8. Ibid.

9. Calvin Trillin, "Atlanta 'Settlement,'" *New Yorker*, 17 March 1973, p. 102. It has been said that one of the power brokers in this agreement was a former Atlantan, a white lawyer, attorney general in President Carter's first cabinet: Griffin B. Bell. As the cliché goes: It is indeed a small world!

10. B. Drummond Ayres, Jr., *New York Times*, 26 April 1973, pp. 1, 20.

11. *New York Times*, 25 April 1973.

12. Bryans, "Jesse Hill . . . ," Atlanta *Journal and Constitution*, 13 May 1973.

13. Figures are taken from Moody's Investor's Service, *Moody's Manuals*, those entitled *Bank and Finance, Industrial,* and *Public Utilities,* which will be abbreviated to the letters *B, I,* and *P.U.* in the page citations to follow: Genuine Parts, *I* (1950), p. 559, *I* (1976), p. 1693; Coastal States Life Insurance Company, *B* (1950), p. 1068, *B* (1978), 2:2070; Life Insurance Company of Georgia, *B* (1950), p. 1423, *B* (1976), p. 2148; Trust Company of Georgia, *I* (1950), p. 1714, *I* (1976), p. 398; Georgia Power Company, *P.U.* (1950), p. 1458, *P.U.* (1977), p. 1769; Atlanta Gas Light Company, *P.U.* (1949), p. 210, *P.U.* (1978), p. 262; Citizens and Southern Bank, *B* (1950), p. 954, *B* (1976), p. 97; Coca-Cola, *I* (1950), p. 1714, *I* (1976), p. 97; Fulton National Bank, *B* (1950), p. 286, *B* (1977), p. 710. All figures are rounded to the nearest million.

Chapter 6

1. Ivan Allen, Jr., *Mayor*, pp. 20ff.

2. Ibid., p. 25. Order of sentences reversed for clarity in our text.

3. Ibid., p. 29.

4. Ibid.

5. Ibid., pp. 29–30.

6. Ibid.

7. Ibid., p. 29.

8. Ibid., p. 30.

9. Ibid., p. 23.

10. Ibid., pp. 30–31.

11. Ibid., p. 31.

12. Alex Poinsett, "From Plasterer to Plutocrat," pp. 84–96.

13. Gene D. Sullivan, "Southern Agriculture," p. 150. See also Federal Reserve Bank of Atlanta, *Monthly Review*, September 1972, appendix on 6th District agriculture, p. 154.

14. Floyd Hunter, Ruth C. Schaffer, and Cecil G. Sheps, *Community Organization*; and Floyd Hunter, "Host Community-Air Force Base Relationships." See also Domhoff's studies.

Chapter 7

1. William Miller, "A Comparison between the Atlanta Plan of Development, 1952, and the Program for Progress, 1972" (mimeographed), in possession of the author.

2. Ibid.

3. Ibid.

4. Central Atlanta Progress 3, p. 7.

5. John McPhee, "Travels in Georgia," *New Yorker*, 28 April 1973, pp. 44–103.

6. Floyd Hunter, *Top Leadership, U.S.A.,* and *The Big Rich and the Little Rich*.

7. Representative Fordney Stark, Democrat from California, was quoted as saying, "The President is supposed to be the leader of our nation, but the Democrats can no longer follow a president who uses poor people to balance the budget, falls short of promises of national health insurance, and fails to convince the nation of the need for

an accelerated, comprehensive energy program." San Francisco *Examiner and Chronicle*, 1 July 1979, World sec., p. 2.

8. Edward Walsh and Martin Schram, San Francisco *Chronicle*, 10 July 1979, pp. 1 and 7.

9. Ibid, p. 7.

10. Ibid.

11. David Broder, "Carter Finds the Moral Tone His Campaign Was Based On," San Francisco *Chronicle*, 16 July 1979, p. 7.

12. San Francisco *Chronicle*, 16 July 1979, pp. 1 ff.

Chapter 8

1. Personal interview, 1970.

2. Thomas Walker, Atlanta *Journal and Constitution*, 19 January 1970, p. 5A.

3. Ibid., p. 51.

4. Personal interview, 1973.

Chapter 9

1. Allen, *Mayor*, pp. 94–95.

2. Clarence N. Stone, *Economic Growth and Neighborhood Discontent*.

3. Ibid., p. 18.

4. Ibid., p. 97.

5. Ibid.

6. Ibid., pp. 191, 192.

Chapter 11

1. Carroll Arnold, "Appalachian Cooperatives," p. 27.

2. This discussion will be based on three works that I will paraphrase in my own terms, i.e., from my point of view as a cooperative participant: (1) Robert Neptune, *California's Uncommon Markets*, (2) *Co-op News. Annual Report*, and (3) California Consumer Cooperatives, "All About Co-ops."

3. "All About Co-ops."

4. Neptune, *California's Uncommon Markets*, p. 131.

5. Ibid., p. 71.

6. Ibid., p. 129.

7. Alastair Campbell and Blair Foster, *The Mondragon Movement*. The description of the Mondragon experience given here is based on this work.

8. Ibid., pp. 3 and 9.

9. Ibid., p. 3.

10. Ibid., p. 4.

11. Ibid., pp. 6 and 10.

12. Ibid., p. 10.

13. Personal interview with Busch, University of Kentucky, Lexington, Kentucky, 1977.

14. Gold Kist *Annual Report*, 1977, Introduction.

15. Ibid., p. 1.

16. *Fortune*, May 1977, list of 500 largest national corporations, 1977.

Bibliography

Articles and Books on Atlanta

"Abernathy Steps Down." *Time*, 23 July 1973, p. 31.

"Alderman Talks About Money, Not People, Says Urban League." Atlanta *Inquirer*, 17 October 1970.

Alexander, T. M., Jr. "Atlanta's Black Leadership?" (letter to editor). Atlanta *Constitution*, 17 May 1973.

Allen, Ivan, Jr., with Hemphill, Paul. *Mayor: Notes on the Sixties*. New York: Simon and Schuster, 1971.

Allen, Ivan, Sr. *Atlanta from the Ashes*. Atlanta: Ruralist Press, 1928.

"Amazing Atlanta." Atlanta *Journal and Constitution*, sp. ed., 18 January 1970.

Ashworth, George N. "U.S. Moves to Prop Up Lockheed." *Christian Science Monitor*, 5 January 1971.

"Atlanta." *Forum*, April 1969, p. 2.

Atlanta Chamber of Commerce. "Atlanta Construction." Atlanta: Chamber Research Department monograph, Winter 1966.

———. "Economic Indicators." Atlanta: Chamber Research Department monograph, December 1969.

———. "Growth Statistic." Atlanta: Chamber Research Department monograph, July 1970.

———. "Office Space." Atlanta: Chamber Research Department monograph, n.d. [ca. 1970].

"Atlanta Cops Acquitted in (Black) Boy's Death." San Francisco *Chronicle*, 17 October 1970.

Atlanta Regional Commission. "Population and Housing" (monograph). Atlanta, 1972.

Ayres, B. Drummond. "Atlanta Strikes an Integration Bargain." *New York Times*, 25 April 1973, p. 1.

Bell, Chuck. "Mrs. King Looks at Progress." Atlanta *Constitution*, 18 May 1973.

Bell and Stanton, Inc. (public relations). *Atlanta Fact Sheet*. Atlanta, 1970.

Bellury, Philip. "Congress Center: $300 Million Plus." *Real Estate Atlanta*, April 1973.

"The Black Middle Class." Atlanta *Journal and Constitution*, 20 March 1973 (reprint of *Wall Street Journal* editorial).

Bryans, Raleigh. "Atlanta Accepts Challenge and Moves Ahead." Atlanta *Journal and Constitution*, sp. ed., 18 January 1970.

———. "Jesse Hill Gets Leery of 'Token Black' Role." Atlanta *Journal and Constitution*, 13 May 1973, p. 14A.

Calhoun, John H. "Forerunners for Present Black Leaders Were Numerous" (Part II of series, "Black Atlanta Reconstruction through the 60's"). Atlanta *Inquirer*, 17 October 1970.

Central Atlanta Progress 3: A Report, Annual Meeting. Atlanta, 27 January 1971.

Central Atlanta Progress 4: A Report. Atlanta, 1973.

"The Central City Crusade of John Portman." *Southern Living* 4, no. 7 (July 1969): 30.

Citizens and Southern National Bank and Subsidiaries. "Report to Stockholders." Atlanta, 31 December 1969.

City of Atlanta. Atlanta: Tech High School Press, 1921. Esp. chap. 2, "History of Atlanta," pp. 9ff.

Coca-Cola. "Portrait of a Business: The Coca-Cola Company." Atlanta, n.d. [circa 1970].

Coffin, Alex. "The System May Be Weak But the Mayors Are Not." *Atlanta Magazine*, July 1970.

Cousins Properties, Incorporated and Subsidiaries. "Annual Report." Atlanta, 1972.

Crawford, Fred R.; Norman, Roy; and Dabbs, Leah. "A Report of Certain Reactions by Atlanta Public to the Death of Dr. Martin Luther King, Jr." (monograph). Atlanta: Center for the Study of Social Change, Emory University, April 1969.

Crawford, Fred R., et al. "A Comprehensive and Systematic Evaluation of the Community Action Program and Related Programs Operating in 1969, Atlanta, Georgia" (monograph). Atlanta: Emory University, June 1969.

Ellis, William S. "Atlanta, Pacesetter City of the South." *National Geographic*, February 1969.

Erickson, Lou. "Portman's Impatience Made Things Happen." Atlanta *Journal and Constitution*, 18 January 1970, sp. ed., p. 8M.

Ezell, Hank. "Maynard's the Man to Beat" (a news analysis). Atlanta *Constitution*, 13 May 1973.

First National Holding Corporation. "Atlanta: Annual Report." Atlanta, 1969.

Freegood, Seymour. "Life in Buckhead." *Fortune*, September 1961, pp. 109–14.

"From the Ground Up." *Atlanta Magazine* 10, no. 3 (July 1970): 47ff.

Galphin, Bruce. "Cousins by the Dozens." *Atlanta Magazine* 10, no. 6 (October 1970).

Garrett, Franklin. *Atlanta and Environs*. 3 vols. New York: Lewis Historical Publishing, 1954. Reprinted: Athens: University of Georgia Press, 1969.

Georgia Power Company. *Annual Report*. Atlanta, 1969.

"Georgia State University Today: A Few Significant Facts, 1973." Atlanta: Georgia State University, 1973.

Goldberger, Paul. "Portman's Formula: Big Spaces, Flamboyant Forms—Buck Rogers in Times Square." *New York Times Magazine*, 26 August 1973, p. 8.

Grady, Henry. *The New South*. New York: R. Bonner & Sons, 1890.

Great Speckled Bird (Atlanta Cooperative News Project) 3, no. 43 (26 October 1970).

Greene, Bob. *San Francisco Examiner and Chronicle*, ed. sec., 8 July 1979, p. 2.

Harris, Joel Chandler, comp. *Life of Henry W. Grady*, New York: Cassell Publishing, 1890.

Hill, Jesse, Jr. "Samuel Williams" (eulogy). Atlanta *Inquirer*, 17 October 1970.

Hutcheson, John D.; and Steggert, Frank X. "Organized Citizen Participation" (monograph). Atlanta: Georgia State University, Atlanta Urban Observatory, Urban Life Center, n.d. [circa 1970].

"Illustrators View 1890 Cotton States Exposition, Piedmont Park." Atlanta *Journal and Constitution*, 20 May 1973.

"Integrating Atlanta's Power Elite." *Business Week*, 24 November 1973.

Jennings, M. Kent. *Community Influentials: The Elites of Atlanta*. Glencoe, Ill.: Free Press, 1964.

Kent, Francis B. "Atlanta Mayor, Eaves Pitted Against Businessmen, Police in Racial Squabble." Los Angeles *Times* dateline carried in Boston *Globe*, October 1974, p. 13.

King, Coretta, editorial on. Atlanta *Constitution*, 19 May 1973.

Lesher, Stephan. "Leroy Johnson Outslicks Mister Charlie." *New York Times Magazine*, 8 November 1970.

Lindsay, Leon W. "Georgia Black Candidate Gains." *Christian Science Monitor*, 4 August 1970.

Linthicum, Tom. "Jackson Would Help Inman . . . If." Atlanta *Constitution*, 5 May 1973.

"List of Victims in Paris Airline Disaster." Atlanta *Constitution*, 4 June 1962, p. 2.

McPhee, John. "Travels in Georgia." *New Yorker*, 28 April 1973, pp. 44–103.

MARTA. "MARTA Board of Directors." Atlanta: MARTA, May 1973.

———. "MARTA Chronology." Atlanta: MARTA, 1973.

———. "MARTA: Voting Record on Rapid Transit Legislation." Atlanta: MARTA, 1973.

Massell, Sam. "MARTA" (Metropolitan Atlanta Rapid Transit Authority), an address to the International Mass Transit Seminar, Los Angeles, Cal., 20 March 1973.

———. "Sam Massell" (biographical data, photocopy). October 1969.

———. "State of the City Address." 2 January 1973.

Merrimer, Jim. "Running the City." Atlanta *Constitution*, 19 September 1974.

Miller, William. "A Comparison Between the Atlanta Plan of Improvement, 1952, and the Program for Progress, 1972" (unpublished paper). Atlanta: Georgia State University, 1973.

———. "Private Power Structure Tally" (unpublished paper). Atlanta: Georgia State University, 1970.

"1952 Annexation Doubled Size of Atlanta." Atlanta *Journal and Constitution*, 18 January 1970.

"Norman Wins Suit Against Officer." Atlanta *Daily World*, 18 May 1973.

Poinsett, Alex. "From Plasterer to Plutocrat: Multi-Millionaire Herman J. Russell Shows 'How the System Can Be Had.'" *Ebony*, May 1973, pp. 84–96.

Raines, Howell. "Johnson Takes After Hill." Atlanta *Constitution*, 17 May 1973.

—————. "Mayor Race Can Cost $400,000." Atlanta *Constitution*, 16 May 1973.

Real Estate Atlanta. "Atlanta in 1976: Downtown, Uptown Clout." *Real Estate Atlanta* 2, no. 4 (April 1973).

Rich, Richard H. "Biographical Data" (mimeograph). 1973.

Rich's, Inc., *Annual Report*. Atlanta, 31 January 1970.

—————. *Annual Report*. Atlanta, 1972.

—————. "Brief History of (Rich's) Store" (photocopy). August 1969.

—————. "Facts About Rich's" (photocopy). August 1969.

"Rich's." *Newsweek*, 6 February 1967.

Schemmel, Bill. "Atlanta's 'Power Structure' Faces Life." *New South* 27, no. 2 (Spring 1972): 62–68.

Shaffer, Albert, and Shaffer, Ruth Connor. *Woodruff: A Study of Community Decision Making*. Chapel Hill: University of North Carolina Press, 1970.

Smith, Edward D. "Biographical Data" (Xerox). October 1970.

Steppe, Diane. Atlanta *Journal and Constitution*, sp. ed., 18 January 1970, p. 2J.

Stone, Clarence N. *Economic Growth and Neighborhood Discontent: System Bias in the Urban Renewal Program of Atlanta*. Chapel Hill: University of North Carolina Press, 1976.

Sullivan, Gene D. "Southeastern Agriculture: A New Dress and a New Girl Too." *Monthly Review* (Federal Reserve Bank of Atlanta), September 1972, p. 150.

Sumner, Gary. "Abernathy Arrested in Protest at Home." Atlanta *Journal and Constitution*, 13 May 1973.

Townsend, James L., Associates. *Atlanta Resurgence: The First Hundred Years of a City's Progress, Promise, and Philosophy*. Atlanta: First National Bank Publication, 1971.

Trillin, Calvin. "Atlanta 'Settlement'" ("U.S. Journal" section). *New Yorker*, 17 March 1973, p. 102.

Trust Company of Georgia. "Seventy-ninth Annual Report." Atlanta, 1969.

—————. "Statement of Condition." Atlanta, 31 December 1969.

"Unfortunate Verdict." Atlanta *Daily World*, 18 October 1970 (editorial about shooting of 15-year-old boy by police).

Walker, Tom. Atlanta *Journal and Constitution*, 19 January 1970.

Watters, Pat. "Atlanta and the Urban South" (excerpted from *The South and the Nation*). *Atlanta Magazine* (December 1969).

General Sources

Abu-Laban, Baha. "Social Origins and Occupational Career Patterns of Community Leaders." *Sociological Inquiry* 33 (Spring 1963): 131–40.

Aggar, Robert E.; Goldrich, Daniel; and Swanson, Bert E. *The Rulers and the Ruled: Political Power and Impotence in American Communities*. New York: Wiley and Sons, 1964.

Aiken, Michael, and Mott, Paul E., eds. *The Structure of Community Power.* New York: Random, 1970.

Anton, Thomas. "Power Pluralism and Local Politics." *Administrative Science Quarterly* 7 (March 1963): 425–57.

──────. "Rejoinder to 'Critique on Power, Pluralism, and Local Politics.'" *Administrative Science Quarterly* 8 (September 1963): 257–68.

Arnold, Carroll. "Appalachian Cooperatives: Economics of the Third Kind." *Appalachia* (Appalachian Regional Commission) 11, no. 3 (January 1978): 27.

Bachrach, Peter, and Baratz, Morton S. *Power and Poverty: Theory and Practice.* New York: Oxford University Press, 1970.

Barnet, Richard J., and Müller, Ronald E. *Global Reach: The Power of the Multinational Corporations.* New York: Simon and Schuster, 1974.

Barth, Ernest A. T., and Abu-Laban, Baha. "Power Structure and the Negro Sub-Community." *American Sociological Review* 24 (February 1959): 69–76.

Berger, Peter, and Luckman, Thomas. *The Social Construction of Reality.* New York: Anchor Books, 1967.

Billings, Dwight B., Jr. *Planters and the Making of a "New South": Class, Politics, and Development in North Carolina, 1865–1900.* Chapel Hill: University of North Carolina Press, 1979.

Black Enterprise Magazine 3, no. 10 (May 1973).

Blankenship, L. Vaughn. "Community Power and Decision Making: a Comparative Evaluation of Measurement Techniques." *Social Forces* 43 (December 1964): 207–16.

Bloomberg, Warner, Jr.; Sunshine, Morris H.; and Fararo, Thomas J. *Suburban Power Structures in Public Education: A Study of Values, Influences, and Tax Effort.* Syracuse, N.Y.: Syracuse University Press, 1963.

Bonjean, Charles M.; Browning, Harley L.; and Carter, Lewis F. "Toward Comparative Community Research: A Factor Analysis of United States Counties." *Sociological Quarterly* 10 (Spring 1969): 157–76.

Bonser, H. J.; Milk, R. G.; and Alfred, C. E. *Local Leadership in Rural Communities of Kimberlin County, Tennessee.* Tennessee Agricultural Experimental Station, Agricultural Economy and Rural Sociology Department Monograph 144. December 1942.

Booth, David A., and Adrian, Charles R. "Elections and Community Power." *Journal of Politics* 25 (February 1963): 107–18.

──────. "Simplifying the Discovery of Elites." *American Behavioral Scientist,* October 1961, pp. 4–16.

Bouma, Donald H. "The Issue-Analysis Approach to Community Power: A Case Study of Realtors in Kalamazoo." *American Journal of Economics and Sociology* 29 (July 1970): 241–52.

Branscome, James. "The Federal Government in Appalachia." New York: Fiels Foundation Monograph, 1977.

Burgess, M. Elaine. *Negro Leadership in a Southern City.* Chapel Hill: University of North Carolina Press, 1962.

Burtenshaw, Claude J. "The Political Theory of Pluralist Democracy." *Western Political Quarterly* 21 (December 1968): 577–87.

California Consumer Cooperatives. "All About Co-ops: A Directory of Co-op Services." Berkeley, Cal., 1976.

Campbell, Alastair, and Foster, Blair. *The Mondragon Movement: Worker Ownership in Modern Industry.* London: Industrial Common Ownership Movement, November 1974.

Clark, Carroll D. "The Concept of the Public." *Southwestern Science Quarterly* 13 (March 1933): 315.

Clark, Terry N., ed. *Community Structure and Decision Making: Comparative Analyses.* San Francisco: Chandler Publishing, 1968.

――――. *Comparative Research on Decision Making,* special issue of *The New Atlantis* 1, no. 2 (Winter 1970).

Co-Op News: Annual Report. Berkeley, Cal., 29 December 1976.

Cottrell, A. H . "Lectures to National Academy of Engineering in Washington, D.C." Summarized in *New Scientist* 38 (1968): 296.

Crain, Robert L., and Rosenthal, Donald B. "Community Status as a Dimension of Local Decision Making." *American Sociological Review* 32 (December 1967): 970–84.

Dakin, Ralph. "Variations in Power Structures and Organizing Efficiency: A Comparative Study of Four Areas." *Sociological Quarterly* 3 (July 1962): 228–50.

Daland, Robert T. *Dixie City: A Portrait of Political Leadership.* University of Alabama Bureau of Public Administration, 1956.

D'Antonio, William V.; Form, William H.; Loomis, Charles P.; and Erickson, Eugene C. "Institutional and Occupational Representatives in Eleven Community Influence Systems." *American Sociological Review* 26 (June 1961): 440–46.

Dash, Leon. "The Small Impact of Black Gains." San Francisco *Examiner and Chronicle,* 4 January 1976.

Dick, Harry. "A Method for Ranking Community Influentials." *American Sociological Review* 25 (June 1960): 395–99.

"Directory of the Largest Non-Industrial Companies." *Fortune,* July 1973.

Domhoff, G. William. *The Higher Circles.* New York: Random House, 1970.

――――. "Where a Pluralist Goes Wrong." Review of *The Power Structure,* by Arnold M. Rose. *Berkeley Journal of Sociology* 14 (1969): 35–57.

――――. *Who Really Rules?: New Haven and Community Power Reexamined.* Santa Monica, Cal.: Goodyear Publishing, 1978.

――――. *Who Rules America?* Englewood Cliffs, N.J.: Prentice-Hall, 1967.

Dreyfuss, Joel. "The Black in the White House." San Francisco *Examiner and Chronicle,* 4 November 1973.

Drummond, Roscoe. "New Industrialized South." *Christian Science Monitor,* 30 January 1970.

Dubin, Robert. "Decision-Making by Management in Industrial Relations." *American Journal of Sociology* 54 (January 1949): 294.

Dye, Thomas R. *Who's Running America?* Englewood Cliffs, N.J.: Prentice-Hall, 1976.

Edwards, Harold T. "Power Structure and Its Communication Behavior in San Jose, Costa Rica." *Journal of Inter-American Studies* 10 (April 1967): 236–47.

Ehrlich, Howard J. "The Reputational Approach to the Study of Community Power." *American Sociological Review* 26 (December 1961): 926–27.

"Executive Suites—A White Domain" (UPI dateline Nashville, Tenn.). San Francisco *Chronicle*, 1 October 1970.

Fisher, Sethard. "Community Power Studies: A Critique." *Social Research* 29 (Winter 1962): 449–66.

Fisher, Titus D. "Minorities Make Economic Gains." San Francisco *Examiner*, 20 December 1970.

Form, William H., and Miller, Delbert C. *Industry, Labor, and Community.* New York: Harper, 1960.

Forward, Roy. "Issue Analysis in Community Power Studies." *Australian Journal of Politics and History* 15 (December 1969): 26–44.

Foskett, John M., and Hohle, Raymond. "Measurement of Influence in Community Affairs." Proceedings of Pacific Sociological Society, published in *Research Studies of the State College of Washington* 25 (June 1957): 148–54.

Fowler, Irving A. "Local Industrial Structure, Economic Power and Community Welfare." *Social Problems* 6 (Summer 1958): 41–51.

Frazier, E. Franklin. *Black Bourgeoisie.* Glencoe, Ill.: Free Press, 1957.

Freeman, Charles, and Mayo, Selz C. "Decision Makers in Community Action." *Social Forces* 35 (May 1957): 319–22.

Freeman, Linton C. *Patterns of Local Community Leadership.* Indianapolis: Bobbs-Merrill, 1968.

Freeman, Linton C.; Bloomberg, Warner, Jr.; Koff, Stephen P.; Sunshine, Morris H.; and Fararo, Thomas J. *Local Community Leadership.* Syracuse, N.Y.: Syracuse University College Paper No. 15, 1960.

French, Robert Mills. "Change Comes to Cornucopia—Industry and the Community." In Robert Mills French, ed., *The Community: A Comparative Perspective.* Itasca, Ill.: F. E. Peacock Publishers, 1969.

Gamson, William A. "Reputation and Resources in Community Politics." *American Journal of Sociology* 72 (September 1966): 121–31.

Gans, Herbert J. *The Levittowners: Ways of Life and Politics in a New Suburban Community.* New York: Pantheon Books, 1967.

Goldman, John J. "Highest Building in the World." San Francisco *Chronicle Sunday Punch*, 24 January 1971.

Guida, Bartholomew F. "State of City Message." *Magazine on New Haven*, 2 February 1970.

Haer, John L. "Social Stratification in Attitudes Towards Sources of Power in a Community." *Social Forces* 35 (December 1956): 137–42.

Haley, Alex. *Roots: The Saga of an American Family.* New York: Doubleday, 1976.

Halverson, Guy. "Few New Blacks Expected to Land Seats in Congress." *Christian Science Monitor*, 31 October 1970.

Hanson, Robert C., and Associates. "Predicting Community Decision: A Test of the Miller-Form Theory." *American Sociological Review* 24 (October 1959): 662–71.

Hart, B. H. L., ed. *Memoirs of General William Tecumseh Sherman.* Civil War Centennial Services. Bloomington, Ind.: Indiana University Press, 1957.

Hawley, Amos H. "Community Power and Urban Renewal Success." *American Journal of Sociology* 68 (June 1963): 422–31.

Hawley, Willis, and Svara, James. *The Study of Community Power: A Bibliographical Review.* Santa Barbara, Cal.: ABC-Clio Press, 1973.

Hawley, Willis, and Wirt, Frederick, eds. *The Search for Community Power.* Englewood Cliffs, N.J.: Prentice-Hall, 1968.

Hays, Edward. *Power Structure and Urban Policy: Who Rules Oakland?* New York: McGraw-Hill, 1971.

Helmreich, William. "Black Militant Organizations and Agents of Social Control. A Case Study," paper presented to the American Sociological Society, New Orleans, 5–8 April 1972.

Herson, Lawrence J. "In the Footsteps of Community Power." *American Political Science Review* 55 (December 1961): 817–30.

Hicks, Frederic. "Politics, Power, and the Role of the Village Priest in Paraguay." *Journal of Inter-American Studies* 9 (April 1967): 273–82.

Hunter, Floyd. *The Big Rich and the Little Rich.* New York: Doubleday, 1965.

———. *Community Power Structure: A Study of Decision Makers.* Chapel Hill: University of North Carolina Press, 1953.

———. "Host Community—Air Force Base Relationships" (monograph). University of North Carolina for U.S. Air Force, Savannah, 1953.

———. "How Blacks Took Over." *Newsday,* 28 October 1973.

———. Review of Robert Dahl's book *Who Governs? Democracy and Power in an American City. Administrative Science Quarterly* 6 (March 1962): 517–19.

———. *Top Leadership, U.S.A.* Chapel Hill: University of North Carolina Press, 1959.

Hunter, Floyd; Schaffer, Ruth C.; and Sheps, Cecil G. *Community Organization: Action and Inaction.* Chapel Hill: University of North Carolina Press, 1956. Reprint: Greenwood Press, 1978.

Janowitz, Morris, ed. *Community Political Systems.* Glencoe, Ill.: Free Press, 1959, pp. 117–45.

Kadushin, Charles. "Power Influence and Social Circles: A New Methodology for Studying Opinion Makers." *American Sociological Review* 33 (October 1968): 685–99.

Kaufman, Herbert, and Jones, Victor. "The Mystery of Power." *Public Administrative Review* 14 (Summer 1954): 205–12.

Key, V. O., Jr. *Southern Politics in State and Nation.* New York: Knopf, 1949.

Killian, Lewis M. "Community Structure and the Role of the Negro Leader-Agent." *Sociological Inquiry* 35 (Winter 1965): 69–79.

Kimball, Solon. *The Talladega Story.* University: University of Alabama Press, 1954.

King, Stephen Clark. "Effects of Socio-economic Status and Linguistic Development Upon Responses to a Social Research Instrument." M.A. thesis, Ball State University, 1975.

Kraft, Joseph. "New Strategy for Black Community." San Francisco *Chronicle*, 22 February 1973.

Kuroda, Yasumasa. "Political Role Attributions and Dynamics in a Japanese Community." *Public Opinion Quarterly* 29 (Winter 1965–66): 602–13.

Leif, Irving P. *Community Power and Decision Making*. Metuchen, N.J.: Scarecrow Press, 1974.

Lindsay, Leon W. "Blacks Widen (vote) Base," *Christian Science Monitor*, 15 December 1970.

––––––. "The Changing Status of the Southern Negro." *Christian Science Monitor*, 2 December 1970.

Linquist, J. H. "An Occupational Analysis of Local Politics: Syracuse, New York, 1880–1959." *Sociology and Rural Sociology* 49 (April 1965): 343–54.

Lowry, Richie P. *Who's Running This Town? Community Leadership and Social Change*. New York: Harper and Row, 1965.

Lundberg, Ferdinand. *America's Sixty Families*. New York: Vanguard Press, 1937.

––––––. *The Rich and the Super-Rich*. New York: Bantam, 1968.

––––––. *The Rockefeller Syndrome*. New York: Kensington Publishing (Zebra Books), 1975.

Lynd, Robert S., and Lynd, Helen M. *Middletown in Transition*. New York: Harcourt, Brace, 1937.

McLuhan, Marshall. *Understanding Media: The Extensions of Man*. New York: McGraw-Hill, 1971.

Martindale, Don, and Gallen, R. *Small Town and the Nation: The Conflict of Local and Translocal Forces*. Westport, Conn.: Greenwood Publishing, 1969.

Meredith, James. "Black Leaders." *Ebony*, May 1973, p. 154.

Merton, Robert K. *On Theoretical Sociology*. New York: Free Press, 1967.

Miller, Delbert C. *International Community Power Structures: Comparative Studies in Four World Cities*. Bloomington, Ind.: University of Indiana Press, 1970.

––––––. "Power, Complementary, and the Cutting Edge of Research." *Sociological Focus* I, no. 4 (Summer 1968).

Mills, C. Wright. *Power Elite*. New York: Oxford University Press, 1956.

"Mortgage Money." *Southern Living* 4, no. 7 (July 1969): 15.

Mosca, Gaetano. *The Ruling Class*, trans. Hannah D. Kahn. New York: McGraw-Hill, 1939.

Moskowitz, Milton. "Black Capitalism—Still Just a Trickle." San Francisco *Chronicle*, 3 June 1973.

––––––. "Black Faces in the Board Room." San Francisco *Chronicle*, 28 July 1973.

––––––. "One Mutual Fund's (Dreyfus Fund) Heavy Trading." San Francisco *Chronicle*, 2 September 1973.

Mulford, Charles L. "On Role Consensus about Community Leaders." *Sociological Inquiry* 36 (Winter 1966): 15–18.

Neptune, Robert. *California's Uncommon Markets: The Story of the Consumer's*

Cooperative, 1935–1971. Richmond, Cal.: Associated Cooperative, Inc., 1971.

"New Style in Public Enemies: The White Collar Criminal." *U.S. News and World Report,* 12 March 1977, p. 53.

New Haven Chamber of Commerce. "South Central Connecticut," New Haven, 1973.

New Haven Redevelopment Agency. "Annual Report, 1972." New Haven, 1 November 1972.

———. "Downtown Development (map)." New Haven, 1969.

———. "Government Assistance Housing in New Haven as of May 1968" (includes map). New Haven, 1968.

Newton, K. "A Critique of the Pluralist Model." *Acta Sociologica* 12, no. 4 (1969): 209–23.

Norbeck, Edward. *Pineapple Town: Hawaii.* Berkeley: University of California Press, 1959.

"Offices in the Suburbs." *Time,* 8 February 1971, p. 53.

Parenti, Michael. "Power and Pluralism: A View from the Bottom." *Journal of Politics* 32 (August 1970): 501–30.

Pelligren, Roland J., and Coates, Charles. "Absentee-Owned Corporations and Community Power Structure." *American Journal of Sociology* 61 (March 1956): 413–19.

Perrucci, Robert, and Pilisuk, Marc. "Leaders and Ruling Elites: The Interorganizational Bases of Community Power." *American Sociological Review* 35 (December 1970): 1040–57.

Pfautz, Harold W. "The Power Structure of the Negro Sub-Community: A Case Study and a Comparative View." *Phylon* 23 (Summer 1962): 156–66.

Pinard, Maurice. "Structural Attachments and Political Support in Urban Politics: The Case of Fluoridation Referendums." *American Journal of Sociology* 68 (March 1963): 513–26.

Present, Philip Edward. "Defense Contracting and Community Leadership: A Comparative Analysis." *Southwestern Social Science Quarterly* 48 (December 1967): 399–410.

Presthus, Robert. *Men at the Top: A Study in Community Power.* New York: Oxford University Press, 1964.

Preston, James D. "A Comparative Methodology for Identifying Community Leaders." *Rural Sociology* 34 (December 1969): 556–62.

Rabinovitz, Francine F. "Sound and Fury Signify Nothing? A Review of Community Power Research in Latin America." *Urban Affairs Quarterly* 3 (March 1968): 111–22.

Reiss, Albert J., Jr. "Some Logical and Methodological Problems in Community Research." *Social Forces* 33 (October 1954): 51–57.

"Rocketing Cost of Farm Land." *U.S. News and World Report,* 12 March 1977, p. 62.

Rossi, Peter H. "Power and Community Structure." *Midwest Journal of Political Science* 4 (November 1960): 390–401.

Salisbury, Robert H. "St. Louis Politics: Relationships Among Interests, Parties, and Governmental Structure." *Western Political Quarterly* 13 (June 1960): 498–507.

Schultze, Robert O. "The Bifurcation of Power in a Satellite City." In Morris Janowitz, ed., *Community Political Systems*. Glencoe, Ill.: Free Press, 1961. Pp. 19–80.

Scoble, Harry. "Leadership Hierarchies and Political Issues in a New England Town." In Morris Janowitz, ed., *Community Political Systems*. Glencoe, Ill.: Free Press, 1961. Pp. 117–45.

Sjoberg, Gideon. "Urban Community Theory and Research: A Partial Evaluation." *American Journal of Economics and Sociology* 14 (January 1955): 199–206.

Smith, Joel, and Hood, Thomas. "The Delineation of Community Power Structures by Reputational Approach." *Sociological Inquiry* 36 (Winter 1966): 3–14.

Smith, Lincoln. "Power Politics in Brunswick: A Case Study." *Human Organization* 22 (Summer 1963): 153–58.

Smith, Ted C. "The Structuring of Power in a Suburban Community." *Pacific Sociological Review* 3 (Fall 1960): 83–88.

Stegner, Wallace, and Stegner, Page. "Rocky Mountain Country." *Atlantic Monthly*, April 1978.

Stinchcombe, Jean L. *Reform and Reaction: City Politics in Toledo*. Belmont, Cal.: Wadsworth Publishing, 1968.

Talbot, Allen. "The Lessons of New Haven, the Erstwhile Model City." *Psychology Today* 2, no. 3 (August 1968).

Thometz, Carol Estes. *The Decision Makers: The Power Structure of Dallas*. Dallas: Southern Methodist University Press, 1963.

Tolchin, Martin. "South Bronx: A Jungle Stalked by Fear, Seized by Rage" (a series of four articles). *New York Times*, 15 January 1973, 16 January 1973, 17 January 1973, 18 January 1973.

United States Department of Commerce. Social and Economic Statistics Administration. *News*. Washington, D.C.: Government Printing Office, 21 April 1972.

Vidich, Arthur, and Bensman, Joseph. *Small Town in Mass Society*. Princeton, N.J.: Princeton University Press, 1958.

Walter, Benjamin. "Political Decision Making in North Carolina Cities." *Prod* 3 (May 1960): 18–21.

Walton, John. "Discipline, Method, and Community Power: A Note on the Sociology of Knowledge." *American Sociological Review* 31 (October 1966): 684–89.

Westby, David L. "The Civic Sphere in the American City." *Social Forces* 45 (December 1966): 161–70.

Wildavsky, Aaron B. *Leadership in a Small Town*. Totowa, N.J.: Bedminster Press, 1964.

Williams, Oliver P. "A Typology for Comparative Local Government." *Midwest Journal of Political Science* 5 (May 1961): 150–64.

Index

Abernathy, Ralph, 57, 70, 76, 77
Accession, categories of, 89
Advisors, presidential, 138. *See also* Presidential confidants
Allen, Ivan, Jr., 41, 46, 49, 52, 53, 64, 86, 114
Allen, Ivan, III, 62
American Farm Bureau, 104
Annexation attempts, 112–15
Aristocracy, money, 30
Arnold, Carroll, 165–66
Associations, human: as manifestations of belief or value systems, xiii; social goals of, xv
Atlanta: physical characteristics, 8–9; as a national center, 9; in national perspective, 117
Attitudes: class, 160; ownership, 160–61
Austin, J. Paul, 21, 43, 62, 79
Ayres, B. Drummond, Jr., 78

Baltzell, Digby, 88
Belief systems: institutional, 16. *See also* Associations, human
Bias: systematic, 125; economic, 147
Billings, Dwight B., Jr., 36
Black power structure: policy goals, 71; role changes, 71; changes in occupations, 71–72; professionals in, 71–72; and leadership roles, 73–74; black-white shifts, 85–86; as a voting force, 115
Bond, Julian, 39, 57, 80, 81
Book-capital, xx, 125. *See also* Capital
Borders, William Holmes, 73, 76, 106
Brockey, Harold, 58, 62
Brown, Thaddeus, 83
Bryans, Raleigh, 79–80
Building. *See* Skyscrapers
Bureaucratic structures, 159
Burge, Lee, 79
Busch, Lawrence (Larry), 173